*For the health and aged care quality professionals, past, present and future.
Pioneers all.*

Published by Arcade Custom publications
Rm 2, Lvl 7, The Nicholas Building
37 Swanston St, Melbourne, Victoria

© Cathy Balding 2011

All rights reserved. Apart from any fair dealing for the purpose of private study, research, criticism or review, as permitted under the Copyright Act, no part of this publication may be reproduced, stored in a retrieval system, or transmitted in any form by any means electronic, mechanical, photocopying, recording or otherwise without the prior consent of the publisher.

ISBN 978 0 9871714 1 2 (pbk.)

Designed by Michael Brady
Printed by Ligare

This book has been researched, written, edited, designed and printed in Australia.

THE STRATEGIC QUALITY MANAGER

A Handbook for Navigating Quality Management Roles in Health and Aged Care

CATHY BALDING

About the author

Cathy Balding PhD has worked in quality improvement and clinical governance for over 20 years. She has held quality management and executive roles in rural and metropolitan health services across acute community and aged care, and worked at state and national levels in policy development and accreditation. Since establishing her Qualityworks consultancy in 2005, Cathy has worked with many health and aged care services and policymakers to build organisational capacity for providing great care for consumers. Her key focus is on supporting quality managers to develop the effectiveness, profile and enjoyment of their roles. Professionally, Cathy holds an Adjunct Associate Professor appointment in the School of Public Health at La Trobe University and is a Fellow of the Australasian College of Health Service Managers. She is also a member of the Board of a large not for profit aged care provider and an accreditation surveyor with The Australian Council on Healthcare Standards.

Visit **www.cathybalding.com** for more information and to access *The Strategic Quality Manager* and other quality manager resources.

CONTENTS

INTRODUCTION 1

CHAPTER 1 – DON'T CALL ME 'QUALITY': Defining the quality manager role and function 7

What makes a quality manager? 8
The changing quality management context 8
Unpacking the quality manager role 9
The quality system jigsaw 10
Quality is not something we 'are' – or 'do' 15
Taking control of the quality manager role 17
Supporting your organisation 20
Headlines: Chapter One 23
References and Further Reading 23

CHAPTER 2 – NAVIGATING PLANET HEALTHCARE: Working effectively in complex systems 27

Health services are complicated – and complex 28
A systems' recap 29
Exploring complex systems 30
Complex systems and the quality manager 36
Headlines: Chapter Two 37
References and Further Reading 37

CHAPTER 3 – THE RULES OF THE GAME: Change in complex systems 41

What's the issue with change? 41
The seven basics of change in complex systems 43
Lead change – and empower others to make it 61
Headlines: Chapter Three 62
References and Further Reading 62

CHAPTER 4 – DEVELOPING A THINKING ORGANISATION: Creating safety and quality in complex systems 67

Creating safety in healthcare – how did we get here? 67
Are we heading in the right direction? 70
Creating safety in a complex system 73
Building resilience to create safety 74
Creating resilient organisations 77
Supporting resilience development 79
Building safety – and quality – requires a thinking organisation 79
Headlines: Chapter Four 81
References and Further Reading 81

CHAPTER 5 – YOU CAN'T DO IT ON YOUR OWN: Leading and influencing great care   85

Leading quality care   86
Specific leadership knowledge for quality managers   92
Adding influence skills to your quality toolkit   94
The influence tools continuum   100
Leadership and influence are required for buy-in – and stay in   102
Headlines: Chapter Five   103
References and Further Reading   103

CHAPTER 6 – PLANNING FOR 'GREAT': Creating a consumer centred quality system   107

Strategic planning for great care – what are we talking about?   107
Six steps to a consumer centred quality system   109
Putting it all together – a framework for creating great care and services   138
Headlines: Chapter Six   140
References and Further Reading   140

CHAPTER 7 – BUILDING YOUR BRAND: The quality professionals' 'essentials' kit   145

Reviewing your current 'quality manager essentials' kit   145
A small slice of the big picture: how we got to here   146
Quality management methods   148
Data and evaluation   150
Building your quality professional brand   156
The last word   160
Headlines: Chapter Seven   161
References and Further Reading   161

APPENDIX 1 Quality Manager Skills and Knowledge Framework   164
APPENDIX 2 Example of Four Pillars and Components of Quality Governance   178
APPENDIX 3 Example Quality Governance Structure and Reporting   180
APPENDIX 4 The Quality Cycle and Tools Map   184
APPENDICES' REFERENCES AND FURTHER READING   185

INTRODUCTION

Let's start with what this book is not. It's not an academic text on managing quality and clinical governance in healthcare – even though relevant research, tools and techniques are discussed. It's not 'the answer' – unfortunately! – and it won't magically turn your role into a dream career. It's not about teaching experienced quality managers how to do their job, and it's not a comprehensive exploration of the ins and outs of quality and risk management.

So, what *is* it? Well, it *is* a book for people like you: managers, directors, leaders and coordinators of quality, improvement, compliance, redesign, risk management and clinical governance in acute, aged, primary and mental health settings (you now understand why I've limited myself to the generic terms 'healthcare quality manager' and 'quality professional' throughout the book!). It is also designed for those who may be considering working in these areas, involved in quality as one aspect of a broader role, or who are managing or mentoring quality managers and would like to better understand and support their role.

Offering suggestions to tackle the complex challenges of the healthcare quality role may seem glib. But it is not intended to be. I don't underestimate the difficulties of effecting change in the healthcare environment. I've lived it. This book is full of mistakes – mine! – and I've tried to take the lessons I've learned the hard way and offer information and ideas for thinking and acting differently that may help others avoid the same pitfalls. *The Strategic Quality Manager* is based on a simple premise: to be successful as a quality manager you need to be clear about your purpose, and strategic and proactive about achieving it. It's about better understanding and navigating the amazingly complex healthcare environment so that you can maximise your effectiveness. It offers information and tips for surviving and thriving as a quality professional. But mostly, this book is about developing and supporting quality managers who want to build on their operational demands to be proactive and strategic leaders in their organisations and in their field.

There are many things I wish I'd known in my career as a quality professional. I've worked across a number of rural health services involving acute, aged and community care; developed and piloted clinical indicators for a national accreditation agency; coordinated the quality system across a large metropolitan healthcare network; been a teaching hospital quality director; and I've developed and tested innovative state-wide quality systems as manager of a Ministerial Quality Council. My needs for information, skills and support have been different at each stage of my career, but there were many things I wished I'd known that would have stood me in good stead across all of these roles (and may have resulted in more people running towards me in corridors, rather than away!).

I remember learning the basics of quality tools and methods through my undergraduate Health Information Management qualification, short courses, conferences and books (pre internet!). I also picked up much useful guidance and handy tips from my peers, experienced quality professionals and mentors, and I will always be grateful for their generosity in sharing their time and hard earned knowledge to give me those much needed boosts. The rest I picked up on the job – much of which was about learning what not to do. The information that would have been most useful took me longest to learn: understanding how healthcare organisations – and the people within them – operate, and the importance of this knowledge in being able to successfully apply quality tools and methods to effect real improvement. I eventually realised that change also requires a specialist set of skills, and that without much formal organisational power I would need to become a master influencer. I eventually went on to postgraduate study where I was able to fill some of my knowledge gaps, and I've enjoyed continuing to learn from quality leaders, mentors and peers and from the evolving research and knowledge base being built in the quality area. But I could have avoided countless brick walls and wrong turns early in my career had I better understood some of this basic information – and the organisations I've worked for could only have benefited.

I've met and worked with hundreds of quality managers over the years. Many are asking themselves the same questions: Why am I not enjoying my job? Am I doing the right things? How can I get things done when I have no formal power? How can I complete all the things that need to be done? Why do my change efforts fail? How do I develop credibility? How can I develop a more strategic approach to quality so the quality system is not just a list of tasks for accreditation? How can I motivate people to do what is needed to improve care for our consumers? How can I be more effective? Why don't I have more support from my organisation? How can I develop my role into a respected part of the management team? Why do people think 'quality' is me?

Having worked as a quality manager myself, I've asked all these questions and more! And the answers to these questions aren't easy to find. Sure there's plenty of material available on quality management, but very little about being a quality manager. Some quality professionals are lucky – or proactive – enough to have access to mentors or a peer group that help smooth the way and can provide guidance. Some information is gleaned through courses, conferences and meetings. Most people, however, particularly those working in isolated areas and/or as a sole practitioner tend to learn how to be a quality manager through trial and error. This can result in a reactive, task-driven quality manager role because your colleagues don't understand what your job is really about – and so they think you're a 'fix all'.

Quality managers are often the people you see running around their organisation, reacting to yet another request for assistance or consumer safety problem. They have little time to think, plan, or develop their jobs to become more meaningful and interesting. Yet the ultimate success of the quality manager in effecting change and improvement largely rests on them developing their abilities and opportunities to be strategic and proactive: not to 'be' quality but to support the creation of quality. This book is therefore aimed at assisting quality managers to develop their role and their organisation's quality system to be something more than a list of tasks with little strategic impact.

The content of this book is a combination of relevant literature, research, my own experience in quality management roles and what I've learned working with quality managers over the last two decades. The principles are common to all healthcare sectors and can be equally well applied across acute, community, aged and mental health services. A range of knowledge, theory and strategies are drawn on, including those you may not find in generic quality management resources, and synthesised and interpreted for application by those in quality management roles. This book is also based on the fact that the quality professional does not exist in a vacuum, but functions in an incredibly complex and challenging environment. Understanding this environment is the first step to operating effectively and proactively within it, and breaking out of a reactive, task-driven quality role. The critical impact of influence on quality managers' effectiveness is explored and a 'quality manager essentials' kit is identified. This book also provides the inside knowledge on how to navigate the traps and pitfalls of the complex, constantly evolving environment in which healthcare quality managers work.

The result is really a conversation about being a quality manager. Whether you are redesigning your role to be more effective or achieve greater job satisfaction, or you're thinking about becoming a quality professional, the material in this book will help you decide if this is the job for you. The chapters cover:

- Exploring the quality manager role
- Understanding complex healthcare systems
- Effecting change in complex healthcare systems
- Creating safety and quality in complex healthcare systems
- Quality leadership and influence
- Strategic quality planning
- The 'quality professionals' essentials' kit

As you can see, it's a mix of macro and micro – from strategy to skills. The chapters build on one another – from defining the role of the quality professional in chapter One to implementing a strategic approach to quality systems planning in chapter Seven.

If what you've read so far has you nodding, rather than nodding off, then this book is for you! As the pressure on our health and aged care services grows, so too do the demands on the quality professional. Continuing to increase the efficiency and quality of healthcare will require new and savvier ways of working. Simply adding more tasks to current positions is not the answer, nor is it sustainable. It will take a proactive response from quality managers to re-shape their roles and redefine them for the future – no one else can do it for us. To meet these challenges, we will need to re-think the way quality professionals operate, identify priorities more strategically, apply skills more effectively and support development and retention of great quality managers into the future by crafting these roles to have more impact – and to be more satisfying. This book is part of that conversation.

Q1 DON'T CALL ME 'QUALITY':
Defining the quality manager role and function

'What you do speaks so loudly that I cannot hear what you say.'
– **RW Emerson**

1. DON'T CALL ME 'QUALITY':
Defining the quality manager role and function

If you have learned to be a quality manager on the job and without a 'how to be a quality manager' manual, you might think that you are missing some fundamental skills and knowledge. This chapter explores the functions of the quality manager role in relation to your organisation's quality system. It offers a generic list of quality manager responsibilities, skills and knowledge, and suggests ways in which you can be more proactive and strategic.

Working to change systems and behaviours to improve care for patients is a fabulous thing to be a part of. And when you get a real win, it's spectacular! But day to day, a quality management role can be a tough gig. It is not a job for the faint hearted. If my memory serves me correctly, working in quality roles used to be more enjoyable. I don't think this is just a sentimental view of the past. In some respects when it was more fun we probably weren't as effective as we should have been, or focused on the right things or rigorous enough in our approaches. The rise and rise of risk and compliance over the past decade has changed the quality role. In some ways this is change for the better: a role that used to be seen as optional is now, mostly, viewed as necessary, as much an integral part of a health service structure as an IT or HR manager. Gone are the days when we use to preach that a good quality manager should do themselves out of a job because they had set everything up so nicely and taught staff all they needed to know. What were we thinking? This is akin to saying that health services no longer require their IT manager when the software is installed, the computers are working and the staff know how to use them. Yes, systems setup is important, but in the dynamic healthcare world, maintenance, improvement and evolution of systems to achieve their purpose is also essential.

Healthcare quality management is also much more than implementing systems for monitoring and improvement. It's about charting a course to take the organisation somewhere better than where it is now, whilst responding to a dynamic external environment and ever increasing consumer and organisational needs. And when it all comes together, there's nothing better than knowing you've facilitated a significant process or outcome improvement for health service consumers – and that their experience of your organisation, their healthcare and even their lives, are better as a result. But this is getting harder to achieve as healthcare increasingly equals seemingly endless demand plus severely constrained resources. This environment requires skilled, proactive and strategic quality professionals to enable governing bodies to fulfil their accountabilities for the quality of care their organisation provides, and to support staff to monitor and improve the quality of care they deliver within a jungle of competing priorities.

This chapter endeavours to help you clarify your role so you're doing more of the things you should be doing to increase your effectiveness and build your credibility, and less of the things that don't add significant value to you or to your health service. It also aims to increase the confidence of those quality managers who are in that 'am I doing what I'm supposed to be doing?' stage. With knowledge and competence comes confidence[1] and this chapter – and book – aims to help quality managers become more confident in their role. In short, it is recognition that this is not a job you choose because it is easy, but because it is challenging.

What makes a quality manager?

Healthcare quality management is more often than not a classic 'learn on the job' role. Many quality professionals don't have a formal qualification in quality management, and have picked up their theory from conferences, short courses and as subjects in postgraduate courses. This is partly because there aren't many formal quality-specific healthcare qualifications around. But it's also because quality managers don't always choose quality management as a career – sometimes it chooses them. One day you're a normal person, the next day you're a quality manager! If you're new to a quality management role and have looked for information that may help you identify the skills and knowledge you need, you'll know there are not many resources around that are specific to this need. If you're in an established role, but think you could be professionally more effective, it can be tricky to find information on how to pursue this. There are plenty of resources available on quality management, but few about being a quality manager.

For many the job is part-time juggle of quality tasks and clinical or management responsibilities. This is becoming less sustainable as increasing societal and political demands for healthcare quality, transparency, compliance and accountability flow on to quality managers, increasing the length of their to do lists and adding to the number of 'hats' they wear. The spotlight on quality has never been brighter. In this environment quality managers want to be more effective and healthcare organisations need them to be more effective. Yet despite this growing recognition that the quality manager position is a key component of any health, community or aged care organisation, quality managers often have to design – and largely support – their own continuously expanding role. It often seems that as long as accreditation and compliance requirements are successfully addressed, there is less attention paid by health service executives and managers as to how these are achieved or how to move beyond this. They are not alone in this. It is easy for quality managers to be so preoccupied with juggling their many tasks that they have little time to stop and think about their role and purpose, and how it might be more effective, let alone how it could be more fulfilling or interesting. And yet the 'how' is key to the effectiveness and enjoyment of the quality manager role and ultimately to the effectiveness of the quality system in improving patient care.

The changing quality management context

As the healthcare environment changes, it is important to revisit the quality manager role and function. The rising profile of consumer safety, in particular, appears to be driving the quality manager role towards the compliance end of the quality spectrum, and there is a danger that quality professionals will have fewer and fewer opportunities to develop their knowledge and exercise their improvement and innovation skills. The establishment of

---

WHAT IS 'GREAT' CARE?

Why am I using the term 'great' care? Why not 'world's best' or 'perfect'? Why not 'quality' or 'excellent' care? Your organisation's strategic plan will no doubt contain some sort of broad aim, goal or statement about providing quality/excellent/best practice care. This is an important piece of the quality jigsaw. But what does it mean? 'Excellent and 'world's best practice' are admirable things to aspire to, but they're difficult to achieve for every consumer at every encounter. After all, there's no point in 5% of your consumers receiving world's best practice care if the other 95% receive average or suboptimal care. Great care is made up of the basics – the things that consumers want and need from each encounter with your health service. Achieving the basics of great care for each of your consumers 100% of the time may sound a little prosaic and not very exciting, but this couldn't be further from the truth. In the complex system that is your healthcare organisation, achieving anything consistently is far from easy. As a professional and organisational goal, it will take all your enthusiasm, skills and smarts to define and pursue. It also takes strategic thinking, robust governance and focused implementation. If we could guarantee a consistently good level of service and care for every consumer every time, it truly would be 'great'.

parallel innovation, redesign and service improvement roles in many health services has also contributed to this. For many quality managers this creates tension between where they are (the inflexible world of compliance and accreditation) and where they'd like to be (transforming healthcare for patients). In this situation, quality managers can struggle to establish a fulfilling role for themselves and may feel unvalued. In the absence of a clear and valued quality systems role, some quality managers take on a personal responsibility for the quality of care delivered, which can be impossible to fulfil.

Quality managers who find themselves in this space often experience frustration and helplessness and may question their career choices. Burned out quality managers are not an uncommon breed. They feel that their job is running them rather than the other way around. There is often little organisational backing for defining and enhancing their role, and they may be unsure how to go about seeking this support. Sometimes this is because the people to whom the quality managers are accountable are unsure themselves about what they want from the quality manager position, or the quality system, so they end up asking for a bit of everything. It is not uncommon for a quality professional in healthcare to be a statistician in the morning, a psychologist at lunchtime, an educator in the afternoon and an investigator in the evening, all in one of the most high risk and complex environments in the world. And many of them deliver! This in itself is not a bad thing, particularly if you enjoy challenge and variety, but it can be easy to lose your way. You require a clear purpose to help you work effectively, maintain your motivation and prioritise your 'hats'.

Unpacking the quality manager role

You may not be able to change the context within which your role operates, but you can change the way you think about it and work within it. You can choose to be more proactive and strategic. You can re-frame the way you (and others) perceive what you do by committing to clarifying your purpose, focusing your efforts, better understanding your environment and applying a few handy tools and techniques.

Let's start by unpacking the key elements of the quality management role. As with everything discussed in this book, there is no single 'accepted' industry template for the components of the role; these will vary from organisation to organisation. There are, however, a few core things that most quality professionals will be expected to do. From my experience, these are the three core requirements of the quality manager role:

1. Assist your executive and staff to define and develop a clear picture of the 'great' quality of care your organisation wants to provide, and a strategic quality plan for achieving it.
2. Define, develop and organise the various components of the quality system into a framework for achieving great care that will motivate staff to fulfil their roles.
3. Support your organisation to achieve this picture of great care by working effectively with staff at all levels of your organisation to implement and evaluate the quality plan and system.

These core areas are a good place to start if you are a first-time quality manager and/or you don't have much organisational support for defining and establishing your role. (If you don't have a clear set of responsibilities in a position description, it is critical that you remedy this with your manager as soon as you can.)

Being unclear about your role and the objectives and processes for which you are responsible creates a number of problems. You may be asked to produce or achieve something you didn't know was part of the role. Your colleagues might be unclear about your role and therefore think you are there to pick up surplus work or anything that can have a 'quality' label slapped on it. But before you can shape your job description into something that is useful, manageable, achievable and – hopefully – enjoyable, you must first have a clear picture of the what, the how and the why of your role.

The quality manager purpose
Few quality managers have the time or the opportunity to take a step back and examine why their role exists, and therefore how they can best add value to the organisation. Yet this is vital to ensuring your role has purpose, achieves what it is supposed to and results in job satisfaction. Both your quality role and your organisational quality system require a purpose and goals to be effective and you have some control over what these look like. You can't be responsible for the quality of care delivered unless part of your own organisational role is care delivery. This is where governance comes in. It starts with the health service's governing body and cascades down the organisation through line management to those who directly provide care, with each level of managers and staff having clear and specific responsibility for their role in providing great care. The technical design of the quality system that assists them to enact these roles is the responsibility of the quality manager. Your job is to provide everyone – from the chair of your governing body to frontline staff – with the tools and approaches to support their responsibilities. This book will help you use your knowledge and skill to create a quality system that supports staff to create and provide great care and services.

So, what is a quality system? For the purposes of this book I'm defining it as a systematic, organisation-wide program of planning, leadership, change, measurement, evaluation and action that achieves and maintains the organisation's vision of great care for each consumer. Without an overall purpose and framework to organise all the components, a quality system is just a list of activities and the quality manager's role just a collection of tasks. To give meaning and life to the quality system you, your manager and your chief executive need to be clear about what all this activity is meant to achieve. I'm not talking about the many and varied KPIs and targets you may be working towards. These are important, but they are a means to an end.

So what is the end goal for your quality system and for your role? This can be impossible to know unless your quality system has a clear definition of quality care. And yet many organisational quality systems are chugging along monitoring, improving, managing and complying without defining exactly what it is that all this work is supposed to achieve, and how it all fits together. All they know is that they're 'doing' quality. This creates a number of problems: staff can't see the purpose of all their auditing, counting and documentation; your quality system is difficult to evaluate when its objectives aren't defined, making it difficult to report on; and accreditation becomes the de facto purpose of the quality system – which makes all of these problems worse.

The quality system jigsaw

Think of all of the components of your quality system as pieces of a giant three-dimensional jigsaw. This jigsaw comprises consumers, staff, policy, monitoring and improvement, systems, leadership and governance, training, care delivery and accreditation. And that's just for starters! To pull all of the pieces together into a coherent whole, you need to see the picture of what you're trying to create. Without this, it is difficult for people in your organisation to play their part in bringing the pieces together and for you to fulfil your role in facilitating this. To effect real and lasting change to the way a consumer experiences your organisation – and the outcomes achieved – you need a vision, some goals and a plan to guide all the 'doing'.

One of the key quality manager responsibilities is to assist the people in the organisation to develop a shared understanding of the purpose of the quality system, and to create the framework to achieve it. Without it, staff can't understand why they should contribute to a quality system, the organisation can't proactively improve care and services, and you will be dependent on your own willpower and your colleagues' goodwill to effect change. Not having a vision and framework of skills, incentives, resources and planning to drive your quality system results in all sorts of barriers and difficulties.[2]

When designing your quality system, you must 'begin with the end in mind'.[3] What are you trying to achieve? This vision is your organisation's definition of the great care it wants for each consumer (Chapter Six discusses defining and planning for this) and the quality system framework provides the instructions on how all the pieces fit together to achieve great care in a planned, coordinated and purposeful way. Some people will be responsible for the 'corner' pieces of the jigsaw; others for gathering certain 'like' pieces together or for particular parts of the 'scenery'. In the end, it takes a shared understanding of the big picture - the vision to bring all the pieces together and complete the picture.

Getting organised – fitting the pieces together
Let's start by putting your current quality system under the microscope. What are the key components? Do they include some or most of these activities?

- processes for meeting accreditation standards
- data collection for monitoring and reporting on key aspects of care and risk
- improvement and innovation priorities and initiatives
- credentialing, scope of practice and competency development system
- risk identification and control, incident and complaints reporting, investigation and analysis
- responding to requests for medico legal and other information
- systems review and improvement
- policies, protocols and guidelines based on evidence and legislation
- audits for monitoring care quality
- consumer participation activities
- customer service program
- meeting government and corporate targets and goals
- training and development

This list is not exhaustive, of course, but is it getting close? Can you see a pattern in these components? What are all these things for? How would consumer care be affected if your organisation stopped doing these things? Can you list the components in order from most powerful through to least powerful in terms of direct consumer impact? This exercise will give you an appreciation of the 'core' components of your quality system, and is also a useful exercise to do with your governing body and executive when prioritising resources. But there's a critical step before this that brings all of the pieces into a coherent whole.

So far we have a list – a list that becomes less and less interesting to staff the closer they are to frontline care. Sound familiar? If it does you are certainly not alone. Organisational quality systems tend to be built around a range of drivers such as policy and accreditation requirements, funding opportunities and leaders' interests. They are rarely designed from the ground up and the various components (sometimes conflicting) are added here and there at various times in response to these drivers. There will always be external imperatives, and internal leaders will always influence according to their particular skills and interests. But that is all the more reason to know you're your quality system is supposed to achieve.

Factors necessary for large scale system change and the consequences of their absence[2]	
Vision + Skills + Incentives + Resources + Action Plan	Change
No Vision + Skills + Incentives + Resources + Action Plan	Confusion
Vision + **No Skills** + Incentives + Resources + Action Plan	Anxiety
Vision + Skills + **No Incentives** + Resources + Action Plan	Gradual Change
Vision + Skills + Incentives + **No Resources** + Action Plan	Frustration
Vision + Skills + Incentives + No Resources + **No Action Plan**	False Starts

Not having a 'box top' vision and framework of skills, incentives, resources and planning to drive your quality system results in all sorts of barriers and difficulties, as seen above[2] – do you recognise your situation here?

When you know what your quality system is supposed to achieve you can identify its core components – those that should not be messed with because they impact on patient care – and the components that are the 'nice to have' because they add interest and enhance knowledge. Knowing what your quality system is supposed to achieve also helps you identify gaps, spot overemphasis on low value-adding activities (that may be taking up a lot of your time) and ensure you have all the levers in place to drive quality care. Internationally, the health services that consistently provide high quality care all share this key characteristic. They have all defined the quality of care they want to provide, and their governing bodies and executives take a strategic approach to achieving this with an effective quality systems framework and system (see Chapter Six on planning a strategic organisational approach to great care).

Some components are non-negotiable, of course. Compliance with legislation and government and corporate policy, managing and reporting on risk and medico legal issues, and meeting accreditation requirements definitely fall into the 'don't mess with' category. These are the first things to identify and bed down with the best system you can develop (or afford). The trick for the quality manager is to find the most effective and efficient ways to manage these 'non-negotiables'. Use of administrative databases for data collection and reporting are essential to this part of your job.

Let's organise the components of the quality system and allocate some tasks to three general purposes, as seen in Table 1. This is certainly better than no structure at all and may be helpful to get your and others' head around the quality system. But this is still just a list of the mechanics of a quality system. This table will be of little interest to most of those at the frontline of care delivery because it doesn't illustrate how these mechanics impact on patient care. A key part of the quality manager's role is to help staff understand their role the quality system – and how it leads to great care. So, a quality system's logic and framework might look something like Table 2. Using a framework and logic for the quality system as seen in Table 2 may help to put it in perspective.

Non-negotiables	Guarding against poor care	Creating great care
Meeting standards	Proactive and reactive aspects of risk management	Improvement and innovation initiatives and tools
Compliance with legislation and government/corporate policy	Policies, guidelines and protocols	Policies, guidelines and protocols
Government and corporate goals and targets	Minimum dataset	Stretch, strategic quality goals
Information requests	Systems review and redesign	Systems review and redesign
Accreditation preparation	Credentialing, scope of practice and competency development	Consumer participation and customer services
	Staff knowledge and skills development	Staff knowledge and skills development

Table 1: Example of quality manager tasks and purposes

Of course the quality manager can't do all these things. Your job is to ensure that staff at all levels are supported with skills and knowledge to understand the left column, contribute to the items in the right column, and that these things happen in a planned and coordinated way. It can be a fine line to tread, however, between enabling others to improve quality through providing them with skills and knowledge, and the work you must do yourself to support quality care. Staff have to be involved in monitoring and improvement as part of their responsibility for, and ownership of, providing care that is consistently good – and getting better. The quality manager role should be aimed at helping them do this by providing an effective quality system.

Quality managers are like the building site project managers who coordinate and advise on the building of a quality house. This doesn't mean that you don't have to get your hands dirty – effective project managers have to apply their particular technical skills as well as planning, monitoring and coordination, and, depending on the size of your organisation, you will have to do some of the building yourself. Some of this will be about transfer of skills and some will be about you working alongside staff to help with the more systems aspects of improvement, such as provision of comparative data, planning initiatives, designing changes and putting in some of the hard change management yards required to implement them. You are also likely to have a key role in preparing for external evaluations or accreditation assessments. But you can't provide the quality consumer experience – your job is to help the managers and staff in your organisation to fulfil their responsibility for creating this.

The most successful quality managers I've seen have a simple and straightforward way of explaining to staff at all levels of the organisation where they fit within the quality system framework. Critically, they are able to successfully explain how what staff do (their actions on the frontline of care and the way in which they monitor and improve those actions) contributes to what the organisation is trying to achieve: great care for each consumer.

Clarifying the connection between the how and the why helps reduce the problem of the word 'quality' becoming synonymous with the quality system mechanics (such as the audits, compliance, data collections and protocols) and focuses on the quality of care being delivered. The more explicit you can make this, the easier it will be for people to see how their jigsaw piece, and all the other jigsaw pieces, come together to complete the picture of great care, and the easier it will be for you to involve them.

We need a quality systems framework to:	The corresponding components of our quality system are:
1. Define 'great care': the level of care the organisation will provide for every consumer, every time	1. Defined vision for great care and corresponding goals, building blocks, priorities, targets and measurable objectives across the dimensions of quality care, linked to the organisation's strategic plan
2. Determine the people and systems that must be in place to make this happen: Structure: what you need Process: what you do Outcome: what you expect	2. Governance to support quality care: leadership, accountability, legislation, standards, policy, protocols, systems, external evaluation and accreditation to support achievement of each dimension of quality care
3. Ensure those people are supported and systems are implemented to achieve the desired quality of care	3. Implementation of systems and governance to support quality care, including clear and supported staff roles, training, resilience, change, sustainability, and spread methods and mechanisms
4. Monitor whether practice and systems are achieving the level of care we have defined	4. Monitoring and evaluation: data collection, analysis and benchmarking across each dimension of quality
5. Improve systems and practice if the desired quality of care is not where it should be and to improve standards over time	5. Applying continuous improvement 'science': planning; tools such as PDSA; systems; redesign; lean; bundling; learning from other organizations and industries; use of policy, protocols, guidelines, prompts and reminders; monitoring and evaluation of process and outcomes
6. Manage and respond to the risk of things going wrong	6. Proactive and reactive risk management: risk planning and register, controls, reporting, response, and safety culture

Table 2: Quality system framework logic and components

Quality is not something we 'are' or 'do'

You will often hear the phrase 'doing quality' in healthcare organisations, and I believe it is one of the most damaging phrases in our health vocabulary. Quality of care can't be 'done'. It is something we define and create. It is how we want to describe the care and services we provide. But we have allowed staff to confuse being involved with quality improvement mechanics – the monitoring, reporting and improvement – with providing quality care. This confusion has all sorts of flow on effects, none of them good. First, it means that 'doing quality' is seen as boring, a chore, extra work or something we 'do' on Tuesday afternoons, often for accreditation purposes. Second, it can create a false sense of security – an assumption that if we have 'done' quality such as an audit or a checklist then the actual care we provide must also be good (similar to the belief that if we have completed a care plan, this somehow guarantees that the plan will be effectively implemented). Third, it makes it difficult for people to understand the quality cycle. If the quality they 'did' on Tuesday afternoon in the shape of an audit, some other data collection, or a meeting, isn't followed up with an evaluation and discussion of the impact it had at the bedside/chairside, how are they supposed to find it meaningful?

> ➡ **TOP TIP**
>
> A quality manager rule to live by: never discuss, develop or implement a piece of the quality system (the mechanics of quality) without clearly showing the link to its contribution to the purpose of the quality system – achieving great care for each consumer.

If a key aspect of the quality manager role is to help staff make the connection between the quality system and the quality of care actually provided and experienced by consumers, then let's stop 'doing quality' and start 'creating quality'. And while we're at it, let's get some action back into the quality manager title. You are not just a quality manager. You are a quality systems manager, or a quality improvement advisor, or a quality governance consultant. Make sure there is a noun and a verb attached to your title that clearly describes what you are responsible for doing in terms of the quality of care provided.

Once staff understand that great quality care is something the whole organisation works together to achieve, they also need to be shown how they are contributing to the 'great' consumer experience described in the organisational quality plan, as seen in Figure 1.

By now, many of you will be muttering darkly that what you are responsible for doing can be summed up in one word: accreditation. If you find your quality system is mostly aimed at preparation for accreditation, it's a fair bet that a large proportion of staff in your organisation are missing the point and see 'quality' as the dull mechanics you are nagging them to engage in. As a result, your quality system may not be achieving interesting or innovative care improvement – or even basic good care for consumers – just compliance with standards, which, whilst improving your organisation's chances of providing consistently great care, does not guarantee this.

If you feel like this, you are certainly not alone! Accreditation is a hydra that devours the time and focus of quality managers and healthcare executives, and often distracts from the real purpose of improving care, the very purpose it purports to support. Accreditation was never designed to be the point of the quality program; it was meant to support good care and provide a means of evaluating it. But we know that it doesn't always translate that way, and that there is considerable work involved in demonstrating that the right things are happening and standards are being met – particularly when your health service has to meet more than one set of accreditation standards.

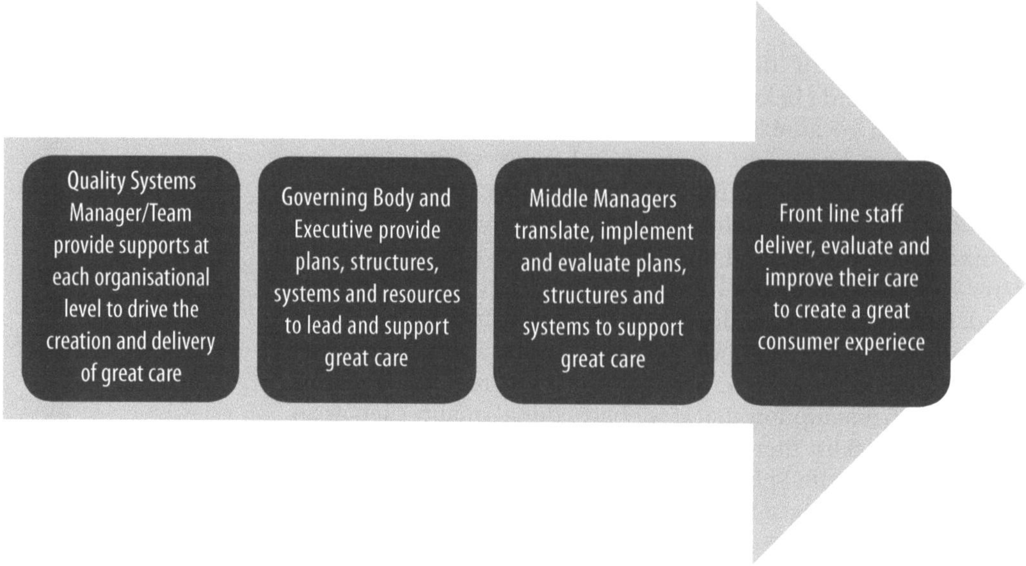

[Arrow diagram containing four boxes, left to right:]

- Quality Systems Manager/Team provide supports at each organisational level to drive the creation and delivery of great care
- Governing Body and Executive provide plans, structures, systems and resources to lead and support great care
- Middle Managers translate, implement and evaluate plans, structures and systems to support great care
- Front line staff deliver, evaluate and improve their care to create a great consumer experiece

Figure 1: Embedding the creation of quality care in organisational roles

Accreditation can be made slightly easier, however, if addressed as part of a broader approach to planning and driving quality care, if it is implemented as part of your quality systems framework. Accreditation requirements are pieces of the jigsaw and play their part in creating the vision for great care. Some standards form the components of great care to be delivered at the frontline while some are components of the governance systems provided by the governing body and executive to support great care. At this point it is important to urge you not to reinvent the wheel! There are many frameworks available for organising your quality system components, including one discussed as part of strategic quality planning in Chapter Six. Whatever framework you use and whichever way you organise your quality system, the important thing is that it works for your healthcare organisation by helping to connect all the tools, standards, governance, roles, data, activities and myriad other jigsaw pieces that make up your quality system, to maintain the things that are good, improve the things that need improving and transform the consumer experience.

A quality system should address three key aspects of quality:

1. Maintenance - minimise risk, maintain processes and standards of care, detect problems, monitor compliance
2. Improvement - identify and drive operational improvements in processes designed to solve problems and improve consumer experiences and outcomes
3. Transformation - develop and pursue a strategic view of consistently 'great' care for every consumer.

Taking control of the quality manager role

This chapter was written primarily for those quality managers who have asked themselves, 'Am I doing what I'm supposed to be doing?' I hope by now that those of you who fit this category can see that, to answer this question, you need to ask another question: 'What is our quality system supposed to be achieving?' When you and your organisation can answer this, it will be easier for you to negotiate your specific responsibilities and win the corresponding support you will require to effectively fulfil them. No one is going to be any clearer on what you are supposed to be doing than you! If you want to shape your role into something more than it is now, it's important that you be proactive in defining it in a way that others can understand and work with.

Once you've clarified your role (or the role you would like to have) in helping your organisation to achieve 'great' care you will know whether you are doing what you are supposed to be doing – and what your new priorities should be!

Responsibilities and tasks

Currently, the key responsibilities and tasks of your average quality manager will include:

- facilitating preparation for accreditation (as previously discussed, for some quality manager positions, this is the role)
- collecting, analysing and presenting data on various safety and quality issues
- alerting governing bodies, executives and external agencies to safety and quality problems
- supporting and sitting on various quality-related committees
- providing technical support for department heads and staff to monitor and improve what they do
- responding to requests for information from health departments, corporate offices, coroners, insurers, lawyers, commissions and councils, patients and the public, just to name a few
- coordinating and leading improvement and innovation projects, investigations and root cause analyses
- synthesising and coordinating all of the quality-related activity across the organisation
- providing training and information on accreditation, risk management and service improvement for staff
- implementing government and corporate policy.

Hmmm – doesn't sound like that much fun, does it? What if we look at the 'how', which includes some of the knowledge and skills required to fulfil those responsibilities.

Knowledge

- accreditation, standards and compliance
- the nature and management of risk, error and human factors
- change management
- improvement and innovation
- motivation and influence
- teamwork
- consumer feedback and satisfaction
- medical terminology, anatomy, physiology and pharmacology (even a smattering of terminology definitely helps!)

- how the health system works: governance, funding, policy, structures and processes, key players, information flow, professional functions, politics and hierarchies
- how healthcare organisations work and understanding complex systems.

Skills
- planning: strategic, operational, project
- relationship building
- influencing and effecting change
- planning and goal setting
- report and submission preparation
- measurement and evaluation: data collection and analysis, validity and reliability, indicators, statistics, presentation
- application of tools for monitoring and managing risk and improvement
- influencing and motivating participation in monitoring and improvement
- facilitating sustainable change
- developing effective teams
- public speaking and presenting
- training
- use of information management and technology
- developing policies and procedures
- organising and chairing meetings
- coordinating and synthesising risk and improvement activities in an organisation.

Phew – that's a lot of hats to wear! Of course, not all quality manager roles require all of these, all of the time. And not everything that every quality manager does is listed here. That will depend on the size of the organisation and the role. The quality manager in a sole position, or even within a two or three person team, requires different skills to those in larger organisations where quality team members are likely to have more specific and specialist quality roles, such as in compliance, improvement and risk.

It is useful to link the skills and knowledge you need to your quality systems framework – remembering that your framework must be a clear and comprehensive description of your organisation's approach to creating quality care! Appendix 1 uses the cycle of improvement and quality governance pillars to identify likely quality manager tasks, and therefore, skills and knowledge, for example:

Planning, creating and monitoring quality care and services
- identify the legislation, policy and standards to be met by the organisation and develop an organisation-wide plan to monitor and achieve them
- help service managers define the quality of care they want their consumers to experience and organise this using the dimensions of quality
- assist department managers and staff to plan maintenance and improvement initiatives:
  - Use data analysis and problem identification tools to identify relevant activities
  - Define the activity purpose
  - Set 'SMART' objectives and corresponding evaluation method
  - Advise on data collection.

Identifying and analysing quality of care status and problems:
- Identify organisational gaps in meeting mandatory requirements and standards
- Assist service managers to identify their quality status and problems, using:
  - Basic quality analysis tools
  - Basic statistics
  - Basic data collection, analysis and presentation, using qualitative and quantitative data (including validity and reliability)
  - Audit design and implementation
  - Simple survey design and analysis
  - Trend analysis of basic risk and quality data
  - Measures of process and outcome
  - Sourcing and use of existing indicators to monitor and identify issues.

On top of all this, it is useful to identify and develop your *modus operandi*. Are you a facilitator? Coordinator? Manager? Facilitator? Teacher? Leader? Influencer? All of the above, probably, which means you may need to develop some specific skills in these areas, and this is further discussed in Chapters Six and Seven.

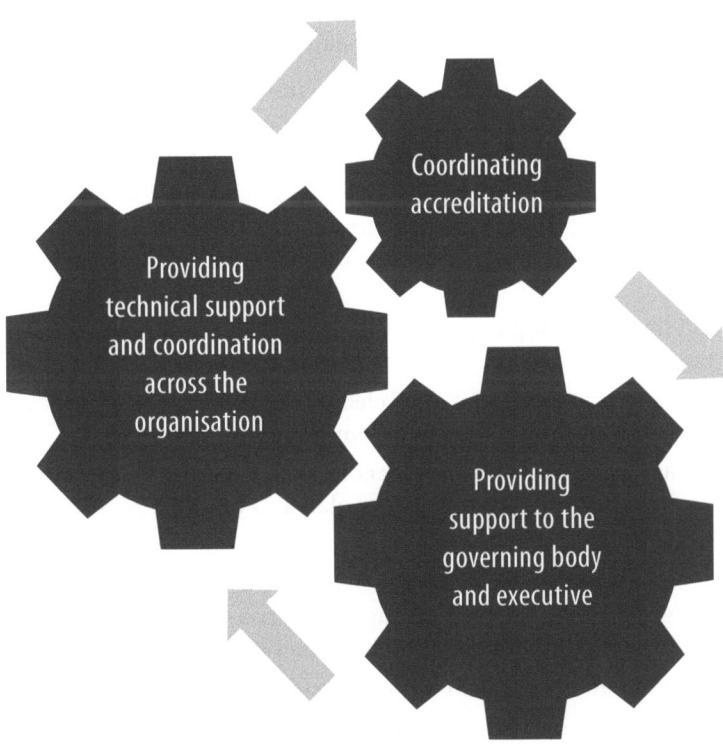

Figure 2: Components of the quality manager organisational support and implementation role

Let's revisit the three core requirements of the quality manager role we identified at the beginning of this chapter:

1. Assist your executive and staff to define and develop a clear picture of the 'great' quality of care your organisation wants to provide, and a strategic quality plan for achieving it
2. Define, develop and organise the various components of the quality system into a framework for achieving great care that will motivate staff to be involved, and which also covers corporate, policy and external requirements
3. Support your organisation to achieve this picture of great care by working effectively with staff at all levels of your organisation to implement and evaluate the quality system.

Supporting your organisation

We've discussed 1 and 2. What about 3? Your job is not to implement the whole quality systems framework – that's a governance function and executive and management responsibility. So what is your role in implementation? You are the ultimate support team – guiding and assisting your organisation to achieve its vision for great care. This role can be described as three interconnecting functions, as seen in Figure 2:

1. Supporting the governing body and/or executive to enable them to fulfil their corporate governance and quality leadership roles
2. Providing technical support and coordination across the organisation for the achievement of strategic quality goals
3. Coordinating accreditation and other compliance activities.

Providing support to the governing body and executive will include tasks to facilitate the governing body and executive to define the quality of care they wish consumers to receive, and to drive a planned and strategic approach to achieving it through:

- developing and implementing organisational governance for quality care through planning, benchmarking governance processes with other organisations and sourcing contemporary information and evidence about effective quality governance structures and processes
- developing and implementing a quality system that plans and drives the achievement of consistently positive consumer experiences at point of care
- enabling line management and staff to be clear about their responsibilities for the quality of care provided and supported to enact them
- supporting management, staff and relevant committees to be informed by valid and robust information and analysis to drive the quality plan and to make good decisions about the quality and safety of care
- meeting corporate and government policy requirements
- identifying, analysing and proactively managing of a risk system that paints a picture of the key risks throughout the organisation and identifies strengths and gaps
- driving effective change in people and systems to support good care
- coordinating the quality initiatives across the organisation and tracking and reporting progress with achieving the strategic quality goals and other quality plan requirements
- seeking opportunities for external project funding and participation in inter-facility improvement initiatives and data comparison.

➡ TOP TIP

Providing technical support for and coordination of the maintenance and improvement activities across the organisation will be easier with a dedicated database. One of the best investments you can make to support you in your role will be to buy or build a quality systems database. Ideally, the database should:

- be organised around your strategic quality goals
- allow departments to record their quality plan and track their contribution to the quality goals
- guide the development of improvement activities through the quality cycle and link them to the organisational quality goals and accreditation standards and criteria
- provide an overview of organisational progress with the strategic quality goals
- give alerts when new activities are inputted, and let you know if your assistance is required in the development of an improvement initiative
- link similar activities across the organisation through keywords to facilitate inter-departmental collaboration and minimise duplication
- monitor high risk areas and flags problems
- link to your incident reporting database to connect incidents and complaints with the improvement cycle
- make it easy to request the reports required for managers, committees and for the purposes of accreditation

If you are a savvy IT person, or have access to one with available time, you can build a database in-house. There are also off-the-shelf databases that fulfil the criteria listed above. This requires an investment, of course, but in my opinion it is one that will pay off immediately. A well constructed database will remove much of the tedium of your role by driving consistency and focus in the way staff go about developing and evaluating improvement activities, and should help you to coordinate and channel the various safety and improvement initiatives across the organisation to achieve common quality goals. In the process, you can capture a lot of required accreditation information, which is an excellent by-product. Please note one warning! The way in which any database is configured and implemented is critical to its success. Work with someone who has done this before, and done it successfully. Design your quality system first and then develop the database to support it – not the other way around; the database should not be dictating the way in which your quality system operates. If a database is not making participation in the quality system easier and more interesting for you and other staff, it's not doing its job.

Providing technical support and coordination across the organisation for the achievement of the strategic quality goals will include:

- coordinating the quality initiatives across the organisation and tracking progress with achieving the strategic quality goals and other quality plan requirements
- ensuring staff understand and are equipped with the knowledge and skills to fulfil their responsibilities for providing great care
- working with divisional and department heads and staff to understand their role in achieving the organisational quality plan goals and objectives and to translate these into local initiatives
- involving staff in ensuring both proactive and responsive risk systems are in place and function effectively to reduce risk and create safety.

Coordinating accreditation and other compliance activities will include all of the above as well as:

- helping managers and staff understand the purpose of accreditation and how it is linked to achieving great care (if you can do this, the other tasks get easier)
- working with the governing body and executive to analyse organisational gaps in meeting the standards, plan the approach to fulfilling accreditation and other compliance requirements, and implement recommendations
- ensuring the accreditation standards are linked to and embedded in the strategic quality goals
- setting up and monitoring a system for ensuring the compliance requirements of accreditation are enacted as part of departmental operational plans where possible
- ensuring accreditation documentation requirements are met
- overseeing the organisational responsibilities for organising and coordinating accreditation visits.

So, what's your role in all this? Developing an agreed purpose and framework for your organisation's quality system can assist you to answer this question. It should help you to redefine and shape your quality manager function and role in relation to the overall quality system purpose in a way that emphasises the importance of your contribution and makes the job more interesting and fulfilling. It should also give you more control over your work, give your role a more strategic flavour and achieve a better balance between reactive and proactive tasks. It will not change the harsh and unforgiving environment on planet healthcare, but it should improve your chances of operating effectively within it. But only you can decide to be proactive in your role – no one else can do it for you.

So where to from here? Spend a few minutes completing the following sentences, taking into account what we've discussed throughout this chapter:

- My current purpose as the quality manager in my organisation/service is to [do what] to achieve [what].
- I would like my purpose as quality manager in my organisation to be [do what] to achieve [what].

Are your two completed sentences very different? This should give you a sense of how much change you want to make to your role and possibly reveal whether this is realistic in your current role. Your 'purpose statement' is also the sentence you should be able to trot out to anyone, quickly and clearly, to give them at least a concept of what you're about when you go to work. This is the statement you pull out when you find yourself standing next to the Chair of the Board in the 60 seconds before the meeting starts, and they say, 'and what exactly do you do?' The quality manager role is changing and evolving, and you might find that your answers to these questions reflect this. In fact, with the rise of compliance that we're seeing in the new century, we may see more specialised quality roles created, and the generalist quality manager who covered the whole quality management spectrum from quality control to innovation to transformation may become a thing of the past. You may find yourself having to decide where on this spectrum you want to focus your career and whether that fits with your organisation's needs.

Once you're clear about the role you want to play in your organisation's provision of quality care, the next step is to enact it with savvy and success. To do that, you'll need to understand the unique characteristics of the healthcare landscape, and how to navigate safely and effectively within it. The rest of this book is designed to assist you on this journey.

Headlines: Chapter One

- The quality manager role in health and aged care requires a mix of strategic and operational skills and knowledge and encompasses a wide range of tasks.
- The core responsibility of the quality manager is to help and support their organisation to create a consistently high quality experience for consumers. This requires the development and implementation of an effective quality system and governance supports.
- One approach to clarifying the role, purpose and components of your organisation's quality system is to think of it as a jigsaw, comprising the picture on the box, the pieces and the instructions.
- Staff will be more likely to engage in creating great care if you can clarify and explain the link between their responsibility to create a quality consumer experience and the mechanics of the quality system you're asking them to participate in.
- Make sure your job title is proactive and dynamic – and live it!

References and Further Reading

1. Argyris C (1996) *Actionable Knowledge: Design Causality in the Service of Consequential Theory.* Journal of Applied Behavioral Science, vol. 32 no. 4.

2. Ragush S, McAuliffe J (2005) *The Quality Improvement Toolbox.* Health Quality Council and National Primary Care Development Team, Canada.

3. Covey SR (1989) *The Seven Habits of Highly Effective People.* Simon & Schuster Inc., USA.

Q2 NAVIGATING PLANET HEALTHCARE:
Working effectively in complex systems

'Expansion means complexity, and complexity, decay.'
– C. NORTHCOTE PRESTON

2. NAVIGATING PLANET HEALTHCARE:
Working effectively in complex systems

Whether you know it or not, if you are working in a primary, acute or aged care service, you are working in a complex system. Your success as a quality manager heavily depends on effectively navigating this challenging environment. This chapter explains what complex systems are, how they work and, most importantly, the impact they have on quality managers' ability to do what they do every day.

'Who am I? I am a significant part of your life. I am brilliant but unpredictable, flexible and responsive to change if you manage me in the right way; but if you don't, I can be stubborn. My goals are clear – to me – but may be a mystery to you. You'll have to get to know me before I'll reveal them to you! If we understand each other, we can work together to achieve something good for both of us. I'm not keen on rigid rules and can generally find a way around them if they don't fit with my personality or interfere with achieving my goals. Narrow right/wrong thinking doesn't work with me – I'm into all shades of grey and prefer people who can see the big picture. I'm fairly social, but choose my friends carefully as they are important to me. I am happiest when working with my team and we'll let you know that we're unhappy if something interferes with our team harmony. There's more to me than meets the eye and you'll have to be prepared to get to know me fairly well if you want me to change as I can create all sorts of chaos if you push the wrong buttons. Without my space and social life, I can be moody and irritable and if you work me too hard for too long I may lose the ability to function altogether. But if you recognise that you too are part of me; support me and my team and give me a bit of space, I'll do my best to produce the outputs you want and will even help you to identify and manage unexpected problems. If you're up to the challenge, I'm sure that together we can achieve great things for our consumers.'

I am your healthcare organisation! – a complex system that is dynamic and continuously responding and adapting to its environment, often in unpredictable ways.[1] While healthcare organisations often feel like factory production lines, and we expect them to behave as if they are, in reality they are more like people – if not quite a human being then a 'systems being'. It's alive! It breathes! This has nothing to do with the size or type of your organisation: large, small, rural or metropolitan, acute, primary or aged. They are all complex due to the nature of the work, the way they are constructed and the myriad of technology, processes and people that have to come together to create a well functioning health service. Understanding the concept of complex systems is critical to better understanding and navigating planet healthcare. Getting to know your organisation as a complex system will take a little homework, as it does to get to know a person, but the effort required is worth it in terms of the significant, positive difference it will make to your role.

Imagine that you are still around in a century or two and that you are part of an advance party to set up a health service for a group of human scientists living on a distant planet. The physical environment is harsh and the planet's indigenous life forms, although friendly, have specific customs and laws that you must abide by. How much study would you do to ensure you fully understood this new world before you arrived? What would you need to know to guarantee your survival and achieve your goals in the difficult and challenging surroundings? What would you observe when you were there? How would you learn and improve your ability to operate successfully in this new environment? There's no need

THE CYNEFIN FRAMEWORK: A LEADER'S FRAMEWORK FOR DECISION MAKING.[4]

The Cynefin framework is a sense-making tool for decision making that identifies five types of decision-making contexts in which leaders can find themselves. These are described as five domains: simple, complicated, complex, chaotic and disordered. Decision making in each of the domains involves a different approach:

- in the simple domain, a best practice solution can usually be found
- in the complicated domain, there is often no single obvious solution, but experts when brought together can usually agree on "best practice"
- in the complex domain, an experimental approach is required in which a diversity of opinions is sought, and a high level of interaction and different types of communication between stakeholders are encouraged
- in the chaotic domain, there is little time to explore possible solutions, and quick action is required with an immediate review of the impact
- in the disordered domain, there are competing agendas and disagreement among leaders. Disorder is best dealt with by breaking the issues down into their component parts and assigning each part to the appropriate domain.

for time travel or warp speed to experience this scenario. You already deal with a challenging and harsh environment every day on planet healthcare. Although you are not likely to experience physical challenges, there are many other difficulties to overcome to survive and to achieve your professional and organisational goals. Yet how much preparation do we undertake before taking on a quality role? How much research have you undertaken to help you navigate the laws and customs and behaviours of the beings around you, on whom your success depends?

Quality managers are often too busy 'doing' to observe, study and reflect on their environment. Facing the triple challenge of gaining people's attention, cooperation and effort (in the face of competing priorities and often without formal power) quality professionals need a range of tools and techniques to do their jobs effectively. Understanding how your healthcare organisation and its population ticks is an essential component of any quality manager's toolkit. There are many ways of approaching this and many of you will already be using approaches gleaned from organisational and management theory. Much of the theory on complex systems arises from and overlaps with organisational and management theory, but there are some characteristics of complex systems, discussed in this chapter, that specifically impact on the pursuit of safe, high quality care and services.

Health services are complicated – and complex

No doubt you have often thought of your organisation as complicated. It is! And it may feel as if it's becoming more complicated every day. Healthcare organisations have particular characteristics that make them interesting places to observe and difficult places to change, including:

- politics and perverse incentives. Health is a key political issue and this adds a number of layers of bureaucracy, interest groups and funding issues that challenge the most well-intentioned improvement efforts. With politics comes funding and related incentives that are not always what they seem, such as payment and reward systems that may appear to be good practice (for example, meeting waiting time targets) but which can create a whole lot of unintended side effects, such as unplanned readmission for some patients discharged early as part of the process of meeting the targets
- complex decision making at the point of care. Staff at the bedside and chairside have a significant impact on the care experienced by the consumer, and yet their decision-making processes are often developed in isolation without input from corporate management
- numerous sub cultures. Slice a healthcare organisation vertically or horizontally and you'll find a web of subcultures comprising professional groups, services and departments. These groups

have different ideas about their purpose and role. For example, nurses may think the focus of the service is care; doctors: cure; managers: control; and boards: the community served by the health service. Bringing these groups together to create a shared focus is extremely challenging

- rapid growth and change due to external forces. Healthcare literature claims that new knowledge in healthcare doubles every 5–10 years – faster than any other complex, high-risk industry
- staffing comprised of autonomous experts working in teams. Health professionals are trained to be experts and we expect them to work well in teams and to follow protocols, but also to deviate from protocols and use their professional judgement when necessary to ensure safe care
- innovation without organisational slack. The organisational slack (or sufficient down time) required to achieve true innovation is generally in short supply
- mismatched funding and costs. With limited budgets supporting endless demand, managing healthcare dollars consumes a significant amount of managers' energy and attention.[1,2,3]

These characteristics – which can be seen in all health and aged care services – mean that basic day-to-day operations management can be gruelling, often leaving little time for creating great care. Navigating the multiple challenges of leading and managing within this environment is not for the faint hearted. Fortunately, most people who work in healthcare organisations are courageous, smart, determined and committed to providing quality healthcare services – and take these difficulties in their stride. They enjoy healthcare because it's challenging. Whether they're on the frontline or in the boardroom, healthcare professionals achieve remarkable things in some very testing environments.

Difficult and complicated is one thing. Complex is another. But what is the difference? An example of 'complicated' is sending a rocket to the moon or creating a multi-course dinner for a large group of people. There are many steps and precise calculations to make, but achieve it once and you should be able to follow the same steps to achieve the same results every time.

'Complex' is more like raising a child. You can apply the same rules and follow the same steps in the same order to one child as you did to their sibling but you may still end up with a completely different result. The rules applied to the first child may not apply to the second, because there are so many factors at play that will influence the result. Complex systems are complex because they comprise so many interdependent and interconnecting components. Over time they adapt to different inputs and develop coping strategies to deal with stress and change, just as a human being would. Do you ever look at your organisation and think that you couldn't (wouldn't!) design it to be this complex even if you tried? That is the hallmark of a complex system – they tend not to be designed but rather evolve in response to internal components, relationships, external pressures and input. So even your most elegantly designed change, if developed in isolation and released into a larger system without regard for how the two will fit together, may be unrecognisable to you if you go looking for it a few months later.[5]

A systems' recap

Our complex healthcare organisations are made up of systems that are a collection of processes, which themselves are made up of tasks. Processes have rules, purposes and functions of their own, but are generally part of something bigger. So, a heart may go through all the tasks it has to complete to maintain an optimum beat, but this is of little use unless it is part of the larger cardiovascular system, and this, in turn, is connected to a body.

Likewise, pharmacists may carefully follow the rules and tasks for preparing a prescription, but to be effective this process needs to be part of a system for ensuring the patient gets the medication when needed, and in the right way. A process for client intake may be very efficient but this does not help the client if they can't get an appointment with an appropriate health professional within the desired timeframe. Processes such as streamlined discharge routines may be developed as part of larger systems to facilitate patient flow, but these must be linked to a system of corresponding initiatives across departments if they are to be effective. Otherwise, improved flow in the Emergency Department will cause headaches for the wards, which must have enough beds for all of the streamlined ED patients requiring admission.

Systems in healthcare are usually designed – or evolve – for specific purposes, such as facilitating patient flow, collecting and organising data or managing tasks into a logical order. A collection of processes are brought together and required to connect and interact effectively in order for a goal to be achieved. Processes that don't connect and work towards common goals are not systems – they are just a collection of tasks. Many staff view the quality system as just a collection of tasks because they don't understand the bigger picture of where their monitoring and improvement actions contribute towards achieving better care for consumers. So 'quality' quickly becomes labelled as extra work with no advantage.

Exploring complex systems

Does your heath service sometimes seem to have a mind of its own? Can you do the same things two days running and get slightly – or extremely – different results? Complex systems have a lot more going on than simple systems. They comprise many components and are subject to many internal and external forces. Your organisation has many of the same complex system characteristics as the transport system, where those of you who commute in a city will know that you can leave at the same time each day and not be able to predict your time of arrival. That's because there are multiple factors, many of which are unpredictable, influencing how that system behaves. Processes in complex systems may have little regard for their specifications and just do what they're capable of doing in a certain situation. As every quality manager knows, 'every system is perfectly designed to achieve the results it gets'.[6] Your systems are only as good as they are designed to be within the circumstances they are designed for – and much also depends on how well the system is implemented. Changes in these systems can have ramifications far larger than the original change. For example, a train may be an efficient way to get to work – until it breaks down. The impact on the hundreds of people on that train – and the one behind it – may range from minor irritation, to missing out on an important job interview, to losing money through having pay docked for being late to work. In the bigger picture, a number of businesses will experience lost productivity. A freeway may be the easiest way to get to work until there's an accident between a car and a truck at the busiest point. The freeway's performance now changes. Unless backup systems have been built into the design, the freeway is not designed to work well when there's an accident, and the results reflect that with traffic jams and extended travel times. Within this chaos human behaviour kicks in. Drivers try to find ways around the problem and make things worse for other drivers on secondary roads as they do so. Road rules become secondary considerations to finding a way around the problem.

In the complexity of healthcare, the consumers who entrust their lives to health professionals add a layer of unpredictability, risk and emotion to the mix that other complex, high-risk industries don't have to deal with. These consumers are entering and leaving the system at different points, with different needs, and relying on the myriad of subsystems and processes and the people working within them, to coordinate and produce a safe, effective, person-centred and integrated experience. And as with all complex systems, healthcare organisations themselves are never static; they are constantly changing to respond to stimuli, which makes it even more difficult to create consistently quality experiences for every consumer.

Complex systems are commonly identified by a number of key characteristics, arranged here into eight 'complex systems factors'. These are not intended to cover every aspect of complex systems, but are the things that are handy for quality managers to know to help them drive change and improve quality in this environment. Here are eight complex systems factors:

EIGHT COMPLEX SYSTEMS FACTORS

1. All complex systems have a goal
2. You can't change a complex system without side effects
3. The outputs and outcomes of complex systems are the result of a combination of factors
4. Complex systems can be both flexible and brittle
5. Complex systems can cope well with unexpected events – or not
6. Complex systems operate on relationships and interdependencies
7. Relationships and interdependencies within complex systems function according to unwritten rules
8. Complex systems are policy resistant.

So, let's take a closer look at each of these organisational personality traits.

1. All complex systems have a goal

All systems have a goal, which may be as simple as survival or maintaining the current situation. Be prepared for push back from the system if you interfere with it achieving its goal. Systems enjoy their status quo and strive to maintain it. If you change one part of the system, this will result in resistance from the other parts of the system it is linked to because it means they will have to change as well. If you stick a pin into one part of the system, another part of it might say 'ouch'. The more parts of the system there are and the more possible connections between them, the harder it is to change and the easier it is to create chaos. Sound familiar? [7]

2. You can't change a complex system without side effects and feedback

Systems, like humans, respond to stimuli. Whenever you take action within a system, there will be side effects. These may be positive or negative, depending on your perspective. You have to be able to predict and observe them to be a successful change agent in this environment. In our health services, we logically expect that effect will follow cause. This is production line thinking and is generally not applicable in a circular complex system. Looking for an effect

SYSTEMS MAKE THINGS HAPPEN

We all use systems every day, often without thinking too much about it. Anyone who's ever gone shopping in their work lunchtime and put their car keys in the fridge with their groceries so they won't forget to take them home has developed and implemented a simple but effective 'forcing' system. Forcing systems are all around us: from the ATM on the street to the PC at your desk that both require passwords to do their job. Other systems have more of a guidance function, such as information systems that provide information and advice on drug prescribing, checklists to remind us about key tasks, and protocols that describe the way a process should be carried out. Systems can also be developed as a backup, such as a having a generator available to take over in the case of a power failure. These forcing, guidance and backup systems are increasingly being implemented to improve consumer safety, although they are not foolproof and still require human beings to think and engage with their surroundings, as we'll discuss in Chapter Four.

closely related to a cause, such as an improvement as a result of a change we make can lead us to draw false conclusions about our effectiveness. We recognise these as false conclusions when we can't then replicate the same result in another part of the organisation. Your result may have been due to the natural variation inherent in every system. Or it may have been due to your intervention – but this intervention won't work the same way in another part of the system. Generally speaking, real change in complex systems requires a lot of different parts of the system to be working towards the same change.

Accepting that making changes will elicit side effects is an important part of managing change in complex systems. Because of the complexity, it is hard to predict the effect your change will have and you may find yourself in all sorts of trouble – or causing trouble for others. This is akin to being stuck in a traffic jam. Somewhere in the road system, something changed and you – or others in your organisation – feel the side effects. As you no doubt will have experienced, sometimes the effect of the changes you make to a system may not be proportional to the intervention or improvement that you have made. Cause and effect are uncertain in complex systems. A huge epidemic can be caused by something as small as a virus. Even in mechanical systems you can get a big effect from a small input, like a surge of power when you put your foot on the accelerator of a car, because the system can amplify the effects of the inputs. This has given many a learner driver a fright!

Conversely, sometimes an action has no effect on the system at all because the stimulus is below the system's threshold for change; the change isn't quite enough of a 'big bang', or it targets the wrong part of the system – and therefore nothing happens. So small changes can have large effects while seemingly large changes may have little effect. For example, a major change management program in an organisation may have little impact, while a conversation among friends at a conference could result in one of them implementing a major change. It is difficult to predict where these leverage points might be within the system, but they are often found embedded in the culture, assumptions and relationships upon which the system is built. Systems can also suddenly and unexpectedly change if just the right combination of actions or leverage occurs. Sometimes this is planned, but sometimes a system changes and we don't know why.[1,8,9,10]

3. The outputs and outcomes of complex systems are the result of a combination of factors

Think of the number of interactions that occur within your health service in the course of an hour. Could you count them even if you wanted to? Then add the interactions between your organisation and external services. The mind boggles. And yet, out of this complex web of interactions, relationships and systems, healthcare produces reasonably good care for most consumers most of the time. So how do we move from good care most of the time to great care all of the time in this environment? Complex systems have emergent properties in the same way that personality traits emerge from human beings, or flavour emerges from fruit. The characteristics we want from our complex system – for example, safety – are evident when the system designed to produce them is working as it is supposed to. To understand these systems, therefore, and get out of them what we need, we need to look at them as wholes, rather than as parts. When you deconstruct a hospital system or department system, you won't find the 'safe' characteristic just as you won't find the 'flavour' characteristic by deconstructing an apple. Safety is created from the synthesis of many processes and people inside the organisation, and is also influenced by relationships between the internal and external environment. When you take a complex system apart and analyse it, it loses its properties. In healthcare, our preferred method for finding out what's going on and attempting to solve problems is by breaking down systems and processes into their component parts. But this does not work as well as we might like in a complex system. In systems thinking, the explanation for effects does not lie in single causes, but in the structure of the system and the relationships and interdependencies within it. (This is an important issue to note in relation to creating safety in complex systems, discussed in Chapter Four.) This means that, to make real and lasting changes, you generally need a combination of strategies, rather than a single strategy, which is discussed in Chapter Three.[1,8]

4. Complex systems can be both flexible and brittle

A complex system acts like a web of elastic bands so that when you pull one piece out of position it will stay there only for as long as you exert force on it. When you let go, you may be surprised and annoyed that it springs back to where it was before. (You've probably also experienced the phenomenon of workplace change only lasting as long as it is policed!) In addition, a complex system may or may not be stable. Stable complex systems that have not been subject to a lot of change become more resistant to change as time goes on. All of us have experienced this in organisations, where one service or department has somehow escaped the force of change experienced by other parts of the organisation. When their turn comes, they find change very difficult. In an unstable system, however, pressure to make changes can cause the system to burst like a balloon. If the system is under a lot of pressure routinely, this may only take a small trigger, just as a small crack in a dam can lead to its collapse because of the constant pressure of water behind it. So if you put an unstable system under enough pressure for long enough, it can suddenly disintegrate.

There is also a limit to how big a system can grow before it becomes unwieldy, hard to manage and prone to breaking down. Every system has an optimum size so growing the number of staff or consumers in a system has an impact on the robustness of the system. Unless it is also strengthened and supported, it may give way under the extra strain. Growth is usually presented as a good thing – but without corresponding attention to the systems that support the growth, it can make things worse rather than better. Providing more hospital beds, for example, is routinely promoted as a positive solution to long waiting lists – but this growth can have catastrophic consequences if more staff and facilities are not provided to support the patients in those extra beds.[5,7]

5. Complex systems cope well with unexpected events – or not

Complex systems can be extremely resilient when unexpected or major adverse events occur, as the system will respond to unexpected change and attempt to restore the status quo. However, a complex system that is based on following set rules created by rigid 'straight line' thinking, or one that is under constant pressure to push beyond its capabilities, can also be brittle when it comes to unexpected events. In this context, the 'resilience' of a system is like a plateau upon which the system performs its normal functions. A resilient system sits on a wide plateau and has a lot of space within which it can wander, with elastic safety walls that will bounce it back if it comes near a dangerous cliff edge. As a system becomes more rigid or is put under increasing pressure, its plateau of resilience shrinks and its protective walls shrink and become brittle until the system is teetering on the cliff edge. Loss of resilience in a system can come as a surprise because, caught up in our busy everyday activities, more attention is usually paid to the system's output than to the way the system is operating. A system's flexibility, innovation and responsiveness – the resilience that acts as a safety net when the system is pushed to the limit – is often sacrificed for purposes of short-term productivity and stability. And then, one day, something happens that the system has coped with a thousand times before and instead of bouncing back, it crashes over that cliff edge into the abyss.[7]

If we want to keep our systems in good working order, and achieving what they are designed to achieve, we have to keep an eye on them. We must understand that systems naturally change and erode over time. They drift from their original direction and purpose. Sometimes, this results in systems that evolve to be more effective than the originals. And sometimes they evolve to better meet short-term needs, but in the process they drift towards failure. The people who work in these systems are often aware of the system changing around them – not coping as well as it used to, getting slower, allowing more mistakes. It is important to take these observations on board when you are getting to know a system. Monitoring the width of systems' plateaus and the degree of brittleness of their boundaries, to identify when we are on the verge of pushing them just that little bit too hard, is preferable to waiting for the plunge over the cliff before taking action.[5,7,11]

6. Complex systems operate on relationships and interdependencies

Systems work because people make them work. But to do this, processes in the system are often changed as the system evolves. And then the relationships between the processes have to change to keep the system working. The relationship between different parts of the system determines how the system overall works, so each process change, however minor, can affect the behaviour of the whole. This is an important point! All processes in a system are interdependent and they all interact. The key to change is not to just focus on one process in isolation, but to look at how it relates to the other processes in the system.

Systems can also become self-organising and can generate their own hierarchies of power and influence. These hierarchies may not be the same as those seen on your organisational chart. Each person, wherever they sit in the system, has the power to affect the way the system behaves. Relationships within each subsystem are denser and stronger than relationships between subsystems. For example, there are likely to be more interdependencies and networks up and down a silo in a health service than across and between silos. Interaction within the silos occurs mainly between members of the same professional group: nurses interacting with nurses, and doctors interacting with doctors. These 'tribes' give the people within them an important sense of belonging but it can be hard to break down the walls and build bridges between them.[14]

There are always certain individuals within organisations who can communicate across these professional subcultures – and they are important players in systems change. For example, the pharmacist plays a key role in providing medication advice to many different health professionals, and may therefore have a broader view of the interdependent processes that make up a system and the views of those who work within them. Junior doctors can be important in bridging or brokering between the senior doctors and the nurses. Clerical staff play an important liaison role in providing help to a range of other staff.[1,7,12,13,14,15] These relationships are central to change in complex systems and will be discussed in more detail in the next chapter.

7. Relationships within complex systems function according to unwritten rules

The networks and hierarchies of power and influence that drive complex systems are likely to operate on a range of simple rules or beliefs that dictate how the system works. But don't expect to see these rules listed on a notice board. They are generally unwritten, unstated, and known only to those involved. This is often described as organisational culture. These rules can be derived from the mental models, or maps, of those who work in the system. These maps are deeply ingrained assumptions and generalisations that influence how we understand the world, what we think the rules are and, therefore, how we act within it. An important implication for change in complex systems is that these unwritten rules are generally much more powerful in driving behaviour than any explicit rules imposed through policies and procedures.[1,7]

Mental models can be simple generalisations such as 'people are untrustworthy' or they can be complex theories such as assumptions about why members of a certain professional group act as they do. Often we are not consciously aware of our mental models or the influence they have on our behaviour. For example, believing that certain people are untrustworthy (whether or not they are untrustworthy in reality) would cause us to act differently towards them from the way we would if we believed they were trustworthy. Mental models are powerful in affecting what we do because they affect what we see. The problems with mental models lie not in whether they are right or wrong, but in the fact that they are usually over-simplifications. They are also usually operating at a subconscious level, so are hard to deal with. Failure to appreciate and identify the mental models at work in any system can affect our ability to understand why the system works the way it does and therefore our ability to effect change in that system.[8,9]

8. Complex systems are policy resistant

Complex systems do not necessarily operate according to the policies of the organisation. On the contrary, complex systems can be exceedingly policy resistant. This resistance particularly arises when an introduced change threatens the goal of the system or when policies are implemented that are not based on the reality and unwritten rules of those having to implement them. We've all experienced policies developed on the run, or even painstakingly over a long period, that have only been partially adhered to by those they were designed for. If there is too great a mismatch between the policy requirements and the way that things really get done or the goals of the system, the policy will generally fail. At worst, people will disregard it; at best, they will work around it to meet their goals of getting their work done in the most effective, efficient and easiest way – a way that has probably been crafted over time and is protected by and embedded in the way the system operates and the unwritten beliefs of those who work within it. The way in which policy is implemented can also influence the degree to which it is enacted as intended. Poor implementation opens up a policy to all sorts of change and interpretation by those using it. This may drive policy enactment to drift away from the original intention.

Policy resistance is not necessarily the result of deliberate scheming to subvert authority, although this can also exist in any organisation. In the context of complex systems, it is the way human beings survive and thrive in demanding, high-risk environments, particularly when those human beings are educated and capable of deciding on calculated risk. Humans are more likely to cause chaos and unpredictability than stability and calm. If policies are not seen to be useful in helping the system run smoothly, or if they work against the system rather than with it, this can pull the system in different directions and reduce its effectiveness as people try to find new ways of making things work and the system drifts away from its original intention, functioning or robustness. Similarly, new technology is often heralded as the solution to efficiency, safety and quality problems, but unless it is designed to fit the environment and is well implemented, it may cause more problems than it solves.[15]

It is easy to see the futility of imposing a new policy, rule or technology on a system that no longer works according to the original policies that created it, without first finding out what has changed on the ground. The trick is to find a way to meet the goals of the participants in the system (usually to get the work done in the easiest and fastest way with an acceptable result) while lifting the overall system performance and meeting the improvement goals. People are more likely to change their individual or group goals if they feel the overall direction of the system is moving towards goals they believe will deliver measurable good, without introducing unnecessary or ineffective steps into their process.[7,13]

Complex systems and the quality manager

So, it appears that our health services are not as logical and machine-like as we would like. As we saw in the 'Who am I?' at the beginning of this chapter, your health service behaves more like a slightly eccentric older relative than an organised collection of infrastructure and people. Your job as a quality manager is to get to know this 'systems being' – its personality, motives and likes and dislikes. No one can ever develop a purely objective view of a system – there are too many components and unwritten rules involved for that to be possible.[5] Most people working within systems can generally only understand their process and perhaps one or two other processes that theirs connects to. But effective change and improvement in a system requires a quality manager to develop the most complete picture possible of how the system works, its relationships, unwritten rules and resilience.

No doubt you are starting to see some of the implications of our rule-based approaches for safety and quality in complex systems. The following chapters will explore strategies for change and for leading and creating high-quality care and services in this environment. We will examine how to plan your approach to creating great quality care so that it complements the way complex systems behave and gives you the best chance of achieving your quality goals.

Headlines: Chapter Two

- Healthcare organisations are complex systems, and behave more like human beings than factories.
- Complex systems demonstrate a number of characteristics, or personality traits, and to be effective in this environment it is important to understand and work with these. Achieving consistent responses and behaviours within this environment is challenging.
- Change in complex systems relies on a combination of factors; there is seldom a simple cause and effect relationship.
- Complex systems can be both flexible and brittle, depending on how much pressure they are under and how much resilience has been built into their operations.
- Complex systems run on relationships and unwritten rules and can resist the imposition of policies and changes that work against these relationships and rules.
- Complex systems are not static. They evolve and can drift from their original design and intention due to the variety of forces on them.

References and Further Reading

1. O'Connor J, McDermott I (1997) *The Art of Systems Thinking*. Harper Collins Publishers, UK

2. Glouberman S & Mintzberg H (2001) *Managing the Care of Health and the Cure of Disease*. Health Care Management Review, Winter, pp. 56–69

3. Boaden R, Harvey G, Moxham C and Proudlove L (2007) *QI: Theory and Practice in Healthcare*. University of Manchester Business School, UK

4. Snowdon DJ, Boone ME (2007) A Leader's Framework for Decision Making. *Harvard Business Review*, vol. 85, no.11, pp. 68–76

5. Dekker S (2011) *Drift Into Failure - From Hunting Broken Components to Understanding Complex Systems*. Ashgate Publishing Company, UK

6. Berwick D (2000) *Institute of Medicine 2000 Annual Meeting*. (Also attributed to Paul Batalden and W. Edwards Deming). www.iom.edu/ObjectFile/Master/7/695/berwickppt (Accessed November 2010)

7. Meadows DH (2008) *Thinking in Systems – A Primer*. Sustainability Institute, USA

8. Plsek P, Greenhalgh T (2001) The challenge of complexity in healthcare. *BMJ*, vol. 323, September

9. Senge PM (1990) *The Fifth Discipline – The Art and Practice of the Learning Organisation*. Century Business, UK

10. Gladwell M (2002) *The Tipping Point*. Backbay Books, USA

11. Dekker S (2006) *The Field Guide to Understanding Human Error*. Ashgate Publishing Company, UK

12. Duck JD (1996) *Managing Change – The Art of Balancing*. Harvard Business Review on Change, Paperback Series, USA

13. Mackay H (2010) *What Makes Us Tick? The Ten Desires that Drive Us*. Hachette Publishing, Australia

14. Braithwaite J, Runciman WB, Merry AF (2009) Towards Safer, Better Healthcare: Harnessing the Natural Properties of Complex Socio-Technical Systems. *Quality and Safety in Healthcare*, vol.18, pp. 37–41

15. Westbrook JI, Braithwaite J, Georgiou A, Ampt A, Creswick N, Coiera E, Iedema R (2007) Multimethod Evaluation of Information and Communication Technologies in Health in the Context of Wicked Problems and Sociotechnical Theory. *J Am Med Inform Assoc*. Nov–Dec; vol. 14, no.6, pp.746–755

Q3 THE RULES OF THE GAME:
Change in complex systems

'There is nothing more difficult to arrange, more doubtful of success and more dangerous to carry through than initiating changes in a state's constitution.'
– **Niccolo Machiavelli**

3. THE RULES OF THE GAME:
Change in complex systems

The ability to change systems and behaviours is central to your success as a quality manager. You can't improve if you can't change – it's that simple. Yet change, particularly in complex systems, is challenging and requires a specific set of skills. This chapter describes a framework to guide you on your journey of change and improvement in healthcare. Chapter Two discussed thinking of your organisation as a person, rather than as a machine, and explored some complex systems rules and the importance of understanding these to work effectively as a quality manager. That discussion laid the groundwork for a systems approach to change, and this chapter aims to fit you out with a complex systems change toolkit that will support and drive your change and improvement efforts.

Imagine this: you win a holiday, but you don't want to go on your own. You need to find someone to go with you at short notice. The person you would like to go with you feels that they may enjoy it, but they are particularly busy at work and they can think of 101 other reasons why they can't go with you. What would you do to persuade them to come on the journey with you?

- Emphasise how much they need this trip – and how much you'd like them to go with you?
- Provide a rich and tantalising picture of the destination of your journey?
- Find out exactly what their interests are and ensure that these are worked into the itinerary?
- Explain clearly how you will get there and what this will involve?
- Identify the barriers to them participating and help them find solutions?
- Give them time to get used to the idea, and come back to them for a response?

You may do one or all of these, but it is likely that the more of these strategies you employ, the greater your chances of persuading them to join you. If you know the person well enough, you will know exactly which strategy to use! Organisational change is also a journey.

What's the issue with change?

People working in organisations are not just passive recipients of change and innovation. They may enjoy a shake-up, or they may need to be persuaded to engage in it. They may worry about it, complain about it, and try to improve it, exactly as they would with any change in their lives. Because our complex healthcare systems are populated by people and not machines, change and innovation implementation is never as clean cut as we would like and is more likely to be often messy, non-linear and involve setback and resistance.[1] As you will be well aware, change is a challenge and one that is central to the quality manager's role. You can't avoid it if you want to be effective, but you can better understand how to manage it. It's not a lack of guidance or ideas that stops us from effecting successful and sustainable change. There appears to be an almost infinite number of change models and tools available. Despite this, we make a lot of mistakes. Part of the problem, in my experience, is that we are optimistic creatures who expect, or hope, that change will be relatively easy – and then get frustrated when it's hard or doesn't work out the way we thought it would. There seem to be as many mistakes to be made with change as there are change models to help us do it right! We may approach change as if a top-down approach of changing policies,

ORIGINS AND DESTINATIONS

The concept of origin and destination can be tricky to nail down, so let's consider an example. The goal of most sporting teams is probably to win a premiership. But their plans to achieve this will be different, depending on where they are starting the season. If the team that finished last year on the bottom of the ladder has an identical plan to the team that finished on top, one of those teams does not have the right plan! The objectives, timelines and strategies will differ between the teams, depending on a number of factors, such as how they performed last year, the skills and experience of their players, the quality of their coach and their financial situation.

procedures and rules will also change behaviours. We under-invest in preparation and planning. We apply changes that are a poor fit for the environment because we don't first develop an understanding of how the system works before we try to change it. We pay for these mistakes at the front end of change with lots of backend work: rehashing and fixing changes that don't 'take' the first time or are half-heartedly adopted, thus not fulfilling their potential; or abandoning the change altogether.

A scan of the extensive literature around the subject of change and innovation makes it abundantly clear that making change requires making plans – good plans – as well as taking a number of other key steps that are almost universally recommended. These 'complex systems change basics', common to most approaches, are set out here as a guide to point you in a positive direction when contemplating change in a healthcare organisation. Before looking at the change basics, let's do a quick stock take of your current approach to change using this list of common organisational change errors:

Error 1: Not establishing a great enough sense of urgency. That is, not having a good enough reason for the change, or not clearly identifying and explaining the problem that needs to be solved

Error 2: Not creating a powerful enough guiding coalition. Not involving the influential people in the system as well as the powerful people

Error 3: Lacking a vision. A vision is a picture of the future that is relatively easy to communicate, helps clarify the direction in which the system needs to move and appeals to staff because it clearly indicates an improvement for them and/or for patients

Error 4: Under-communicating the vision by a factor of 10

Error 5: Not identifying and removing obstacles to the new vision

Error 6: Not systematically planning for and creating short-term wins

Error 7: Declaring victory too soon

Error 8: Not anchoring changes in the corporation's culture. This step involves clearly demonstrating the connections between the changes made by the people involved and the improvement gained.[2]

By now you may be thinking that a career change looks like a good option! But when executed skilfully, achieving a significant, lasting change that results in a clear improvement for consumers and/or staff is one of the most satisfying things you can do in your professional life. Neither does it hurt your career advancement and credibility. And when you work with the rules of complex systems, you might find that change becomes a little easier than in the past, and becomes an interesting, and even intriguing, challenge for your professional skills.

Having identified some of your opportunities for improving your approach to change, let's have a look at the 'complex systems change basics' for some hints and tips on developing your complex systems change toolkit.

The seven basics of change in complex systems

There are a number of essential steps for carrying out successful change in a complex healthcare environment. Here, they have been synthesised into seven key elements for a guide to change. Each one will be explored in detail with tips on how they can be applied in a healthcare organisation. The majority of this discussion focuses on how to develop a successful change plan, as that is the lynch pin to making any change, and is often the skipped step in healthcare.

THE SEVEN COMPLEX CHANGE BASICS

1. Create the need for change
2. Gather your preplanning intelligence and create a mud map of the current situation
3. Develop the vision for change into SMART goals
4. Develop a change plan that includes both people and process change strategies
5. Get the project roles and governance right
6. Test the change with short cycle pilots
7. Reinforce, embed and spread the change

Let's look at these change basics in detail.

1. Create the need for change and develop a rich picture of how the change will be better than the status quo

One of the most critical preconditions for change is the development of a shared vision, based on dissatisfaction with the current situation. By 'vision' I don't mean the organisation's vision and mission statement, I mean the development of the rich picture of how things will look after the change. How will things work differently day to day? What problems will this solve? How will things be better for consumers and staff? The more people who share the development of this vision and see the benefits for themselves in it, the easier it will be to get the change off the ground. The value of having a destination for your 'change journey' is closely followed by the importance of having an origin; that is, knowing exactly where you're starting and who and what you're starting with. Clarifying the origin and destination is the first step to mapping your change journey.[3,4]

People need to understand where the change will take them and their role in it, and be able to see that their investment in the journey will be worth it. A lack of understanding can swiftly relegate your idea for change to the too hard basket. Change should be challenged; testing and discussion acts as a safety net for the potential damaging effects of inappropriate change. In healthcare we have the advantage of the majority of change participants being interested in improving things for consumers, so this always makes a good general basis for your destination – but, where possible, focus on change that solves a specific problem or makes things faster and easier. Accept that there will be a creative tension between the destination, or the vision for how things will be different as a result of the change, and the current reality. Just stating that we would like things to be different from the way they are immediately creates a different energy in the system. This can lead to positive feelings for those who are enthusiastic about change, and negative feelings for those who would like

> **TOP TIP**
> **SPOTTING THE MENTAL MAPS**
>
> The words 'ought', 'should', 'have to' and 'must', when used by staff involved in the change, are your keys to understanding the current situation. They indicate the strong possibility that an unspoken system rule and belief underpins what they are saying and may be anchoring them to the current situation. Even replacing these words with 'could' may assist in a more constructive conversation. Any other absolute words at this point such as 'all', 'every', 'never', 'always' and 'no one' also indicate simple rules and assumptions underlying the attitudes of those involved, and act as alerts to barriers to achieving your change goal. Tease out and name these assumptions and models, as they can drive or hinder your change. Which ones must be kept? Which are old habits that even the system participants would agree have outlived their usefulness?[6]

things to stay the same. That is why it is important that the vision be as detailed as possible, so it includes how the day-to-day actions of each of the participants will change. This helps allay fears of the unknown and identify potential problems before they turn into obstacles.[3]

2. Gather your preplanning intelligence and create a mud map of the current situation

In a complex system you need to understand what drives current processes before you can achieve a change in outcomes. So dust off your binoculars and prepare to do a little field work. Observe the humans in their natural systems environment. This may be the most important of all the 'change basics' steps – and one of the least practised. With the goal of determining organisational fit and readiness for change, you can look for systems factors such as:

- the degree to which the system participants perceive the change as beneficial
- who and what drives the current system
- the key relationships between processes and people
- the degree of fit between the goals of the system and the goals of the change
- the timing and context of the change. What else is changing or happening in this system?
- the perception of the need for change
- personal attitudes towards change generally, and past experiences with change in the organisation
- the social and values anchors that are important to the change targets and that maintain the status quo. Which of these are non-negotiable?
- aspects of the current situation that the change targets don't like. Can these be eliminated or improved as part of the change?
- driving and restraining forces for change and the degree to which it looks like the drivers outweigh the restraints.[5]

This should help you build an informative picture of the current situation. What has to change to achieve your vision? Work policies and practices? Physical surrounds? Emotional ties? Cultural norms? The context of the change will also influence where people enter the continuum of engagement, and how they are likely to travel along it, as seen in Figure 1.

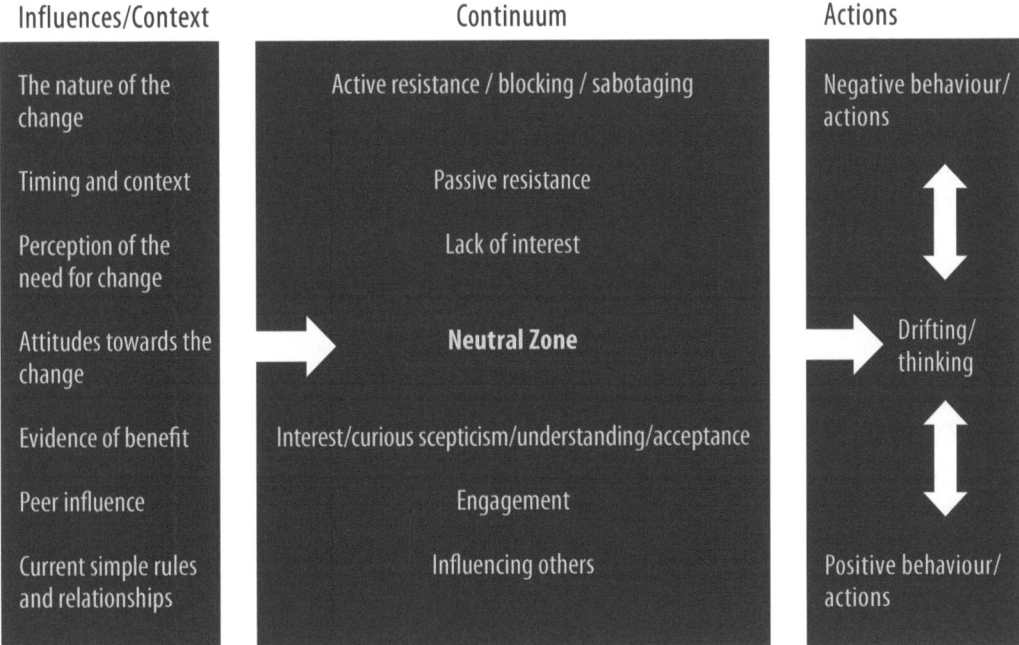

Figure 1: Pathways for moving through and around a change process [2,3,4,5,6,17]

Of course many people do not logically flow through this continuum in one direction from negative to positive behaviours. If only! They can get stuck, go backwards and dig in at a particular point. They are likely to have a period of drifting at some point too. Much depends on where they enter the continuum and on the influences and context at play when you commence the change journey with them. This is why your initial observation and mud map are so important, and where your knowledge and skill as a change agent comes into play as you lead from the front and nudge from the back, and guide the change in such a way that people will move towards the positive end of behaviour. The rest of this chapter discusses your role in supporting people through this journey.

It is often the beliefs of the people in the system that are the most critical leverage points because beliefs are often what sustains a system.[6] As discussed in Chapter Two, many beliefs arise out of the mental models and unwritten rules that underpin the way the system works, but some will arise out of traditional policies and procedures that may or may not be useful. Directly challenging these beliefs as outdated or no longer useful is likely to lead to them being defended vigorously, and you may lose the buy-in of your change targets before you even get started.[7]

Using empathy

Empathy is a powerful yet under-utilised change technique. It can assist with staff engagement in change, and enhance the change's sustainability and spread. Using empathy requires you to identify staff who need to change their thinking and behaviour in order to effect the required change. You will need to understand their current situation and perspective, and engage with their agenda before you ask them to engage with yours. So, ask those involved: 'what will stop us achieving this goal?' 'What is stopping us from moving to where we want to be?' 'Can we find a common goal in this change that helps both of us achieve something?'

EXAMPLES OF UNWRITTEN RULES AND SYSTEM GOALS AND THEIR FLOW ON EFFECTS

Unwritten rule/System goal	Flow on effects
No patients can be discharged from Ward X without the NUM's OK	Delays in discharges and bed block contribute to long waiting lists and waiting times in the Emergency Department
The staff in Clinic Y always have lunch together	Long waiting times for consumers arriving for appointments around lunchtime lead to complaints, and the afternoon staff have to stay late to catch up on the backlog, and claim overtime
Health professionals should make all important decisions about clients' care and treatment regimes in the ABC Community Health Service	Ineffective implementation of client participation policy; limited opportunity for clients to make choices about their care; reduced client understanding of and commitment to treatment regime; complaints about poor communication
The staff can have a longer morning tea break and always finish on time if residents are showered before breakfast in the Sunrise Aged Care Facility	Residents are woken early and deal with rushed and stressed staff leading to a number of falls and incidents related to showering

These unwritten rules and their implications are probably not the result of any particular decision, but have arisen from small changes over time which have evolved to have a big impact. This is classic complex system behaviour. The processes in each of these services are likely to be organised to achieve these goals and fit with these unwritten rules than with the aim of running an effective and efficient service. And not even those working in these areas may realise that this is how the situation has evolved.

Imagine you are the quality manager leading improvement projects to reduce the bed block in Ward X, improve waiting times and finishing times in Clinic Y, implement a client participation policy in the ABC Community Health Service, or change the showering times in the Sunrise Aged Care facility. Change strategies that don't address these unwritten current system anchors are unlikely to shift the status quo very far. The plan for change must be rooted in the way the current system really works, rather than how it should work or how we would like it to work.

This observation and interaction should also give you valuable insight into the relationships and power bases operating in the system you wish to change. These relationships will also include relationships between staff and consumers, who are all part of the complex systems relationships web. Observing these will tell you a lot about the culture and unspoken norms of a department or service. All staff groups, depending on the change, have the potential to drive or sabotage the change either actively or passively. How many changes in policy and process have disappeared without trace because there was not enough preparation of the ground before the change seeds were sown? Managers and team leaders deserve your particular attention. They often hold more power and influence than their titles suggest, and their attitudes and behaviours strongly influence the way their staff work and interrelate. They are also likely to be the key implementers of your proposed change – so your relationship with them is critical. They require your support in times of change – and you require theirs.[8,9]

It is also useful to look beyond the immediate staff group that will be impacted by the change. There are very few changes in the complex web of a healthcare organisation that can be implemented by just focusing on one group. Clinical staff are reliant on administrative staff, who are reliant on the support of IT staff, who are reliant on managers for hardware and software decisions, and on it goes. As part of your observation, look for the gaps in communication between these tribes, the way in which they describe each other, the lack or presence of trust. This will tell you a lot about how they operate and about potential pitfalls for your proposed change.[10] Identify and cultivate the messengers: people who work across professional clusters and networks, such as administrative and allied health staff. These staff are valuable links between otherwise insular groups.[10, 11]

Understanding and working with the current culture is critical to success – even if that culture is the very thing you want to change. Use your mud map of the current situation to assess, identify and build on what currently works. 'Appreciative inquiry' is a process of identifying something that works consistently well within a system and finding out how this happens. Have you ever performed a root cause analysis on something that works to find out why it works well? This makes a nice change from looking at things that don't work well, which is a more common approach in healthcare. Tools such as process mapping, direct observation and conversations with the various players are useful here to tease out the positive characteristics of the current system that will help anchor the changed system. Not only will this help inform your preplanning, but you will be laying a foundation for buy in.[4]

3. Develop the vision into SMART, attractor goals that align with the system goals and are anchored in reality

Complex systems work towards attractors. These are like magnets that pull the system in a certain direction. Building attractors into your change goals will help move people towards achieving your change and lessen the amount you have to push! Attractors that engage systems participants can be difficult to identify, however, as in a complex system they are not always obvious, nor predictable, and change efforts based on the wrong attractors often fail. Change agents can make the mistake of assuming that because they want something, everyone else must want it too. We think that the things that are attractors for us are attractors for everybody. But remember the 'complex systems factors' about complex systems and sub-systems having minds of their own and their own goals? This is where developing your mud map of the current system's rules and goals before introducing your change (possibly with all the finesse of a freight train) is time well spent. Attractors are further discussed in Chapter Six in the discussion on leadership and influence.

A decision to go with a change is ultimately made by individuals in a complex system according to their personal mental models about such things as the benefits and risks associated with the change. As you will have experienced, even when those with positional power within a hierarchy believe that they can implement change, individuals in the system retain their own right to decide for themselves how they will react. In a complex system such as a healthcare organisation, where individuals have significant freedom to act autonomously, coercive strategies for implementing change are of limited value. Successful change is not so much about overcoming resistance (pushing people) as it is about understanding and working with the natural attractor patterns in the system (having them drawn towards something).

In healthcare, the current goals and attractors of the system you are trying to change may include things such as sustaining a professional group's autonomy and enhancing its image with patients. Doctors, in particular, may reject what they see as rigid and bureaucratic approaches that they perceive are not helpful within the complexity of healthcare. As difficult as it may be at times, we know that gaining medical buy in is critical to change associated with safety and quality. Medical staff practices and attitudes strongly influence the quality of care delivered in health services. The relationships and interdependencies that they have with others in the complex system may well be critical to the success of your change. Building relationships with medical staff is essential to gaining their engagement in change. One of the reasons for this is that they often do not have the same relationship with your organisation that you do and therefore view organisational change from a completely different perspective. Many doctors want the health service to efficiently support them to look after their patients – and that's it. Organisational processes, hierarchies and initiatives may be of little interest and therefore are not good attractors. Even managers with a medical background maintain a strong connection to their clinician role and tend to have a weaker affiliation with organisational goals than other clinician managers. As with any group, it's important to find out what motivates them, what it is about a change that could be beneficial to them and engage them in building the rich picture of what you want to achieve through implementing change.[13]

If the goals and objectives of your change are not seen to be helping the participants in a system achieve their goals, or are not drawing them towards new goals, your change efforts may struggle to gain traction. So identify and attach some magnets to your change goals. For example, balancing patient care, organisational interests and doctors' needs has been found to cause job related stress and reduced job satisfaction and performance for many medical managers.[10,11] Quality managers who assist and support medical managers to juggle their hats are well placed to develop collaborative relationships that will support change.

Setting clear goals

People are attracted to ideas they feel they are involved in generating. Involving the staff affected in developing the goals for change can help create both buy-in, and the goal clarity that people need before deciding if and how they will participate. Goal clarity appears to be another problem area in creating change. If you aim at nothing in particular – or something ambiguous – that's probably what you'll hit. And yet it is not uncommon to see changes and improvements implemented with only a vague idea of what they will achieve and no clear objectives against which to measure success. The goals for your change must be SMART: specific, measurable, achievable, realistic and time-bound. Goals are about turning your vision into something achievable. Goals are not tasks; goals describe the desired future achievement. A SMART goal will encompass: How well? By when? How will we know? These are then broken down into objectives and the key tasks or stepping stones that have to be traversed, depending on where you're starting from, to achieve the final goal. One of the most valuable skills a quality manager can offer an organisation is the development of clear and measurable goals, and this is discussed in more detail when we look at planning for quality in Chapter Six.

4. Develop a change plan that includes both people and process change strategies

When developing your action plan for change, remember that people, relationships and processes are vital elements to effecting change in a complex environment. If you've developed your mud map of the system you want to change, you'll have a good idea of how the people and processes in the current system work together to achieve the current results. You'll know that each part of the system cannot be analysed or changed in isolation, but only in relationship to the other parts and processes that create the whole, and that change in one part of the system will affect the other interdependent parts of the system. And, ideally, you will have identified the people in the system who are more open to change than others.[3]

No matter what the change, there will be people who love trying different things. These people are the innovators and early adopters who will be happy to be involved. They generally comprise about 20 per cent of your population. Then there are the 'early and late majority' making up about 60 per cent of the population. Finally, there is the 'laggard' 20 per cent who don't much enjoy change – even when it's something they want![4] As tempting as it is to label, try to keep an open mind about the 'laggards'. Someone who is a 'laggard' on one new idea may be an early adopter of a different idea, depending on where they sit in the organisation and the impact of the change on them, their relationships and mental maps at the time. The message across the change literature is that if you engage 20 per cent of your target population, the majority will eventually follow if they see the first 20 per cent having a positive experience. Focus your attention on the first 20 per cent rather than feeling the need to convert those less enthusiastic. You can waste a lot of time and energy on converting and find yourself burnt out – a quality manager occupational hazard.

Try to supply some magnets to draw the first 20 per cent and second 60 per cent of people towards your proposed change, rather than threatening them with the negatives of not being involved. Laggards will require a different, long-term strategy. Some in the laggards category will be quite comfortable with being told what to do. In fact, this may be their preferred style of engaging, particularly if they have a natural tendency to follow directions and rules.[5] The observation of and engagement with the key players as part of your planning and preparation for the change should assist you to identify who fits into which category and, therefore, which strategy is required. And in the end, despite your best efforts, different personality types will also respond differently to change and require varied approaches to be engaged. Understanding this aspect of change is useful knowledge for quality managers to have in their quality toolkit, and discussed in Chapter Six.

Behaviour change is half the story

Many of the change initiatives I've observed in health and aged care organisations appear to be based on a set of activities that is so consistent I've named it the PACEM change model: policy, awareness, communication, education and meetings. Whilst each of these components is useful within a comprehensive change plan, they do not comprise a powerful strategy. PACEM largely relies on people to choose to alter their behaviour, and by itself this is a weak strategy for change. A comprehensive approach is required, comprising activities to guide behaviour change and support it with modifications to the systems that underpin practice, as seen in Table 1.

Operational dimensions of change	People dimensions of change
1. Business need for change identified	1. Awareness of the need for change
2. Project is defined	2. Desire to participate and support the change
3. Business solution is defined	3. Knowledge of and input into how to change
4. New policy and systems are developed	4. Ability and capacity to implement the change
5. Solution is implemented and evaluated	5. Support to embed the change and monitor effects

Table 1: Operational and People Dimensions of Change[16]

CHANGE IS ABOUT HABITS

When we're asking people to behave differently, essentially we're asking them to change their habits and we all know how difficult that can be. If you want cyclists to take a detour because their usual path is being re-surfaced, you can ask or tell them to do it, but awareness – and even education – alone won't cut it. Even if they remember to take the alternative route the first time, they are likely to revert to old habits fairly quickly unless you provide other supports and incentives for them to continue their changed behaviour. It's going to be easier for them to change their behaviour – and you are going to achieve more compliance with the change – if the signage is clear, the other path is closed off and the alternative path will get them to their destination just as easily - if not easier! And if they were the ones that decided in the first place that they wanted their path re-surfaced, they are going to *want* to use the detour, as it is part of achieving their goal. Success!

The process change plan will describe concrete steps and timelines, the ways in which these will be tracked and reported, who needs to do what when and some quick initial wins to get things rolling. Usually the process part of change involves new policy, procedures, software, equipment or location. This is the relatively easy part compared to addressing the cultures and behaviour that you want to change, but both are important; systems need to change to support new ways of doing things and people will not suddenly behave differently without being offered new drivers, supports or incentives for doing so.

Your strategies for change will be based on your mud map of the current situation, particularly the anchors keeping the current situation in place, and represent the 'flight plan' for how to get to your goals from where you are. Where possible, learn from others who have introduced the same or similar changes, whilst adapting their strategies to your own environment. There is no guarantee that strategies that have been successful elsewhere will work as well in your organisation due to the many layers of interactions that make your system unique. Change, transformation and improvement cannot be delivered through the adoption of an imported recipe or formula without adapting it to the current environment (that is what distinguishes complex systems from complicated systems, as we saw in Chapter Two).[5] This is akin to the team at the bottom of the ladder adopting the same plan to win a premiership as a team in the top three – without any alteration to take into account their different cultures, players, contexts and relative positions.

If you introduce a new procedure, software system, data collection or form on a Monday morning without investing in preparing and equipping the people who will use the innovation, it is unlikely to be automatically adopted. The process may have changed, but the people haven't – they are the same as they were on Friday afternoon. Process change is not the same as people change. Process change is transactional and concrete. People change is transitional and involves a psychological process to come to terms with a new situation and change behaviour to enable the new situation to occur. Unless transition is well managed, change will not work and things can get stuck. Even with obviously positive changes, there are transitions that begin with having to let go of something and there will be push back because your change adds to the staff 'to do' list and new behaviours take longer, both of which result in lost time. At worst, staff are losing something they are strongly wedded to and may actively resist or get stuck in a neutral zone where they are aware of the change but not actively engaged – a sort of change no man's land. The failure to identify and be ready for the endings and losses that are the consequences of change causes many of the problems that organisations encounter when attempting change, particularly in complex environments where the endings, the transitions and the people change may be difficult to pinpoint.[17]

Levers for behavioural change

As we have already discussed, within a complex system, changing the rules does not always change behaviours. People behave as they do for many reasons that may have little to do with organisational policies. There is no lack of material available on people change as a subset of change more generally. Rather than attempting to rehash the breadth of this, let's have a look at the news headlines about motivating people to work with you, rather than against you.

First, back to your mud map of the current situation. Where are the levers for behavioural change in this system? Common drivers for the behaviour of people in healthcare organisations include:

- perceived personal benefit
- opportunities to make things better for patients and staff
- habit
- whatever makes work easier and faster
- doing things they are good at and that they have some control over
- the way people perceive they are measured and rewarded
- what their manager wants
- opportunities to learn and develop
- role clarity and perception of support to enact their role – now and when changed
- local and organisational culture.[18]

As you can see, these drivers are a mix of benefit to the individual, the group and the environment they inhabit. Identifying tradeoffs and benefits, and building these into your change plan, is a significant part of effecting people change. You need them to change, but what can you change for them in exchange? For example, will changing the shift handover system result in clinicians spending less time on the phone answering questions from junior clinicians uncertain of a patient's care plan? Will the boss view the staff engaged in the change more favourably? Always come armed with your background information on what problems the change might solve – and try to make the change about a real problem for the staff involved, not just something you think might be a problem or is a problem for you.

It can be harder to find benefits for some staff groups than others, of course. Health professionals have considerable autonomy and discretion as their work involves the application of specialist knowledge and expertise to complex problems, and they are likely to be supportive of change that maintains this.[19] They are generally loyal to their profession and committed to their clients and seek quality work based on internalised values, beliefs and aspirations developed through their work and experience, rather than being based on formal bureaucratic controls.[20] Clinical staff, in particular, often seek data-based evidence before engaging in change, and respond to audits and feedback, rewards for change, and triggers and reminders, all of which help them change their behaviour. So yes, they are a challenging group at times, but we can't make positive changes at point of care without them! I often hear quality managers complain that they can't 'get' staff – particularly doctors – involved in change. This betrays a strong quality manager mental model! It's likely that the more people feel they are being forced to do something the faster they will retreat. Changing this language will help change the underlying attitude that goes with it.

Health professionals such as doctors work largely autonomously, attached to informal networks within the organisation. These informal networks respond poorly or not at all to conventional management or control measures and generally exert a powerful influence on how things really work and where the power sits behind the formal organisational charts.

So what are some of the ways to approach change in this context? Triggers for change within clinical networks include persuasive individuals, memorable messages and peer involvement that fit with their mental models of how things should work. Clinicians are more likely to respond to change where respected clinical leaders are involved in the design of the change, and where the change makes it easier to do the right thing and harder to do the wrong thing. The messages regarding the change need to be embedded in the environment so that they deliver cues and reminders. This can include forcing functions built into IT systems and peer group regulation to reinforce the new behaviour. Clinicians work best when they gather in groupings of their own interest and preference, are empowered rather than directed, and influenced by their peers rather than controlled by others. They are likely to become more involved in promoting safer and better care if invited, rather than compelled, and encouraged to participate in voluntary collaborations with their fellow clinicians. One of the simplest approaches to engaging health professionals in change is to ask them for advice – they are experts, after all – and most will enjoy engaging in a process that recognises and uses their expertise, and where their input results in action that is good for their consumers – and/or themselves.[12]

FIVE ACTIONS FOR ENGAGING DOCTORS IN CHANGE[21]

1. Set the scene
- invest in your relationship, nourish professional networks and structures
- listen and attend to their complaints, be empathic
- say what you mean and do what you say
- be prepared to give and take.

2. Make the case
- why are we doing it?
- who will benefit?
- what is the time/aggravation cost?
- is it clinical or bureaucratic?

3. Find a leader
- find a credible advocate amongst the clinicians who will help them embrace the change.

4. Be flexible
- be prepared to modify the change and respond to reasonable requests, keep them informed, acknowledge the problems.

5. Reinforce the message
- did it work?
- congratulate and thank those involved – whether it worked or not, they gave you their time and energy!

It is important to remember that all staff feel that they are doing their best for each patient. The way you frame your request for change should not suggest otherwise, so avoid the high moral ground and 'we have to do it for accreditation' lines. These approaches are unlikely to act as magnets for staff commitment. Change for improvement should always be presented as something that helps good practitioners achieve even more. Doctors in particular are primarily interested in achieving stability and predictability of clinical outcomes and may perceive any change as posing a threat to this focus.[21] They may maintain that their only desired benefit of change is improved patient outcomes and these, of course, are likely to take some time to become apparent after the initial change.

So what are some of the short-term benefits of change, or magnets, you can use to get people's attention? Is it that the change can form part of an action research project and that you can assist them to write it up for a journal or a conference paper? Will it help them access more useful data about their clinical outcomes? Does it increase their expert status and make them more influential with their peers? Does it count as professional development points for their college or professional association? Can a process be made more efficient and simpler as part of the change? Can you save them time and money?[12]

Help people to change old habits and learn new ones

The issue of habit is one not often considered when we are proposing a change. And yet change projects often require a change in habit, which takes commitment, energy and support. This in itself creates a barrier to change. Reminders, forcing functions (such as software or equipment that will not 'allow' people to do it the old way) and regular discussion and review are key factors in helping people adapt a new way. Name it. Acknowledge how hard it is. And most importantly, remove the old way. At no time are people more creative than when protecting a process they are wedded to – as anyone who has tried to introduce a new form would know!

Learning a new skill, such as a new procedure or software package, can also be a major barrier to participation. Learning something new and applying it becomes more difficult as people become more entrenched in their expertise, and as they get older. No one likes to look foolish, and fear of this has destroyed many a fine change initiative. Wherever possible, play to people's strengths when introducing a new technique or process. The 'conscious competence' model explains the process and stages of learning a new skill (or behaviour, ability, technique etc) and is a useful guide for both raising awareness of this aspect of the change journey and for guiding people through it. The four stages are:

1. Unconscious competence – when people don't know what they don't know and are blissfully unaware of the gap between where they are and where they need to be
2. Conscious incompetence – when they become aware that they have to change and learn something new because they currently can't do it or can't do it well enough. This causes feelings of frustration, embarrassment and resistance
3. Conscious competence – when people have learnt the new way, but they have to think about every step as it does not yet come naturally. This is very tiring and frustrating and slows the work rate down considerably
4. Unconscious competence – this is where the new skill is part of the way they do business every day and is integrated into the way they work. This is akin to driving to work and not being able to remember the journey. There are advantages insofar as you don't have to use too much mental effort to make it happen, but there are risks insofar as you may not be as focused and attentive to the task as you should be.[22]

The learner or 'trainee' always begins at stage 1, 'unconscious incompetence', and (ideally) ends at stage 4, 'unconscious competence', having passed through stages 2 and 3: 'conscious incompetence' and 'conscious competence'. A common problem is that change agents such as quality managers often assume that trainees – those learning the new skill – are starting at stage 2, and focus effort towards achieving stage 3, when often trainees are still at stage 1. If the awareness of the personal need for change is low or non-existent so that the learner is at the unconscious incompetence stage, but this is not specifically addressed, the learner will simply not see the need for learning. It's essential to establish awareness of the need to learn something new or do something differently (create conscious incompetence) prior to attempting to impart the training or skills necessary to move trainees from stage 2 to stage 3. People only respond to training when they are aware of their own need for it, and the personal benefit they will derive from achieving it. So the 'awareness' component of the PACEM model is important in this context. The competency framework is a useful reminder that people need to be given sufficient time to achieve stage 4 and that they will experience frustration and fatigue on their journey. Many change efforts have come undone because the change managers have underestimated the time and empathy required to support staff to move through these stages.

It has been suggested that a fifth stage should be added – 'reflective competence' – as a step beyond unconscious competence. This is the stage in which people are conscious of their own unconscious competence, and understand the dangers of complacency or carelessness, particularly relating to competence in high-risk situations.[22] Stage 5 is particularly relevant in the area of consumer safety, but also relates to quality, as unconscious competence in providing care can diminish our capacity to observe and be sensitive to consumers' changing needs.

Develop the new processes, role expectations and tasks with those who will enact them

Developing a common goal for the change and then allowing the various participants within the system to create their own ways of achieving it is a powerful change approach in complex systems. People support what they help create.[23] I call this 'freedom within a framework' and it's an approach advocated in much of the research into successful change. It also fits well with the characteristics of complex systems and health professionals, such as resistance to top-down approaches to change that don't fit with the rules and relationships within the current system. The plan for change has to be anchored in reality and developed in conjunction with those who know how the current situation really works day to day.

One way to approach this is to conduct a force field analysis with the staff who work in the system. Write the goal for the change on a whiteboard and underneath it draw two columns: drivers and barriers. The staff will quickly point out the barriers, but even if this column is three times longer than the 'drivers' column, it gets the potential roadblocks on the table early so you know what you're dealing with. It also gives the staff an opportunity to be heard and engaged in developing potential solutions. The added bonus of this approach is that it may reveal the 'players' (those who hold the formal and inform power in the system you are trying to change) and indicate who needs to do what to make the change.

As can be seen in Figure 2, both current and desired drivers and current and potential barriers can be identified – although they should be written separately so it is easy to tell which is which. Part of the change strategy is then about how to consolidate and build on current drivers to get some of the desired drivers, and how to manage the current barriers and prevent the potential problems from forming.

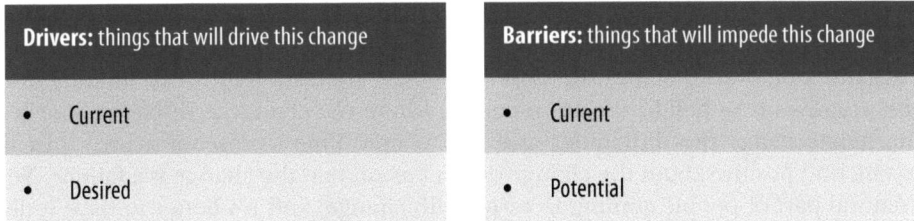

Figure 2: Force Field Analysis [24]

Another tool that is useful for working with staff to develop the new processes and roles is process mapping. Mapping the current steps with the system participants will quickly alert you to the reality of how the system works every day and will help you identify the goals, anchors and leverage points of the system that need changing – and those that don't. Use the '5 whys' for each step of the process, and keep asking 'why do we do it like that?' until you understand each step of the current process.[22,23,24] There will be some very good reasons for some steps and you shouldn't mess with these! And for others there will be weak reasons, or no reasons at all. Some steps exist because some influential person at some point in history just wanted it done that way. What new simple rules will be required to support the new way of doing things? How will they be developed and who should be involved in this process? Like the team whose goal it is to win the premiership, a combination of observation, data, process mapping and force field analysis will guide the strategies and timelines you'll need to achieve your goal.

Empower staff to run the new system and work towards achieving the goals

Within this framework, as far as possible, give people the freedom to devise their own ways of achieving the goals, based on their intimate knowledge of their own systems. I'm not advocating bowing out, yelling 'good luck!' and leaving them to their own devices. I'm suggesting a practical approach to empowerment. Empowerment is not just saying 'make it so' and then being disappointed when they don't come up with the goods. Empowering people to change in complex systems is not straightforward. But there are some common actions that have been shown to be essential in assisting people to take ownership of a task or change, as defined in the DKRS empowerment model, as seen in Table 2.

For the DKRS model to succeed, each of these four components must be present to fully enable people to take ownership of the task or a change. We often see one or two of these employed in healthcare change but it is unusual to see an individual or team supplied with all four.[9] Empowerment does not mean abandonment. Giving people permission to do something differently is not helpful if they are unable to do it. That permission just sets them up to fail. Setting the context for change means preparing the players, understanding what they know and don't know, working with them, watching their performance, giving them feedback and creating an ongoing dialogue with them.[23]

It may be more effort at the front end of a change to work with staff to ensure they have all four components, but it will save you a lot of time and trouble at the back end of the change if they are able to embrace, own and run with the change in their local environment. To take ownership of a change, people should be very clear about their role in the change. Within a complex system this can easily become blurred and even conflict with their system role and relationships. Although each component is important, support is 'first among equals', and perhaps the one we do least well in healthcare in the midst of our pressured and stressful environment. Providing feedback and coaching on how people are enacting their roles in the change is essential to support their ownership and ongoing involvement in the change.[5] Active support can also provide an opportunity for staff to legitimately express the negative emotions that go with most changes. A good strategy for facilitating discussion of the negatives is to build this into meetings where the change is discussed and feedback given. Acknowledge the difficulties and give people time to discuss them.[15] Just because everyone isn't positive about the change doesn't mean that the change is a failure. Negativity is a natural part of people coming to terms with change, and it's better to have it discussed openly. This also helps identify the level and type of support different people need to participate in and own the change. Such discussions require careful chairing and facilitation but it is an important way to acknowledge people's feelings and help move them through the mental transition they need to go through to embrace the new way.[25]

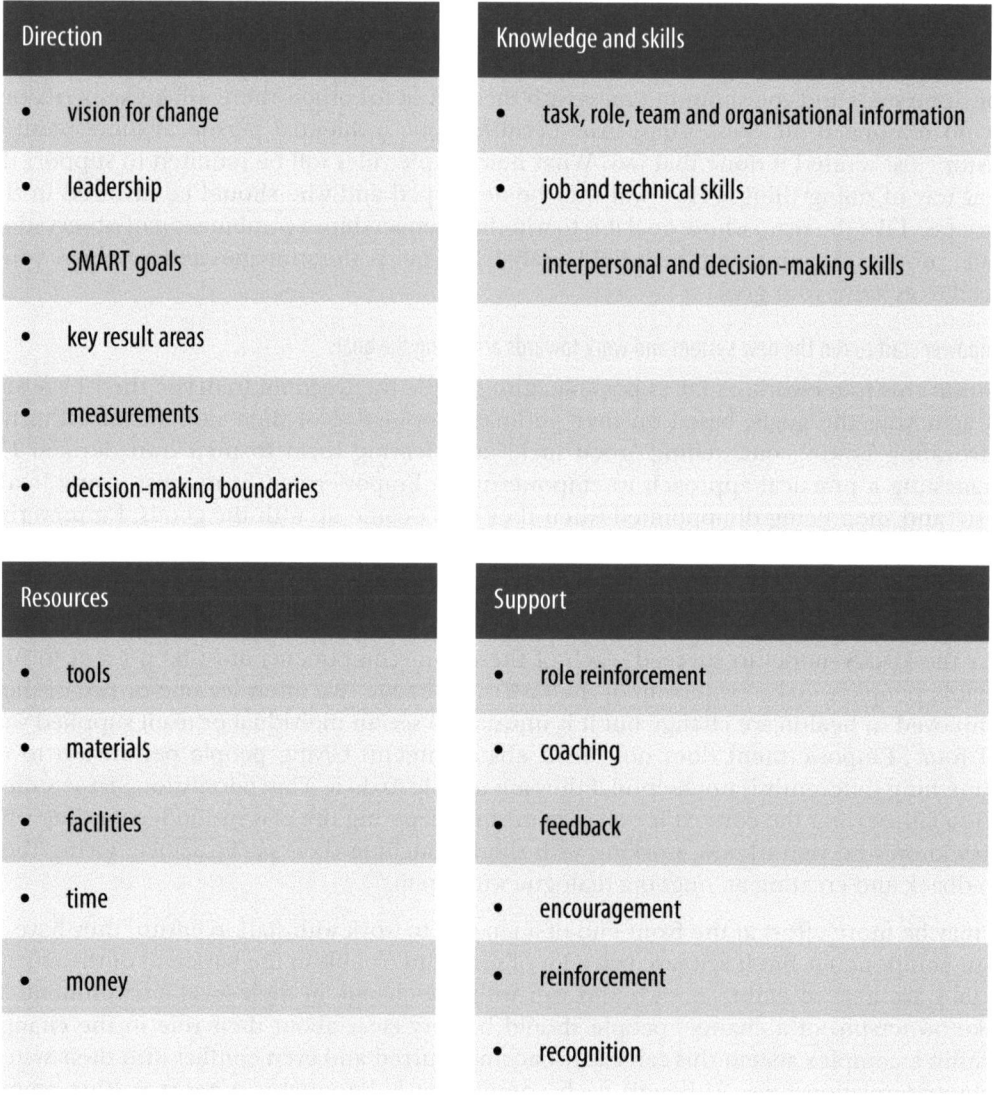

Table 2: *The DKRS (Direction, Knowledge, Resources and Support) Empowerment Model*

5. Get your project roles and governance right

Governance is central to effective project management. The change plan should describe various roles in the change, the committee to whom the project reports and how it is linked to strategic and operational plans and other similar projects. The more the plan demonstrates ways in which a change initiative will help the organisation achieve strategic and operational priorities, the easier it will be to get support for it. It generally also helps to get the initiative onto the agenda of a relevant organisational committee to start to embed it in the fabric of the organisation. This also assists in gaining input from influential players. Clearly identifying change roles is vital to gaining stakeholder buy in. Responsibilities for change are often described ambiguously and this can cause confusion, delays and incomplete project tasks. Change roles should describe the outputs of the key players; not just what aspects of the change they are responsible for. In any change there are at least four key player roles, as seen in Figure 3.

➡ **TOP TIP**

If you have not yet invested in some training in project management – do it! If you are fortunate enough to work with a master project manager, bring them on board to help you plan and execute your changes. These skills are an invaluable part of managing both the people and process aspects of change.

Change sponsor

The sponsor will usually be a senior person who has the authority to legitimise and resource the change, and promote it at senior levels. This leadership is central to the success of your change. Good leaders have a capacity to build and hold a shared picture of the future you seek to create. Strong leadership and genuine vision, particularly in a goal-seeking complex system, helps people move towards the change, not because they are pushed, but because they are attracted by it.[3] The messages must be consistent, clear and repeated, however. When the leaders are so sick of talking about the change that they can hardly stand it, and people are begging them to stop going on about it, you will know that the message is finally starting to get through.[25,26] The best change sponsors can see the positioning of the change within the overall system, advocate for and get involved in the change, provide resources, bring credibility to the process and know how to steer a line around and between the complex system icebergs.

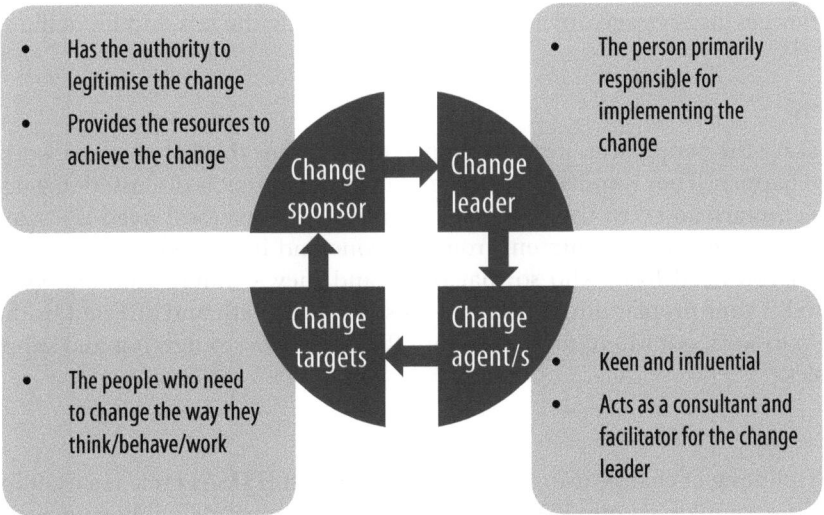

Figure 3: Four 'key player' roles in change[25,26]

Change leader

The leader is the person primarily responsible for implementing the change. This may be the quality manager, or the manager of a department or service. These people must be crystal clear about what is trying to be achieved and why, the steps that will make it happen (both process and people), and how progress is measured. If they are not an excellent project manager, they should ensure someone on the change team is! As a cheerleader for the change, it is imperative for them to understand that different groups will require different messages that are framed and delivered in different ways. They should be able to describe the purpose and the end result of the change in a couple of simple sentences, and be skilful at managing buy in and negative responses.[25,26]

Negative responses (or attack strategies) to the change proposal are inevitable, as we have discussed, but although they may take many forms, they can generally be categorised as one of four types: fear mongering, delay, confusion and ridicule. Expectation and preparation are probably your best defence, and having some response strategies is essential, such as:

- Preparation: prepare for the likely attacks and negative responses
- Don't see negativity as failure – it is part of getting your proposals heard. Be surprised if people aren't negative: does this mean people aren't interested or don't see your change proposal as important?
- Give clear, simple, and commonsense responses. Respond to the content of the questions, not the attitude that comes with them
- Show respect to your questioners. Don't fight, collapse or become defensive. As hard as this is at times, it will serve you well in the longer term, and helps focus the discussion on the proposal, not the argument
- Keep your eye on the whole audience. These are the people you have to convince. Don't be overly distracted by the detractors. [2,27]

Change agents

The agents are the players at various parts of the system who are keen and influential. If you have correctly identified these 'players' through your preplanning preparation, they will act as consultants and facilitators for the change leader to spread and influence the change. They get the message out and support it by walking the talk and modelling required behaviour.[25,26]

Change targets

The targets are the people who need to change the way they think, behave or work to make the change happen. They require the front-end investment that is discussed throughout this chapter to embrace and own the change. It is unlikely that you will need the same level of behavioural change and commitment from everyone and it is important to be clear about exactly what you need from who so that you – and they – don't waste energy where it's not required.[17] Your preplanning work with those involved with and affected by the change should help to work out where to direct your efforts and how to develop and support them in their roles.[25,26]

6. Test the change through short cycle pilots

Rapid cycle piloting of change using the Plan Do Study Act (PDSA) cycle is a useful approach to change in a complex system. PDSA fits the changeable and adaptable nature of complex systems and enables you to test ideas under a variety of circumstances.[14] It's also a good way to pick up on the feedback and side effects of your change – the living, breathing, 'system being' that is your organisation will definitely tell you how it feels about the change and you are likely to experience some form of pushback from the system, as discussed in Chapter Two. This model also includes the possibility that the change being tested will not be successful, but because these tests are done on a small scale the risk of failure can be kept to a level that's manageable. PDSA also helps achieve quick wins, even if small, that are integral to gaining stakeholder acceptance of change. Success on a small scale builds confidence, which allows larger risks and changes. Pilot projects work best under the following circumstances:

- Pilots are limited to small samples and short cycles of change with the people who want to be involved (the 'early adopters')
- They use solutions that have worked for others, but are adapted to fit the local situation
- The easiest change with the most leverage for the biggest impact is made
- An action learning process is used to frequently review progress and the change leader stops to ask: 'how did we go?', 'what did we learn?', 'what were the unintended consequences and side effects?' and 'how should we do it differently in the next cycle?'
- Participants are not afraid to stop a test change that's clearly not working. This is part of change in complex systems. [14,15]

The pilot is your 'audition', if you like, for the later, larger-scale change. Staff will be watching, judging and weighing up whether or not to hitch their wagon to the new way. It is imperative that your process has credibility. When you pilot a change, use a simple but rigorous project management approach and do exactly what you have promised. If you want to change people's beliefs about how things should be done, you must change what they see. A memo or an email about doing something differently will not make it happen. If you want people to believe that changing their behaviour will result in a certain positive outcome, that outcome must occur. If you commit the leadership group to behaving in a different way, they must behave in that way. This is where many change initiatives break down: we make the plan and say what will happen, but don't follow through.

> ➡ TOP TIP
>
> It can be tempting to try to do too much with pilots. The purpose of a pilot is to test the change in the real world to get an idea of its strengths, weaknesses, side effects and the way in which it interacts with the systems around it. Although the change you are testing is no doubt designed to improve something, using the pilot to solve a broad range of problems rarely works as well as it sounds! It is best to test your innovation in an 'average' service – one that reflects real world operations –but not where there are entrenched issues and difficulties, either generally or specific to the area you are trying to improve.
>
> This does seem slightly counter intuitive, of course, and testing an innovation in the service with the most related problems to be solved is often presented in organisations as a smart use of time and resources. But situational readiness is a significant predictor of the success of innovation and change. A good improvement initiative will not fix a poor context![20] Trying to kill two birds with one stone by testing changes – be it new computer software or a revised communication process – in a dysfunctional service may result in the creation of even more problems. You might also get a false reading on the improvement potential of the change.
>
> Run the pilot in an 'average' service, evaluate the outcome, revise the innovation as indicated, possibly test again, depending on the scope and risk associated with the change, and then implement it. This helps separate the issues with the innovation from the issues associated with a problematic service.

Early wins are required to show that change is possible and can have positive outcomes. Action sends a strong message, more than any memo ever could. Don't be surprised by unexpected or negative outcomes, and don't expect a linear cause followed by effect chain with your change. Look for the unintended negative side effect of your change. For example, if you have streamlined the new consumer registration process, does this leave clients feeling that they have been hurried and not heard? Don't ignore or downplay these negative side effects – they are not failure, but the way of the world in complex systems. Recognise them, name them and re-think the strategy to try to avoid or mitigate them. [23]

7. Reinforce, embed and spread the change

Creating buy-in is one thing. 'Stay in' is something else altogether. Systems need a constant supply of new energy to survive and, until your new change starts to create its own energy, it requires yours! Sustainability is a process, not an ending.[4] Many managers want to get everything up and running on auto pilot as soon as possible, but this is the antithesis of what actually sustains change.

In complex systems, sustainability and spread are dynamic processes that need focus and attention. So, define sustainability. What do you mean by it? What do you want to still be happening in one/three/six months from now? People need to be reminded of the goal and the vision, and the way in which these are achieved requires monitoring and course correction in a shifting complex environment. Involve people in developing solutions to overcome the unexpected problems that arise, ensure they are equipped for their role in the change and reinforce where their contribution to the change makes things better for patients. Use the sceptics to help you identify the problems and the roadblocks and show you value their input. Arguing with them will not change their mind and you may lose valuable information.[15]

Sustainability will be less of an issue if those affected have been involved in planning the change and empowered to implement and test it. Once you've got the change right, embed it in job descriptions, policies and procedures, competencies and performance reviews. Reinforce it. Remove the old way – if you don't, people will cling to it because it's familiar, and it will make the new way seem like an extra, rather than a replacement. Keep the change on meeting agendas as a specific review item for at least six to twelve months, depending on the size of the change. Appoint a 'keeper' of the change – someone influential whose job it is to keep an eye on the new way of doing things and the people involved, and to identify regression and unintended side effects. Ensure it continues to be linked to broader organisational initiatives.

If you've done a good job of your change process by giving the participants a positive experience, ensuring the change is an improvement for patients and staff and finding those quick wins, the initiative should have its ownership and should just about spread itself. This is the 'tipping point' concept, which provides a useful summary of spread.[28] The 'law of the few' and the 'stickiness factor' are tipping point concepts, which provide us with direction on how to go about reaching the point where the change takes on a life of its own. The law of the few means that a few influential, popular people can effectively spread a message, and even better if some are 'exceptional' people.[28] Use the people who have influence – the 'players' in your complex system – and also the people who just get around and talk a lot.

Stickiness means that a message has impact: you can't get it out of your head, it sticks in your memory. Are your messages 'sticky' or dull and forgettable?[28] Are they presented in the language of the people – or in complex bureaucratese? Don't be afraid to market! Reminders, colourful tools, awards, interesting and engaging information, and high visibility all help to spread a change. And nothing beats a good old fashioned chat so provide plenty of opportunity for people to talk about it! You want your positive change to go viral.

➡ TOP TIPS FOR LEADING COMPLEX SYSTEMS CHANGE, AND EMPOWERING OTHERS TO DRIVE IT

- Identify and explain the good reason for the change, set a clear vision and goals and know your origin and your destination.
- Develop clear and appropriate roles to achieve the goals.
- Start where they are: identify the mental maps, assumptions and relationships currently holding the current system as it is.
- Plan your steps involving those affected, build on what works and accept the chaos of change in a complex environment.
- Ensure first steps are achievable, and build in some early quick wins.
- Empower people to drive the change by providing direction, knowledge, resources and support.
- Use short cycle pilots to test the change, learn from their outcomes and use rapid briefing and course correction to reach your destination.
- Measure what you want to change.
- Communicate until people beg you not to.
- Reinforce the change by developing policy, roles, systems and mental models to support and spread the new way.

Lead change – and empower others to make it

The 'complex systems change essentials' discussed in this chapter do not constitute a comprehensive review of the copious literature on effective change. Rather, they highlight the consistent themes running through the literature on change, complex systems and high performing organisations that I have found useful. Hopefully you have also found some useful tools and tips to add to your change toolkit. Perhaps the most salient message is that humans, not robots, implement change, so more often than not it will be messy, non-linear and less than logical. You can do much to make the journey easier by applying a few of the strategies discussed in this chapter. Your greatest strength, however, is your ability to anticipate these difficulties and enjoy rather than resent the challenge of using your skills and knowledge to overcome them.

An ancient Chinese saying puts it best: 'Go to the people, learn from them, love them, start with what they know, build on what they have. And of the best leaders, when their task is accomplished, their work is done, the people will remark, 'we have done it ourselves'.[29]

Headlines: Chapter Three

- When planning a change in a healthcare organisation, keep in mind the complex system factors as a guide to your approach
- Change in complex systems is unlikely to be straightforward but will be easier if you invest in gathering intelligence to understand the pre-change situation
- Learn from the literature and from experience – don't make common change mistakes
- Build magnets into your change goals
- A change plan must include strategies for changing both systems and behaviour
- Involving people in developing the change roles and goals empowers them to own the change.

References and Further Reading

1. Greenhalgh T, Robert G, Bate B, Kyriakidou O, McFarlane F, Peacock R (2004) *How to Spread Good Ideas: A Systematic Review of the Literature on Diffusion, Dissemination and Sustainability of Innovations in Health Service Delivery and Organisation.* NCCSDO, UK

2. Kotter J (1996) *Leading Change – Why Transformation Efforts Fail.* Harvard Business Review on Change HBR Paperback Series, USA

3. Senge PM (1990) *The Fifth Discipline – The Art and Practice of the Learning Organisation.* Century Business, UK

4. NHS (2002) *The Improvement Leaders Guide to Managing the Human Dimensions of Change: Working with Individuals.* NHS Modernisation Agency, UK

5. NHS (2004) *Engaging Individual Staff in Service Improvement.* NHS Modernisation Agency, UK

6. O'Connor J, McDermott I (1997) *The Art of Systems Thinking.* Harper Collins Publishers, UK

7. Mackay H (2010) *What Makes Us Tick?: The Ten Desires that Drive Us.* Hachette Publishing, Australia

8. Young S, Bartram T, Stanton P, Leggat SG (2010) High Performance Work Systems and Employee Well-being: A Two Stage Study of a Rural Australian Hospital. *Journal of Health Organization and Management*, vol. 24 no. 2, pp. 182–99

9. Balding C (2005) Strengthening Clinical Governance through Cultivating the Line Management Role. *Australian Health Review*, vol. 29, no. 3

10. Braithwaite J, (2010). Between-group Behaviour in Health Care: Gaps, Edges, Boundaries, Disconnections, Weak Ties, Spaces and Holes. A Systematic Review. *BMC Health Serv Res*, vol. 10, no. 330 (Accessed January 2011)

11. Fitzgerald A, Dadich A (2010) Organisational-Professional Conflict in Medicine, in Braithwaite J, Hyde P and Pope C (eds) *Culture and Climate in Health Care Organisations.* Palgrave MacMillan, UK

12. Frankel A, Leonard M, Simmonds T, Haraden C, Vega K (eds) (2009) *The Essential Guide for Patient Safety Officers.* Joint Commission on Accreditation of Healthcare Organisations and Institute for Healthcare Improvement, USA

13. Davies HTO, Harrison S (2003) Trends in Doctor-Manager Relationships. *British Medical Journal*, vol. 326

14. Reason J (2008) *The Human Contribution.* Ashgate Publishing Company, England

15. Haines SG (1998) *Systems Thinking and Learning.* HRD Press, USA

16. Adapted from La Marsh J & Potts R (2004) Sustain the Change. *Industrial Management*, vol. 46, no. 3

17. Bridges W (1997) *Managing Transitions.* Addison Wesley Publishing Company, USA

18. Tyson S & Jackson T (1992) *The Essence of Organisational Behaviour*. Prentice Hall International UK

19. Eccles M, Grimshaw J, Walker A, Johnston M, Pitts N (2005) Changing the Behaviour of Healthcare Professionals: The Use of Theory in Promoting the Uptake of Research Findings. *Journal of Clinical Epidemiology*, vol. 58, pp. 107–112

20. Boaden R, Harvey G, Moxham C and Proudlove L (2007) *QI: Theory and Practice in Healthcare*. University of Manchester Business School, UK

21. Levitt M, (2010). Presentation at the 8th Australasian Conference on Safety and Quality in Healthcare. Perth, Western Australia

22. Nonaka I (1994) A Dynamic Theory of Organizational Knowledge Creation. *Organization Science*, vol. 5, pp. 14–37, as noted by David Baume, May 2004 on www.bradfordvts.co.uk (Accessed January 2011)

23. Meadows DH (2008) *Thinking in Systems – A Primer*. Sustainability Institute, USA

24. Tague NR (1995) *The Quality Tool Box*. ASQC Quality Press, USA

25. Duck JD (1996) *Managing Change – The Art of Balancing*. Harvard Business Review on Change, Paperback Series, USA

26. Adapted from Cameron E, Green M (2004) *Making Sense of Change Management*. Kogan Page Limited, Great Britain.

27. Kotter J & Whitehead L (2010) *Buy-in: Saving Your Good Idea from Being Shot Down*. Harvard Business Review Press, USA

28. Gladwell M (2002) *The Tipping Point*. Backbay Books, USA

29. (Source unknown) Two thousand year old Chinese poem

Q4 DEVELOPING A THINKING ORGANISATION:
Creating safety and quality in complex systems

'For every complex question, there is an answer that is clear, simple and wrong.'
– H L MENCKEN

4. DEVELOPING A THINKING ORGANISATION:
Creating safety and quality in complex systems

In this chapter we examine the way that safety and quality can be best achieved in the complex healthcare environment. We consider healthcare's traditional rules and standardisation approach to safety and quality, and draw on the discussions of previous chapters to suggest a 'double headed' approach that combines people and systems.

Creating safety in healthcare – how did we get here?

Total Quality Management (TQM) was derived from manufacturing and introduced to healthcare in the 1980s. Despite adding a number of useful tools to health service quality programs, an unintended consequence of TQM was that quality programs in health services began to be positioned as having a management, rather than clinical, focus. The move to TQM alienated many clinicians who had been auditing and improving their own work in their own way. But the trouble with the individual approach to monitoring and improvement was that care and outcomes depended almost solely on who your health professional was.

The introduction of TQM into healthcare also coincided with a change in the way healthcare services were organised. As hospitals got bigger and more expensive to run they transformed from cottage industries run by matrons and medical administrators to large bureaucracies run by chief executives, many of which did not have clinical backgrounds. Accreditation and compliance also emerged as key activities in the management of healthcare.

Not all healthcare professionals are equal. We're human, after all; our skills, knowledge and approach to care vary – and will continue to do so throughout our careers. TQM, with its focus on consistent quality, was hailed at the time as a way to even out this variability through a more systems-oriented, less person-dependent approach to care. Whilst those of us involved in quality at the time learned a lot from Total Quality Management, it's unlikely that we realised the importance of adapting it for the healthcare environment and many potential benefits may have gone unrealised due to poor implementation. TQM in healthcare has gradually evolved into a more generic quality improvement approach, still using industrial approaches such as Six Sigma and Lean Thinking, but adapting them more successfully than our earlier TQM efforts to better meet the unique needs of healthcare organisations.

A few years after the introduction of TQM, the first large-scale studies of adverse events in the acute sector were undertaken in the United States and Australia, with many other countries subsequently following suit. The results of these studies galvanised the quality movement – as well as politicians, managers and clinicians. For all our previous efforts, and with the best intentions, we were still harming our patients, and the concept of patient safety became an almost instant healthcare priority. We now know that somewhere between 10 per cent and 30 per cent of patients in hospital are harmed or killed by iatrogenic factors.[2,3] It's not that people who work in healthcare are more prone to mistakes than those in other industries, but that their environment is alive with risk and the potential to make mistakes.[4] It is also challenging for health professionals who are trained to be as perfect as possible to have to come to terms with the fact that they are fallible and will make mistakes. Healthcare organisations are still struggling to find effective ways to support clinicians to manage this ambiguity. Since those first adverse event studies, there have also been many high-profile

MODELS FOR WORKING WITH COMPLEX SYSTEMS

There are many different ways to think about systems and how they can best be managed to create safety and quality. Hard systems thinking believes that systems will act rationally and can be controlled. Soft systems thinking understands that, as much as we would like organisations to act like machines, not everything can be controlled – so achieving organisational goals relies on a mix of rational and organic systems. Complexity engineering understands and works with systems as organic beings and uses simple rules and attractors to nudge organisations towards their goals. Moving towards organisational goals depends on local actions and relationships.[1]

This chapter proposes a mix of these models for creating safety and quality in healthcare organisations.

inquiries into poor care and harm in health services, as society demands more transparent and accountable healthcare. These inquiries found that most of the instances of poor care under scrutiny were not caused by poor practitioners as much as by poor systems letting practitioners down. The findings of the public inquiries and adverse event studies changed the focus of our quality approaches from review and improvement to consumer safety and risk management. The pendulum has swung from dependence on fallible humans to get everything right all of the time to a risk, systems and reliability approach to achieving safety and quality.

The shift to reliability

One of the positives of this pendulum swing from people to systems is that we now seek ideas and knowledge from other high-risk industries such as nuclear power plants, deep-sea oil rigs, mining and aviation. The concept of 'high reliability' from these industries has been particularly promoted as an approach that will support and drive safer healthcare. High reliability organisations take a systems approach to creating consistently safe, quality output. They standardise systems and procedures wherever possible, use memory aids such as checklists to ensure important tasks are not missed, and discourage staff from innovating or moving outside the standardised approach on the job.

A high reliability approach aims to reduce variation in the way things are done. But healthcare professionals have a lot of work to do to reduce variation. A recent study examining the extent, type and causes of failures in reliability across five clinical systems revealed that unreliability was usually the result of the same factors. These included a lack of feedback mechanisms (for individuals as well as systems), poor communication, and a widespread acceptance on the part of clinical staff that systems were going to be unreliable and that this was not their responsibility.[5]

Reliability approaches in healthcare safety are still evolving and focus on developing systems to protect processes that are at risk of error and problems. This has been most famously described in Reason's 'Swiss Cheese Model of Error Causation' where, if a barrier to error is breached, there is another system in place to catch the error before it becomes an adverse event.[4] This approach to improving safety is based on reductionist thinking; that is, breaking down a system into component parts to find the high-risk areas, usually in response to an incident, fixing the problem part and developing systems to prevent future problems. This is the logic upon which the majority of clinical risk management systems are based.

When we think about our organisations as machines or factories, it is natural to think that variation is undesirable and that people and systems should operate in line with established protocols.

Many of the standardised high reliability systems being introduced into healthcare, such as checklists, decision support and patient identification processes, will help reduce many of the common errors in patient care. For issues where there is a high degree of certainty about the outcome from an action and a high degree of agreement among those who will take the action, it is possible and appropriate to think in machine terms and to aim to reduce variation.[7,8]

> **➡ TOP TIP**
>
> Every change you wish to make will require a range of approaches. Beware the 'one stop shop' solution. In a complex system you will need at least three different strategic pressure points for change: systems, skills and beliefs.

But is a high reliability approach the whole answer? Is it even a good fit in a complex environment? The quest to improve patient safety has achieved a great deal over the past decade, but progress seems to have slowed. The percentage of patients harmed in healthcare appears to have settled at around 10 per cent for the past few years, despite enormous investment in error reporting, analysis and response. This aspect of safety has been the focus of most of our safety efforts thus far and is the reactive side of the safety coin; responding to incidents, adverse events and root cause analyses by developing systems and standardisation to plug the holes in the Swiss cheese.[4] But is this working? Incident reporting is claimed by many authors to be ineffective in detecting safety problems, with claims that the real levels of harm in healthcare are two to three times more than those detected by incident reporting alone.[3,9] Deriving our knowledge and understanding of safety only from incident reports can also give a biased view of the causes of adverse events and may channel our remedial efforts in the wrong direction.

The other side of the safety coin is a dynamic approach to creating safety through the interplay of systems and people; to minimise hazards and to respond appropriately when unchecked hazards pose a threat to patient safety.[4] In healthcare we are trying to create safety in complex organisations – not factories – so we need an approach that fits with the way our health services operate as living 'system beings', as discussed in Chapter Two. A comprehensive approach to tackling patient safety in this environment requires a double-headed proactive and reactive strategy. Health services are increasingly recognising this and are actively pursuing solutions over and above incident reporting and analysis by developing staff to better meet the challenges of creating safety in a complex environment. But the double-headed approach is by no means yet universal, and many quality and risk managers are still kept well occupied by counting, trending and analysing adverse events, and are less involved in actually doing something about them.

Improving communication and relationships, feedback on errors and near misses, enhancing the quality of staff decision making and promoting patients' involvement in their own care have all been identified as vital and proactive components of safer and better care.[8] Progress, however, has been slow in these areas – possibly because they require more planning and resourcing than reactive risk approaches. To be effective, these proactive strategies require us to understand and work with the natural variation, which emerges at the interface between the social and technical components of complex systems. As discussed in Chapters Two and Three, the way staff behave in your organisation is more likely to be governed by beliefs and relationships than by policies. A technical solution alone cannot solve a poor process or a socio-cultural problem, and a new protocol is not enough to guarantee behaviour change. If not well designed and implemented, automation and protocols may even further embed existing problems or make things more complicated.[6,8,10,11,12]

Are we heading in the right direction?

So, what does this all mean? Do we have to throw out our current safety and risk management systems and start again? Definitely not! They are a crucial part of the quality and safety puzzle. Improving reliability through systems that force and guide safe decisions, provide backups, remind staff of preferred behaviour and catch fallible humans when they make a mistake, are key aspects of creating safety. In fact, their use is in its infancy in healthcare – compared to other high-risk industries – and there would probably be significant benefit in fast-tracking the implementation of proven safety systems. Rule-based decision making, such as the use of protocols and checklists is also extremely useful in many situations; for example, by inexperienced practitioners who are learning standard procedures for frequent high-risk situations. Standard procedures can be useful for experts as well – particularly if they find themselves in a situation that they do not often experience.[13]

Not all aspects of standardisation and reliability are foolproof, however, and there is danger in thinking that they are a 'set and forget' solution to safety. There are many reasons for this in a complex system. Remember the 'policy resistant' aspect of complex systems from Chapter Two? Complex systems – and the people working within them – do not always respond well to overly restrictive rules, and they may react in unexpected ways. Creating a standardised approach, unless based on a forcing function, does not guarantee that it will be followed. And yet, we often go straight to the policy book when we want people to behave differently. And forcing functions, while useful in creating safety, can give rise to complacency and a lack of staff alertness. So let's look at some of the reasons why standardisation is *one* answer to improving safety and quality, but not the *only* answer.

You can't have a protocol for everything
We often find that there is such a strong emphasis on procedures, checklists and protocols that organisations attempt to write one for every eventuality. But it is almost impossible for a procedure to be written for every situation in a complex system, and unlikely that staff will refer to all procedures if there are too many of them.[13] Reliability in high reliability organisations is accomplished by standardisation and simplification of as many processes as possible. But your health service is a dynamic organism with a high level of variability, production pressure, professional autonomy and rapid creation of new knowledge. Not everything can be fixed and standardised so when trying to reduce variability and improve reliability, it is better to focus on the variation that is creating real problems, rather than variation more broadly. All safety policies have a natural lifespan as the context around them is constantly changing. Nowhere is this more apparent than in healthcare.[14] The challenge of creating and maintaining safety within this context requires a mix of standardisation and proactive, flexible, thinking solutions.

More rules may equal less thinking
Over reliance on rule-based decision making may cause a degree of skill decay; if an unexpected and unfamiliar situation arises and no rule exists, will the person making the decisions be able to formulate an effective course of action?[13] Protocols too may reduce or discourage the ability of people to be proactive, practice situational awareness, identify deviations from normal situations – in short, to think for themselves.[16] Bad decisions can also occur in rule-based situations if the wrong rule or protocol is selected. It is human nature to prefer a familiar rule, whether or not it is the right one to match the situation that the decision-maker finds themselves in.[13]

CREATING SAFETY IN ANOTHER COMPLEX ENVIRONMENT – THE ROAD SYSTEM

The road system is also a complex system and requires a mix of systems and people, working together, to create safety. You may create safety by ensuring that you and your car are in good working order, sticking to the road rules, choosing to drive on well-constructed roads and actively using your experience and skill. But because of the complexity of the road system, you know that these are not the only factors determining the outcome of your journey. These are the things you can control. But there are many factors you can't. You may encounter many risks on your journey, some of which can be anticipated, such as road works and weather, and some which you cannot. You are heavily dependent on other drivers to also stick to the rules, concentrate and not be affected by alcohol, fatigue or stress. When a hazard causes an adverse event on your journey you may have to deviate from the rules to protect your safety and the safety of others. If you are mindful and alert, you may have a good chance of avoiding an incident in front of you. Other times, however, a major event unfolds rapidly and avoiding it is beyond your control or capacity. In other situations it may be you who is the hazard as you are distracted, tired or stressed. Safety on the roads is as difficult to get right as safety in health and aged care and is a good analogy to use when explaining complexity to staff.

Protocols and checklists are based on a rule-based, mechanistic view of the world

As discussed in Chapter Two, your organisation is a 'systems being' and behaves more like a human than a machine. A mechanistic rule-based approach to safety is based on the premise that safety is the result of people following procedures. But, as we have discussed, compliance, even with proven safety procedures, tends to vary.[12,16] Developing checklists and protocols in response to risks may provide a sense of action having been taken, but can send the message that reliable, safe care requires nothing more than insisting upon routine standardised procedures. Nothing threatens safety like the belief that the problem is solved.[8]

Checklists in particular, even if based on rigorous evidence, have not yet penetrated medicine in the way they have in other high-risk complex industries. The reasons for this appear to be primarily cultural as many clinicians feel that checklists undermine their claims to expertise and autonomy and are an unnecessary impediment to decision making. They are also often poorly implemented, which limits their uptake and effectiveness. Implementing a checklist in a health service requires the same planning and change effort as required with all change in complex systems: opinion leaders, an understanding of the anchors that keep the current situation in place, working with the system's relationships and power, clear communication, and an awareness of the system and subsystem goals. Where checklists have been successful, teams have been allowed to customise the implementation of the evidence locally. This allows staff to create the new norms and mental models to adapt the checklist to their environment. There is little doubt that standardised approaches are useful tools to improve performance and safety, but effective implementation is essential to their success.[3,6,8]

WHICH PROTOCOL IS WHICH?

Proposed protocols should be tested with those who will be using them:

- Do those who are going to use it have doubts about its usefulness?
- Is it easy to violate?
- Are extra rules required to comply?
- Are extra resources required to comply?
- Are there likely to be negative side effects of implementation on system goals?
- Could it conflict with other policies and priorities in certain situations?
- Will it work better for some shifts, or parts of the service, than others? [15]

Answering 'yes' to most of these signals a high likelihood of non-compliance, workaround and drift, and you might want to rethink the approach.

Smart people work around dumb protocols

'Workarounds', where staff bend, adapt or avoid the rules and protocols to solve a problem or get a job done more efficiently, are common in healthcare. Workarounds are driven by production pressures, heavy workloads, and poor protocols that are often based on how we would like work to be done rather than how it is really done.[12] The trouble with these workarounds being informal and often concealed is that they become the norm without the organisation realising it (the system 'drifts', as discussed in Chapter Two). Workarounds and non-compliance is likely to occur when the evidence for a new rule is weak or there appears to be little consequence to not following it. For example, it is estimated that 'intentional non-compliance' by aircrews accounts for 45 per cent of all errors and violations, but only six per cent of these affect flights.[17] Half of the checklists on planes are incorrectly completed because of interruptions and poor checklist design.[18] As standards of practice gradually change and erode, this may have catastrophic consequences. To ground safety in reality, we must accept that workarounds do happen and that it may be a short journey from this to systems failure because the work practices no longer match with the original rules developed to prevent hazards turning into errors.[4]

Workarounds, or deviations from the rules, can create a false sense of security when everything is going well, but they also create an opportunity for error through:

- Normalisation of deviance. Certain problems, defects or workarounds become so commonplace and so apparently inconsequential that their risk is gradually downgraded until they are accepted as being a normal part of everyday work.
- Doing too much with too little. As people adapt and become more efficient, they may increase their workload as they are able to do more, but in fact their resources and backup are thin and unable to respond when hazardous situations occur. The plateau on which the system is operating is shrinking without anyone realising.
- Forgetting to be afraid. Because bad events do not appear to happen very often, at least from the limited perspective of the individual, health professionals can lose sight of the way in which apparently minor changes can combine unexpectedly to cause major tragedies.[4,7,14,19]

Some studies estimate that around 20 per cent of people comply with rules, five per cent avoid complying with rules altogether and 75 per cent comply if the avoiders are seen to have to face the consequences of non-compliance. For things that people think are really important, there will be 60 per cent compliance. For things that people think are not important, there will be 10 per cent compliance. So there is no point having protocols for the things that people don't think are really important. Relevance is one of the key reasons for compliance or non-compliance with a rule, closely followed by leadership, peer pressure and support.[14,15,20]

As discussed in Chapter three, observe the systems in action in your health service and you will find some of the history and relationships that explain and anchor compliance and non-compliance. These are foundations of the way complex systems function. Imposing rules to improve safety may be at odds with staff perceptions of what they require to provide safer care.[21] Observing work as it is really done is an important component of developing safety solutions suited to the complexity of daily situations, as well as identifying the perverse incentives in the system that force people away from safe practice to fulfil other organisational priorities such as efficiency.[12]

Patient safety is often a casualty of governing body and management pressure to prioritise targets and budgets, with not enough attention paid to staff pressures and patient risk. Standards and policies erode as they are buffeted by the heavy weather of efficiency drives, staff shortages, heavy demand and active resistance. Safety is risked in the process.[22] Being aware of this gives organisations an opportunity to identify when safety might be at risk of being compromised so that they can take corrective action.

Creating safety in a complex system

As befits systems thinkers, we don't take an either/or approach to safety. It's not systems versus people, but systems and people. Developing systems to support safe practice is an essential part of creating safety; and the easier you can make it to do the right thing, the greater the chance of it being done. Protocols, checklists, forcing functions, risk management, root cause analyses and incident reporting have doubtless saved many lives and prevented much harm. But their success rests on the way in which these systems are developed and implemented within the complex healthcare environment. Healthcare operates in the real world – a world that is messy, difficult to control and far from ideal. The better that quality managers understand and accept this, the better positioned they are to assist their organisations to understand and practise real world safety. A quality manager skilled in understanding complex systems can guide their organisation's safety efforts far more effectively than one who takes only a mechanistic view. This is not about unlearning everything you know about safety, but adapting it and adding to it to fit a complex systems context.

For example, classic risk management tools such as incident reporting can be supplemented and strengthened by a proactive audit or concurrent screening system that detects adverse events from patient records or datasets. This supplies data that is less open to interpretation of what a deviation is and helps to develop the rich picture of how a safety system is working in the real world and where best to focus change efforts. It has been claimed that indicators and voluntary reporting can miss more than 90 percent of the adverse events identified through record screening. And if we could have someone watching every patient around the clock, we'd probably pick up many more.[3] A risk register is also a valuable risk management tool, but let's ensure that our risk controls and treatments are active and based in reality. And when we undertake root cause analysis to take a complex systems view we understand that, in a healthcare organisation, there is unlikely to be one 'root cause' – instead, a variety of factors, at least one involving relationships, is likely to be involved.

Fewer, better rules
When developing safety policies and protocols, it is better to give staff fewer rules that can be reliably followed around the clock than to write 'perfect' protocols based on ideal conditions that require workarounds to fit the situation at 11pm on a Saturday night. Try to resist the pressure to develop a new rule in response to every adverse event or root cause analysis finding because you'll end up with a mix of 'should follow' and 'must follow' rules that will muddy the safety waters. 'Should follow' rules that have little credibility or apparent consequence are unlikely to be followed in a messy, high-risk, high-stress environment, so why bother?

Erosion of compliance with 'should follow' rules can, in turn, negatively influence compliance with the more important 'must follow' rules. When people are violating a protocol, find out why! It may be for a good reason and may give you an insight into what's going on in practice – and what's required to improve. Use observation and discussion to work out what's really happening. And when introducing a new protocol to reduce a risk, do the troubleshooting around whether or not it's likely to be followed before it's implemented and people's lives depend on it. Quality managers who understand and can explain the value of not constraining the system any more than necessary, and who encourage challenging a new protocol with 'why won't it work?' and 'how are people likely to work around it?' are more likely to effect positive change in their organisation's approach to safety and quality than those obsessed with rules.

Safety will always vary
Finally, the 'real world safety' perspective requires an understanding of variation. This is discussed in Chapter Seven as an essential quality manager tool. As we've discussed, all complex systems will have some variation, which can make it difficult to know whether or not you are doing well. But the concept of variation is a critical one in healthcare organisations where there are a large number of processes. Focus on reducing the variations with the greatest negative impact on the quality and safety of care.

Building resilience to create safety

So far we have explored current approaches to improving safety, such as systems and rules, and error reporting, analysis and response. But creating consistently safe care and services for consumers also requires people power. This aspect of safety – and quality more generally – can be described in many ways and using many theories, but for the purposes of this discussion, they can be neatly wrapped up in the concept of resilience.

What is resilience?
Resilience engineering is a concept derived from human factors engineering – the discipline that studies the interface between machines and systems and human beings, and improves design so that humans can operate safely and effectively. From a human factors perspective, resilience refers to the ability, within complex and high-risk organisations, to understand how failure is avoided and how to design for success. It describes how people learn and adapt to create safety in settings that are fraught with gaps, hazards, tradeoffs and multiple goals. Resilience can be described as a property of both individuals and teams within their workplace.[23] It fits well with James Reason's observation that his 'Swiss Cheese Model of Accident Causation'[4] requires another slice of cheese – cheddar, not Swiss – at the end of the line. This slice represents humans as the final barrier and defence against unsafe situations turning into harm, when all other systems fail.[4] Practising resilience requires organisations to investigate how individuals, teams and organisations monitor, adapt and act effectively to cope with system failures in high-risk situations, and to apply and develop these lessons.

CREATING RESILIENT TEAMS

Building a resilient team requires more than just gathering a group of resilient individuals. Their strengths will vary. For example, one member might be more focused and organised while another is more proactive. As with all teams, some development is required to develop a collective intelligence that combines the skills, experience and resilience of the individuals. Creating this requires commitment and effort, however, and a planned program of development that includes:

- identifying and valuing the experience and resilience strengths of the individual team members
- developing and clarifying individual roles in responding to change and unexpected events, and building resilience skills into team norms such as team goals, priorities, values, communication methods, decision making processes and ground rules
- practising these roles in a coordinated approach to addressing a crisis or unexpected change. This may involve using simulation, brainstorming potential problems in care, observing other teams and using case studies to reflect on team performance and apply lessons learned
- developing the specific skills required for effective response, such as situation awareness, communication, teamwork, leadership, managing stress, coping with fatigue, understanding human factors and the nature of human error, and decision making. [13,23,28]

Although it is a relatively new concept to healthcare, resilience is well accepted in other high-risk industries. A key component of building resilience is appreciative enquiry, which asks 'why do things go right?' as well as 'what went wrong?' Appreciative enquiry allows us to identify and build on the strengths in our safety systems. Resilience is a good fit in healthcare settings because it acknowledges and addresses healthcare as a complex system that resists over-standardisation and rules, and relies heavily on relationships, mind maps and empowerment to get things done. Resilience views humans as capable of not only defending against failure, but of creating safety through their mindfulness, skills, experience and proactivity.

Resilience also complements high reliability. Using both allows organisations to standardise the systems that lend themselves to a mechanistic approach, respond when systems become brittle and fail, and deal with the issues that resist standardisation.[22,23] In short, a mix of both approaches creates safety and quality through proactive people being supported by sound systems.

Characteristics of resilient organisations and teams
Resilience is a form of control that kicks in when systems control fails. Standardisation attempts to minimise unwanted variability but it cannot eliminate it because variation inevitably occurs. These organisations know the difference between unsafe and annoying variation, and they will focus on identifying and responding to the variation likely to cause harm.

Resilient staff and teams are aware that their system is not perfect, and is operating on a safety plateau. They learn to observe, recognise and respond when organisational pressures are shrinking that plateau. A resilient organisation is one in which staff are supported to anticipate failure and restore safe conditions during or after unexpected or crisis events. Resilient organisations encourage and develop situational awareness, proactivity and effective interactions to enable decision making outside the realms of the protocol when required.[23,24]

WHEN RESILIENCE GOES MISSING

Healthcare is not alone in having an over reliance on policy and rules to create safety. This has never been more apparent than in two major disasters over the past few years: the 2010 oil rig explosion in the Gulf of Mexico, responsible for the death of 11 workers and the biggest environmental disaster in US history; and the 2009 'Black Saturday' Victorian bushfires which resulted in 173 deaths.

The Victorian Bushfire Royal Commission discussed the lack of resilience present in the bushfire response without ever mentioning the word:

> *Government fire services furtively developed their doctrinaire rules then enforced them with mindless zeal. Fire and emergency supremos were provided with limitless authority to bend citizens and communities to their rigid controls without effective scrutiny or supervision. What emerges is a layer of self-styled bureaucratic intelligentsia devising policies that become sacrosanct in themselves regardless of their original purpose. Ideological processes left no room for common sense, pragmatism or compassion and opportunities to help vulnerable people were wasted. Directions, strategies and resources were issued and controlled by executives far removed from the horrific reality that their edicts and regulations created.*[30]

Similarly, the *New York Times* investigation into the Deepwater Horizon oil rig disaster claimed:

> *The disaster ... occurred because every single defence on the rig failed. At critical moments on the night of April 20 members of the crew hesitated and did not take the decisive steps needed. Communications fell apart, warning signs were missed and crew members in critical areas failed to co-ordinate a response. The result ... was paralysis. The paralysis had two main sources: the first was a failure to train for the worst ... [the other was] the sheer complexity of the Horizon's defences and by the policies that explained when they were to be deployed ... [E]mergency protocols often urged rapid action while also warning against over-reaction.*[32]

Resilient organisations expect to be surprised so they develop their staff to be prepared for, and to respond effectively to, these surprises. In short, resilience supports safety in the real world.

A side effect of developing resilience is that staff may be more likely to improvise with all of their protocols. So, situations in which resilient responses may be required need to be clearly delineated. This requires the input of experienced, senior staff to identify high-risk situations and formulate appropriate responses in the face of systems failure.

Resilient organisations also know that experienced staff with situational awareness can be found across all levels of the organisation's hierarchy. These staff need to know that they play an important role in creating safety.[12] Some people call their ability to spot a potential hazard or unexpected change 'intuition'. This is essentially pattern recognition. Experienced staff know instinctively when a situation is not quite right, even if they can't put their finger on why. They can tell that the normal pattern is wrong, or changing, even before they can consciously identify what's going on. No doubt you have experienced this. Resilience attempts to capture and use this know-how.

The challenge for organisations is to keep these two in balance; to develop rules and protocols to support safe practice, and also to keep an eye on work as it is really done and situations as they really occur. It is not necessarily easy to identify, train and encourage staff to understand that new and unexpected situations will arise tomorrow and that their skills and experience in effective decision making will be required and valued. This is where the use of simple rules, as discussed in Chapter Two, may prove most useful. Teams attempting to build their resilience may agree on key principles, rather than long lists of tasks, to guide their actions in high-risk situations. For example, simple rules for the treatment of heart attack have been widely promulgated in recent years, such as:

- ensure patient receives thrombolysis within sixty minutes of chest pain
- the thrombolysis can be administered in any environment by a properly trained individual.[26]

Of course, simple rules must be thoroughly tested before being implemented. And if they're to be embraced, they must provide a simple but effective way of managing a complex situation. When effectively developed and applied, simple rules pay dividends – both in improved safety and job satisfaction and developing resilience more broadly can support job satisfaction by providing acknowledgement of hard earned knowldege and flexibility and empowerment to use experience and expertise to resolve difficult situations.

Creating resilient organisations

The rapidly expanding literature in this area identifies the following key strategies implemented by resilient organisations to build resilience and improve reliability.

Train staff to develop a preoccupation with failure

Resilient organisations train their staff to be situationally aware and work with them to build up an inventory of the failures that have happened as well as the failures that may happen. They understand that small lapses and little problems can add up to big problems and catastrophic failure. Staff are vigilant about the inevitable erosion of policies and protocols in a complex environment that lead to unsafe practice, and know how to respond.

Involve staff in building rich pictures of how work is really done

Resilient organisations build rich pictures of difficult situations rather than attempting to over simplify and reduce everything to its root cause. We know in a complex system there is unlikely to be only one cause of problems and adverse events; they are generally the result of the interaction of many parts of the system. Resilient organisations develop detailed scenarios of difficult situations where things have gone wrong and of high-risk situations where things might go wrong. They engage the staff likely to be involved in this process and tap into their perspectives and experience. This approach is a good fit for effecting change in complex systems.

Build an understanding of frontline operations

These organisations are attentive to the frontline where the real work gets done. They develop mindfulness in frontline people so they can make the continuous adjustments within a changing environment that prevent errors from accumulating and enlarging. These organisations are aware of the close ties between sensitivity to frontline operations and sensitivity to relationships within a complex system. They understand that to get the real picture, you have to ask the real people.

Foster a realistic view of their own safety capability and continuously improve it

Resilient organisations understand that none of their systems is able to completely prevent errors occurring. All complex systems will be resilient in some ways and brittle in the face of other challenges. Managers and staff work together to identify the weaknesses in the system. Resilient organisations proactively seek and observe systems that support high-risk procedures to see how they perform when pushed near the boundaries of the safe operation plateau. [25,27]

➤ TOP TIP – WHY QUALITY MANAGERS SHOULD WANT TO PROMOTE RESILIENCE

- Resilience requires clear roles and responsibilities – which is just as important for quality as for safety
- Resilience recognises and values people's strengths, no matter what their place in the organisational hierarchy
- Resilience requires individuals and teams to understand short and long-term quality goals and empowers them to take action to achieve them
- Resilience invites individuals and teams to contribute their experience in achieving consistently high-quality care and services
- Resilience teaches and empowers staff to be observant and responsive, to use their initiative and make good decisions when faced with unexpected situations. From a quality perspective, this could include changes in a patient's condition, a 'left field' request from consumers and families, observing when a client needs another five minutes attention or identifying a resident who is unhappy or dehydrated.

The chief characteristic of these organisations is not that they are error free, but that the errors don't overwhelm them. They develop capabilities to detect, contain and bounce back from the inevitable errors and weaknesses that are part of any complex organisation. They understand that resilience is a combination of minimising error and improvising smart workarounds that allow the system to keep functioning when difficult situations arise. Resilient organisations understand that when a system has been stretched in response to an incident, even if it has been managed well, that the system may not be as robust and elastic as it once was and may not perform as well next time.

Cultivate roles, responsibilities and mindfulness for safety

Resilient organisations reward and cultivate different skills and ways of thinking. Rigid hierarchies have their own special vulnerability to error and rarely reflect how the organisation really works. In difficult situations in resilient organisations, authority migrates to the people with the most experience and expertise, regardless of their rank. All of this requires mindful management on the part of those responsible for the safety of organisations. A good example of an organisation practising this mindfulness and resilience is an aircraft carrier (often described as the most dangerous 4½ acres in the world). It is indeed a complex environment where many unexpected and uncontrollable factors such as the weather and the sea, life and death scenarios, high-risk activities, stress and fatigue combine. Everyone on a carrier is expected to be mindful and to initiate appropriate action in the face of unexpected events – from spotting a bolt on the deck to dealing with a sudden wind shift when a number of aircraft are coming in to land in the middle of the night.

Invest in training and support to help people deal with unexpected change

Adapting to or assimilating change calls on our personal resources, including mental, emotional and physical energy. Everyone has a certain capacity available to adapt to change at any given time. Resilient organisations support staff to consciously expand their capacity for responding to sudden change.[25] Unexpected events show themselves in many forms such as:

- when an event that was expected to happen fails to occur
- when an event that was not expected to happen does occur
- when an event that was completely unanticipated happens. [24]

Decision making skills are key to resilience – and safety

Effective decision making, particularly at point of care and in high-risk situations, is a critical element of using resilience to create safety and this skill cannot be assumed. A number of decision making models and training methods, including the use of simulation and virtual environments, can be adapted from other high-risk industries, and these are increasingly used to develop skills in healthcare. The Cynefin Framework[29] outlined in Chapter Two, also offers decision making processes matched to the complexity of the environment. In the complex domain, an experimental approach is required in which a diversity of opinions is sought, and a high level of interaction between stakeholders is encouraged. In the chaotic domain, there is little time to explore possible solutions, and quick action is required with an immediate review of the impact. A resilience model for creating safety in high-risk situations fits well with the 'chaotic' domain.

Supporting resilience development

So how can you develop resilience in your health service? Quality managers and other organisational leaders can support and build organisational resilience by valuing resilience and recognising its place in creating safety in the complex healthcare environment, alongside the use of policy and systems. Individuals and teams must be engaged in real world protocol development and empowered to respond to unexpected events and know where their boundaries are in terms of decision making.[23,24] Healthcare safety is created from maintaining a picture of the way things really are, and identifying the risks by listening to staff and consumer stories, challenging small workarounds before they become big ones and being alert to language that downplays risk.[12]

Building safety – and quality – requires a thinking organisation

At its most basic, development of safety in a complex system requires the application of complex system rules. These are well represented in a resilience engineering approach to safety, which does not take a mechanistic approach to solving problems but works with the mental models, relationships and interdependencies of the players within a complex system. It is critical that we continue to build safety nets in our systems to catch our errors before they become adverse events and drive desired behaviour and decisions. It is also important to develop our people to be capable of stepping in and overriding these systems when they prove inadequate. Creating safety in the dynamic healthcare environment demands that we develop thinking organisations that understand and manage the cycle of systems development, erosion and drift, as seen in Figure 1.

We cannot expect to eliminate human error and systems failure, but we can develop organisations that are more resistant to their adverse effects. Achieving this balance within a high-risk and ever changing environment is a critical challenge for healthcare managers and staff. But this approach reflects more realistically the environment within which we work every day.

An environment that cultivates both systems and people not only supports the creation of a safer environment, but improved quality of care and services more broadly. Building resilience may not have the same direct and immediate connection to quality that it does to safety, but its alignment with improvement in complex systems means that it is also a key tool for the quality manager toolkit.

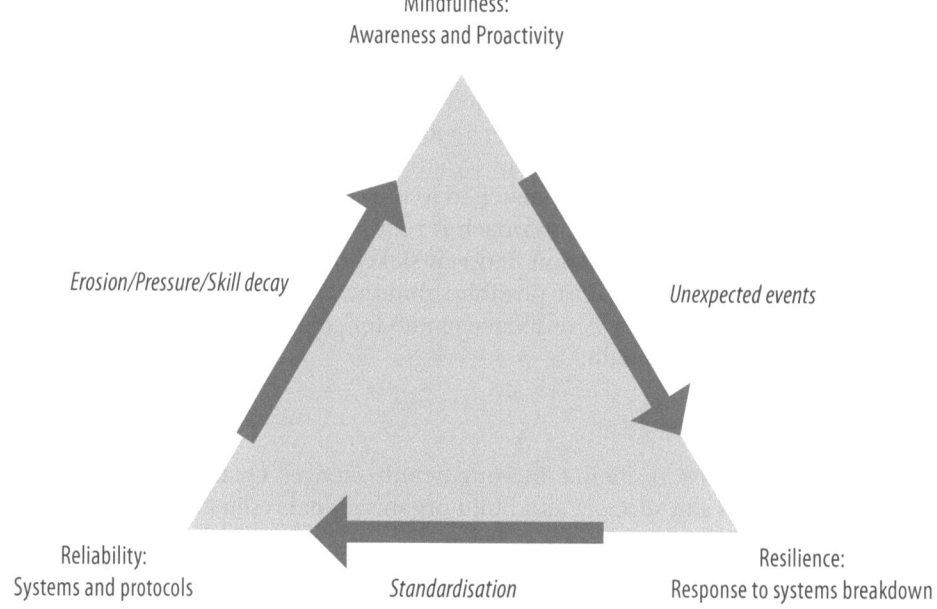

Figure 1: A Systems Development, Erosion and Recovery Safety Cycle [4,8,9,12,13]

In the end, rules don't create safety – people do. Quality care and services are created by systems and standardisation, and also by proactive staff working in partnership with consumers to create the organisation's vision for great care. Building resilience is a component of this approach that combines elements of creating safety, human factors, high performing teams, job satisfaction and empowerment in a way that may assist with winning the hearts and minds of the staff at point of care. These are the staff we ultimately depend on to create and deliver the safety and quality of care we want our consumers to experience every day.

Headlines: Chapter Four

- Safety and quality policies and protocols should be based on work as it is really done, not work as we'd like it to be done in an ideal world.
- Too many rules, rules that interfere with system goals, and rules that are not supported by leaders and peers are likely to be worked around.
- Working around rules leads behaviour and systems to drift away from their original intention, creating unknown threats to safety.
- Creating safety requires a mix of reliability and resilience that fits with the characteristics of complex systems.
- Resilience supports staff to use their skills, experience and mindfulness to identify and deal with unsafe situations.
- The provision of safe and quality care and services requires a thinking organisation.

References and Further Reading

1. Kernick, D (2011) in Swanwick T and McKimm, J (eds) *The ABC of Clinical Leadership*. Blackwell Publishing Ltd, UK

2. Braithwaite J, Coiera E (2010) Beyond Patient Safety Flatland. *JR Soc Med Volume*, vol. 103, pp. 219–225

3. Classen et al (2011) 'Global Trigger Tool' Shows that Adverse Events in Hospitals may be Ten Times Greater than Previously Thought. *Health Affairs*, vol. 30, no. 4, pp. 755–763

4. Reason J (2008) *The Human Contribution*. Ashgate Publishing Company, UK

5. Burnett S, Cooke M et al (2010) *How Safe are Clinical Systems?* The Health Foundation, UK

6. Frankel A, Leonard M, Simmonds T, Haraden C, Vega K (eds) (2009) *The Essential Guide for Patient Safety Officers*. Joint Commission on Accreditation of Healthcare Organisations and Institute for Healthcare Improvement, USA

7. Plsek P (2003) *Complexity and the Adoption of Innovation in Healthcare*. Conference Paper for the National Committee for Quality Healthcare January 27–28, USA

8. Bosk CL, Dixon-Woods M, Goeshel CA, Pronovost PJ (2009) The Art of Medicine: Realty Check for Checklists. *The Lancet*, vol. 374, August 8

9. Vincent C (2007) Incident Reporting and Patient Safety. *BMJ*, vol. 334, vol.51

10. Westbrook JI, Braithwaite J, Georgiou A, Ampt A, Creswick N, Coiera E, Iedema R (2007) Multimethod Evaluation of Information and Communication Technologies in Health in the Context of Wicked Problems and Sociotechnical Theory. *J Am Med Inform Assoc.* Nov–Dec; vol. 14, no. 6 pp. 746–755

11. Baysari M, Westbrook JI, Braithwaite J, Day R (2011) The Role of Computerized Decision Support in Reducing Errors in Selecting Medicines for Prescription: Narrative Review. *Drug Safety*, vol. 34, no. 4, pp. 289–298

12. Dekker S (2011) *Drift Into Failure – From Hunting Broken Components to Understanding Complex Systems*. Ashgate Publishing Company, UK

13. Flin R, O'Connor P, Crichton M (2008) *Safety at the Sharp End – A Guide to Non-Technical Skills*. Ashgate Publishing, UK

14. Amalberti, R, Vincent, C, Auroy, Y and de Saint Maurice G (2006) Violations and Migrations in Health Care: A Framework for Understanding and Management. *Qual Saf Health Care.* December 15 (Suppl 1): i66–i71. (Accessed November 2010)

15. Amalberti R (2010) Presentation at the 8th Australasian Conference on Safety and Quality in Healthcare. Perth, Western Australia

16. Dekker S (2005) *Ten Questions About Human Error.* Lawrence Earlbaum Associates Inc, USA

17. Degani A, Wiener E (1993) Cockpit Checklists: Concepts, Design and Use. *Human Factors.* 35: 345–359

18. Shojania KG, Duncan BW, McDonald KM (2001) Making Health Care Safer: A Critical Analysis of Patient Safety Practices. *Evidence Report/Technology assessment No 43*

19. Hughes C, Travaglia JF, Braithwaite J (2010) Bad Stars or Guiding Lights? Learning from Disasters to Improve Patient Safety. *QHC Online*, 8 April. (Accessed from qualitysafety.bmj.com, February 2011)

20. De Saint Maurice G, Auroy Y, Vincent C, Amalberti R (2010) The Natural Lifespan of a Safety Policy: Violations and System Migration in Anaesthesia. *qualitysafety.bmj.com*, 8 March, (accessed December 2010)

21. Braithwaite J, Westbrook M T, Robinson M, Michael S, Pirone C, Robinson P (2011) Improving Patient Safety: The Comparative Views of Patient Safety Specialists, Workforce Staff and Managers. *BMJ Quality and Safety*, vol. 20, no.5, pp. 424–431

22. Williams MD, Smart A, (2010) Patient Safety: A Casualty of Target Success? *Int J Pub Sector Management*, vol .23, no. 5, pp 416–430

23. Jeffcott SA, Ibrahim JE, Cameron PA (2009) Resilience in Healthcare and Clinical Handover. *Quality and Safety in Healthcare*, vol. 18, pp. 256–260

24. Weick KE, Sutcliffe KM (2007) *Managing the Unexpected.* John Wiley and Sons Inc, USA

25. Conner D R (1992) *Managing at the Speed of Change: How Resilient Managers Succeed and Prosper Where Others Fail.* Villard Books, USA

26. Plsek P, Wilson T (2001) Complexity Leadership and Management in Healthcare Organisations. *BMJ*, vol. 323, no.7315, pp. 746–49

27. Hollnagel E, Woods D, Leveson N (eds) (2006) *Resilience Engineering: Concepts and Precepts.* Ashgate, UK

28. Hoopes L and Kelly M (2004) *Managing Change with Personal Resilience.* MK Books, USA

29. Snowdon DJ, Boone ME (2007) A Leader's Framework for Decision Making. *Harvard Business Rev*, vol. 85, no. 11, pp. 68–76

30. Cutcliffe T (2009) Self-serving Know-alls Fuelled Fires in a Burning Nanny State. *The Australian*, 24 June

31. Bachlard M (2010) Should the Fire Threatened Stay or Go is Still the Question. *The Age*, 2 May

32. Barstow D, Rohde D, Saul S (2010) *Deepwater Horizon's Final Hours: A New York Times Investigation. AFP Summary.* http://coastalcare.org/2010/12/a-new-york-times-investigation-deepwater-horizon%E2%80%99s-final-hours/ (Accessed December 2010)

Q5 YOU CAN'T DO IT ON YOUR OWN:
Leading and influencing great care

'Leadership is influence'.
– JOHN C MAXWELL

5. YOU CAN'T DO IT ON YOUR OWN:
Leading and influencing great care

This chapter explores two essential quality manager skills: leadership and influence. Leadership is discussed from the perspective of quality managers acting in a quality consultant role and supporting others to be leaders as well as being leaders themselves. As many quality managers have to exercise leadership without formal positional power, the discussion also covers the often overlooked skill of influence and its role in a quality manager's effectiveness. The intent of this chapter is to add some useful tools to your quality toolkit, while trying to avoid presenting these skills as overly simplistic or easy. This chapter offers some strategies to navigate leadership and influence as a quality manager, but these don't include any magic wands, unfortunately. A large part of the quality manager job is to persuade and support a whole organisation to think, behave and collaborate in harmony to achieve a set of common goals. Remind yourself of the enormity of this occasionally, set yourself realistic goals for leadership and influence and try to enjoy this fascinating and frustrating aspect of organisational life.

To achieve consistently high-quality care you need strong leadership. But what is leadership? How do leaders effect change in complex systems? Quality managers often complain about a lack of leadership for quality care in their organisations. The executives, clinicians and managers in your organisation may want to lead great care but not know how to go about it. If you can help guide them by suggesting concrete actions, you will be helping them, your organisation and yourself.

The information discussed in this chapter is aimed at highlighting some of the key issues to do with leading and influencing the achievement of consistently safe and quality care. Follow up the references throughout this chapter if you want to explore leadership more deeply.

In general, people follow leaders who are:
- credible and know their stuff
- honest – say what they mean and do what they say
- forward looking – have a clear view of the future as a better place and are prepared to do the planning and work to get there
- inspiring – can engage people's imaginations in the view of the future and make it seem achievable
- competent – good at what they do
- empathic – are clear about their own values and also accept that others may be driven by different values.[1,2]

You may not be able to develop these leadership traits in others – individuals themselves have to decide to do this. But as a quality manager, you have control over the extent to which you develop these in yourself. In a role where control is hard to come by and you have to rely on influence to get things done, developing these qualities can be a source of satisfaction and make it easier to get yourself heard – and followed. It is also useful to think about leaders you admire and have been happy to follow, and model some of your leadership style on theirs. Not at the expense of your own individual style, of course, but it can be useful to watch other successful leaders in action to get a few tips on what works.

One of the essential requirements of leadership is having a goal – something to achieve. People like to follow leaders who know where they're going. One of the reasons we don't see as much active leadership as we would like in creating great quality care is that great quality care – as a destination or goal – is often not defined. That's why Chapter Six is dedicated to quality planning; so much rests on creating the vision for great care that captures hearts and minds and gives people something positive to engage with and move towards.

Leading quality care

There is a body of literature on the specific actions and knowledge required to lead staff in the creation and delivery of quality care. Unfortunately, the evidence surrounding the efficacy of specific leadership actions is relatively weak, due to methodological issues.[3] But there are common themes. We know that leaders in high performing health systems:

- keep the consumer at the centre of the quality system and develop the quality system as a core business strategy
- understand that engagement and relationship skills are fundamentally important to leading change and improvement in complex systems
- know that if you aim at nothing, that's probably what you'll hit; so develop and drive a definition, strategic goals, priorities and measures for providing great quality care for every consumer, every day, that are aligned with the organisation's strategic goals and direction
- drive, support and monitor progress with achieving the quality goals
- understand that the quality and safety of care are dynamic and will vary, welcome all information about the consumer experience, and are not afraid of bad news
- make obvious their role in supporting the quality of care delivered at point of care. Leaders walk around, observe the quality of care in action, seek staff input on improvements, attend meetings, give feedback, reward desired behaviour, provide resources, and remember that no one will take the safety and quality of care more seriously than they do – or appear to do
- get the right team on the bus. That is, they know how to choose the right people for the right jobs, particularly in terms of leading the creation of quality care
- agree what is expected of operational leaders, clinicians and staff in relation to safety and quality, clarify this in job descriptions and help them achieve it with direction, knowledge, resources and support
- provide incentives to improve quality and develop the links between high quality and efficiency, including making the Chief Financial Officer a quality champion
- build improvement culture and capability. Leaders understand what motivates individuals and develop positive relationships to support staff to take the actions required to provide great care
- recognise that, even with the greatest quality system in the world, in complex systems people will make mistakes, systems will fail and circumstances will change: it's how you respond to this that's important
- understand the difficulties of creating consistently great care in a complex system and recognise and manage conflicts between everyday demands and improvement work.[4,5,6,7]

In short, the research demonstrates that quality improvement is dependent on leaders to clarify the overall mission and strategy, create a commitment to change and set organisational structures that empower staff to drive great care in their own areas.[8,9,10] If you can tick all of these off as part of your personal approach to quality, and you can develop a small group of leaders in your organisation who model these behaviours, you would start to build some momentum. Developing leadership for great care is a deliberate, proactive process, and should form a part of the 'how' of any quality plan.

As we've discussed so far throughout this book, successful leaders and quality professionals take into account the specific challenges inherent in their organisation and think strategically about these challenges rather than attempting to bend the organisation to their will. They also empower staff to work together to use their experience, skills and relationships to create great care locally that also contributes to the organisational goals. This is a good fit with the way in which complex systems work – but may not be a popular idea with those organisational leaders who prefer a top-down approach to getting things done.[4]

Successful leaders and quality managers also know that staff do not necessarily welcome change, no matter how good it might be for consumers or the organisation, and initiatives handed down through a hierarchy are even less likely to be welcomed at the frontline of care, particularly if they are seen to mess with the goals and norms of subsystems. The less employees or managers are able to control their own work and how the organisation around them functions, the more concerned they are likely to be with their own rewards and conditions of employment, rather than with the greater good of the system.[5,8]

The organisational and values complexities within healthcare organisations do not make it easy to develop and drive a shared, system-wide organisational view of what constitutes quality care and how it should be achieved. Strong and focused leadership is not a nice to have, it's a must have. This includes leadership from the top of the organisation, at the local clinical microsystem level, from quality managers and everyone in between. Middle managers are particularly important in setting the agenda in their departments and services and, with appropriate support, are the natural leaders of achieving great care at a local level.[6,7] Leaders who do not proactively support and lead great care can certainly constrain improvement, and there is evidence that their actions or failure to act is associated with harm to patients and poor quality care.[4,11] It is in quality professionals' interests to develop themselves as leaders and help develop leadership in other influential individuals throughout the organisation. Without this, their capacity to drive real change and achieve great care will be limited.

Allocate and support specific leadership roles

As I've mentioned several times already – and not by accident – people need to be clear about a role before they can enact it. It may sound like I'm stating the obvious, but I'm constantly surprised at how little effort goes into helping individuals understand their specific responsibility for the safety and quality of the care and services they provide or support every day. Not all leaders have formal leadership roles, either; they will be scattered throughout the organisation and at all levels. There are many models of quality leadership and Chapter Six sets out suggested leadership and governance roles in great care at each level of the organisation.

Developing quality leadership knowledge

As we have seen, leading quality requires a particular set of actions and roles. It also requires a little well-placed knowledge around some key aspects of quality so that planning, and systems and decision making are well targeted and prioritised in this busy, resource-stretched environment. We know more than we used to about what makes high-performing health services tick, and this knowledge is an essential component of effective quality leadership. A number of studies have reviewed high-performing health systems and their characteristics, and these provide a guide for healthcare leaders to consider when planning to lead and create great care. It is important to note that no single healthcare system type was most associated with high performance; high-performing healthcare organisations can be large or small, regional or urban. Nor did any one factor stand out as the essential ingredient to high performance. Success depends on a range of actions.

High performing health services create a shared sense of wanting to be better, and drive towards transformational improvement. They pursue this through short-and long-term goals for the quality of consumer experience they want to create, which are linked to strategic, operational and financial goals. Goal achievement is structured and supported as a partnership between managers, clinicians and staff at every level of the organisation, and service-level interpretation and pursuit of the goals is viewed as critical to success. Quality goals and their achievement is embedded in executives' and leaders' job descriptions and tied to their evaluation and incentives. Clinical directors and managers accept accountability for quality, safety and service on their units, and are willing to be measured against external standards. Innovation at the unit level is supported by evidence, encouraged and celebrated. Staff are supported to provide good care through leadership development and mentoring, effective workforce design and computerised decision support systems. Data and measurement are also organised to support and drive the achievement of the quality goals. Local data is presented as event counts (ie, numerators) and rates in percentages, as frontline staff often find information based on actual numbers of consumers – their consumers – more meaningful than higher level aggregate data. Staff relate well to specific data about their consumers and services – such as what happened to their clients and patients last week – as well as being interested in longer term local and national benchmarking to identify problems and trends in practice. A little healthy competition between departments and services doesn't hurt either! Developing and spreading effective practice is seen as a priority in these services and is embedded through systems and cultural change.[12,13,14,15]

Know the warning signs of poor performing systems

Quality leaders, including quality managers, should be aware of some of the 'red flags' or indicators of problems with quality systems or culture. A useful set of quality red flags was identified through analysing the outcomes of various inquiries into poor healthcare conducted in a number of countries since the late 1990s. The findings of these inquiries found a number of common organisational issues, which serve as a useful alert system for any health service. They include:

- a culture of blame in which critics are ignored or abused
- adverse events are seen as opportunities for blame rather than learning
- problems caused by a lack of teamwork
- patients and families seen as peripheral to the process of care and not included as part of the healthcare team
- a lack of credentialing, training and support for staff
- monitoring and improvement processes that don't achieve clear results
- known problems with care and quality allowed to continue over long periods of time. [18,19]

The majority of strategies put in place to address quality problems in these organisations involved new policies and protocols, and increased monitoring, discussion and education. This is not too different to the popular but often ineffective PACEM approach (policy, awareness, communication, education, meetings) to change, discussed in Chapter Three. Quality and organisational leaders can use this research to scan and analyse their environments for issues that may create big quality problems. How many of these red flags do you see in your organisation? Part of the quality plan strategies of any healthcare service will be to fix these problems if they exist, monitor for their appearance and develop defences to guard against them. This is further discussed in the next chapter.

Understand what the frontline needs to create great care

An organisation-wide systems approach to quality is essential to laying the foundations for great care. In the end, though, high-quality care results from the effective practices and interactions of care givers at the front line. These frontline 'microsystems' involve care givers, consumers and support staff, as well as inputs such as policy, procedures, teamwork, resilience, and technical and communication skills. As we have seen, high-performing health services work with the rules of complex systems by empowering those close to the frontline to create great care and supporting this with effective systems and a positive culture. Improvements at the local level depend on leadership and action at higher levels, and successful leaders support local leadership and provide them with resources, including:

- permission to make changes and to take the initiative
- a reliable flow of useful information
- education and training for staff in improvement theory, methods and techniques
- an understanding of change management necessary to change core processes
- the alignment of strategic organisational incentives and improvement goals
- the development of a common purpose and collaboration to improve outcomes based on the language and mental maps of the local culture
- practical governance supports such as useful data, resources to backfill clinical roles and development of improvement skills. [14,20]

In short, you're unlikely to get quality action at the frontline without an investment in DKRS: Direction, Knowledge, Resources and Support (as discussed in Chapter Three). The effort it takes to empower staff to take on the creation of great care is worth it in time saved in the long term, or sustainability of the change. From the quality manager's perspective, this should mean fewer reminding encounters with managers and frontline staff, and hopefully fewer occasions where staff try to avoid you! Unsurprisingly, these DKRS organisational resources for frontline staff are reflected in the actions and processes often described as key clinical governance supports, as discussed in Chapter Six.

Creating great care requires a mix of front of house understanding, capacity and desire, combined with active and robust backroom organisational and governance supports. These are interdependent elements for creating high-quality care and services; neither on its own can achieve sustained lasting benefits for patients. Healthcare governance, and clinical/ quality governance in particular, is not just a list of things to do and systems to put in place; it provides a supply line to staff on the frontline and is the foundation of safe, quality care. Quality leaders reframe governance as a dynamic element of the executive and managers' responsibility, rather than a set of extra tasks on someone's to do list.

Perhaps the most powerful action in leading quality care is for the leaders to get out and about, develop relationships with staff and observe the care. If I were currently a quality manager in a health service, I would try to spend less time in my office and more time observing, listening – and supporting other leaders to do this. Oral reports of 'out and about' sessions should be part of quality meetings – and the finding used in the qualitative aspect of quality reporting. Bureaucracies inevitably increase the distance between technical and managerial staff, and one way of closing this is to decrease the geographical gulf between the two groups.

LEADING THE CREATION OF A GREAT CONSUMER EXPERIENCE

The specific research on characteristics of organisations that provide a high-quality consumer experience echo the characteristics of high-performing organisations more broadly. There is no single path to success, but some common elements have been identified, including:

- A senior figure in the organisation has the vision and drive for creating a great patient experience, and the skills to communicate these to others.
- Change is effected across the whole organisation rather than in one corner.
- Patients and their families are engaged in care and those experiences are viewed from the users' perspectives.
- There is an emphasis on continual feedback from patients, families and carers, and staff, and regular measurement for improvement.
- Policy and resources are provided to change the model of care.
- There is a consistent, integrated program of activities, including staff capacity building, rather than a series of small random projects.
- There is recognition of the importance of embedding desired values and behaviours across the organisation (beyond paying lip service to a mission statement), and corresponding incentives.
- Staff are accountable for and enabled to deliver excellent patient experience, and are empowered to make changes themselves.
- There is clinical engagement in and professional empowerment for meeting consumers' needs.[16,17]

Link finance and quality

One aspect of creating great care and services that requires more attention from leaders is making a link between finance and clinical quality. Many forms of improvement are good for the financial health of an organisation. We need to be smarter about helping those who deliver care to achieve what they want to achieve while improving the financial bottom line. Fortunately we now know a lot more than we used to about the cost of poor quality care. Here are just a few statistics:

- Health care-associated injury adds between 13 and 16 per cent to hospital costs.
- There are approximately 190,000 medicine-related hospital admissions in Australia each year with an estimated cost of $660 million.
- If nothing is done to slow the current rate of patient falls, the total estimated cost attributable to falls-related injury in Australia will increase almost threefold from $498 million per year in 2001 to $1,375 million per year in 2051.
- In the US, avoidable post-operative sepsis can cost up to $57,700 per patient, reopening of a surgical incision costs $40,300 per patient in excess charges, infection due to medical care costs $38,700 per patient, and the average cost of one hospital pressure ulcer was $37,288 in 1999.
- It has been found that common complications and adverse events can increase the case cost for those cnsumers seven times.[21,22,23]

Saving money while improving quality is perhaps the strongest driver for quality programs that we have and yet we use this driver poorly or not at all. This may stem partly from healthcare's traditional philosophical basis that we should be improving quality based on principle, not on cost – but the two are not mutually exclusive.

Determining whether a quality improvement saves or makes money depends in part on how quality improvement is defined. Some quality-related activities improve care and services for patients and some improve efficiency and save money. Every quality system should include a smaller, but critical, subset of activities that achieve both. Quality leaders should ensure that quality systems include activities that save money and reduce waste as part of the 'efficient' quality dimension. These are the results that will attract senior level support for the quality system. Making savings depends on how much of the cost the health service bears – who is paying for the poor quality in the first place, and who is paying for the intervention? The broader context of whether the service providers are rewarded or penalised for poor quality in the first place also has to be taken into account. There are published examples of cost savings from quality improvement interventions (although these can be difficult to quantify for a variety of reasons) such as reducing deep surgical wound infection rates, reducing practice variations in peripheral bypass surgery, improved approaches for caring for ventilation dependent patients, reducing operating room cancellations and delays, earlier patient discharge, reducing delays in the pathology specimen reception, and reduced readmission.[24]

Quality leaders who initiate discussions between clinicians, managers and finance personnel can help drive funding and support for the quality system. As you would expect in a complex system, however, linking cost and quality is not always straightforward. For example, when improved processes start producing a certain level of consistent quality care and services, it becomes increasingly more expensive to improve to the next level, thus the return on investment drops. At a certain point, it may be cheaper to accept a certain error rate in a system than it is to try to prevent all errors. So the cost of quality also depends on the consequences for the organisation and for the consumer. But we may also argue that in a complex system such as healthcare, with so many factors impacting upon it, it is impossible to eliminate all errors. Some events, such as Stage 3 and 4 pressure ulcers, should be able to be eliminated because there are clear warnings if the consumer already suffers from a Stage 1 or 2 pressure ulcer. Eliminating falls may be difficult without going to extreme lengths to restrain consumers' freedom, which may be counter-productive in its own right. Infections could be eliminated completely, but at what cost? And at the expense of which other risk management processes?[26]

THE QUALITY/COST DIVIDE MAY BE ABOUT LANGUAGE

Quality managers and leaders can sometimes act as if improving quality should be above budget constraints and this does not win them any fans in the finance department. And yet efficiency is an acknowledged dimension of healthcare quality and, in my experience, quality managers are as focused as anyone on trying to create a great consumer experience within the context of shrinking budgets and resource pressures. So it makes sense for finance and quality leaders to work together. Berwick suggests three ways of considering how cost and quality can be viewed as partners that may help translate this language divide, using the Japanese 'Kano' system:

• Kano Type 1: improvements that reduce defects, which in turn reduces expenditure on fixing them. For example, reducing the rate of preventable pressure ulcers

• Kano Type 2: improvements that achieve reductions in cost while maintaining or improving the experience of the person you are serving. For example, reductions in duplication of tests reduces consumer stress and inconvenience, and saves money

• Kano Type 3: innovations and new initiatives that cost more money than the old way of doing things, but are funded from savings gained in Kano Types 1 and 2 activities.[25]

Even within this context of 'buts' and 'ifs' it is still worth attaching a ballpark cost implication to improvement initiatives as this is a sure-fire way to get management attention for your efforts. Seek help from the finance manager in your organisation – they should be the quality manager's greatest ally rather than the deadly enemy they often are! In developing this relationship, you and your finance manager might find these tips useful:

- Choose improvements already proven to make services better for patients and reduce costs, especially those that come from a similar service to yours.
- Do your quality sums. Make your own estimates of the current poor-quality costs before you commence the intervention, calculate the intervention cost for a 50 per cent improvement, calculate when the intervention costs will start paying for themselves, and calculate the annual potential savings. Then track these costs. Research has shown that this can be done well enough for practical purposes using routinely available data.
- Adapt change from other organisations, and manage the implementation – especially the people aspect – using the methods, expertise and experience of others. Don't spend time, effort and money reinventing.[24]

And when you do achieve a real cost/quality benefit in your organisation, publish your experience so the rest of us can learn from it!

Specific leadership knowledge for quality managers

Quality managers need a robust, well-stocked quality essentials toolkit to do all the things they need to do. This is discussed in Chapter Seven. But there are also some specific behaviours you can model to be recognised as a leading quality manager. Here are seven suggested quality system leadership actions:

1. Know and implement the research on effective quality systems.
2. Understand the big picture of what you are leading and how all of the components of the quality system come together to create quality care; that is, be able to construct the 3D quality system jigsaw puzzle.
3. Influence and manage upwards to ensure your organisation's strategic agenda for quality of care drives operational improvements at point of care.
4. Understand the complex high-risk environment in which care is delivered and the various tools, techniques and approaches for providing safe and quality care in this environment – including the fact that standardising systems does not necessarily standardise behaviours.
5. Support the executive, managers and staff to demarcate what constitutes ideal care and what constitutes unacceptable care. Work hard to keep the care provided between these two extremes.
6. Support and guide your colleagues and staff to provide quality care in a difficult environment by using your knowledge, skills, empathy and relationship building.
7. Get out and about: listen, observe, learn and treat this qualitative information as seriously as your quantitative safety and quality data.

And if you're already doing all of these, you'd probably want to add an eighth: share your knowledge and experience through publication and presentations.

If you're responsible for leading other quality managers, you will be mindful of the quality professionals' perception of their role. Surveys of quality managers suggest that it is not the content of the quality manager position that affects quality managers' satisfaction as much as the way in which it is regarded and supported within the organisation. Those responding to these surveys come from different health systems on different sides of the world, but appear to want the same things from their organisations: respect for their work, a strategic role in advancing the quality system, and resources to support their activities. Quality managers reading this who already enjoy the support of committed and empathic senior management should rejoice – but don't let that lead you into complacency! These supports, once won, must be actively nurtured and maintained. And if you are a quality manager currently working without these supports, you must cultivate them, using your leadership and influence.

FINDING – AND KEEPING – QUALITY MANAGERS

A survey of quality managers across 97 acute care hospitals in Ontario showed that many quality managers were new to their role, due to high turnover. The quality improvement systems in these hospitals were not well resourced, and many quality managers had no support staff but were responsible for multiple portfolios. Respondents to the survey thought that the quality objectives of their organisations should be less subject to the changing demands of hospital executives, boards, government and accreditation bodies and not as reactive to adverse events. They felt that quality managers should be supported to take a more proactive role in developing quality plans with a strategic focus and engaging executives and clinicians in their implementation. Those with Masters qualifications and greater experience tended to be more involved in more proactive approaches.[27]

Similarly, a large private healthcare organisation with multiple facilities across Australia regularly surveys the quality managers across their network to gain an understanding of how they view their role, particularly with regard to issues of retention. They have found that many of their quality managers had not sought a quality role but had the quality portfolio added to their existing role, or were asked to fill in for a vacant position. The surveys identified the most common reasons for leaving a quality manager role:

- the demands of accreditation
- not enough time to do the job
- the job was not what they expected
- lack of managerial support
- they were promoted within the organisation.

Factors influencing quality managers to stay in their jobs were:

- challenge, variety, sense of achievement, constant learning
- flexible work environment: family friendly, autonomy, suitable hours
- loyalty, dedication to role, pride in work, capacity to influence change and make a difference
- work colleagues, being involved in a team
- support and leadership from managers, peers and the organisation.

The most important of these factors were reported as management support, senior leadership and staff co-operation with the quality agenda and quality manager.[28]

Adding influence skills to your quality toolkit

> **TOP TIP**
> Sometimes, out of sheer frustration, quality managers act as if they do have control of those who influence organisational behaviour, and resort to demanding their participation in improvement activities. But demanding or preaching the need to be involved in quality improvement is unlikely to get you anywhere but alienated. Everyone in your organisation, whether it is obvious to you or not, believes they are doing their best and providing good services for consumers. Influencing is a much more strategic approach.

As a quality manager, your ability to lead great quality care is largely dependent on your ability to influence great quality care. Sometimes, your influence is all you'll have to get the quality agenda happening. Many quality managers have a limited capacity to use hierarchical authority to tell people what they must and must not do. Even if you are in a position to do so, this is generally not a sustainable approach to systems and behaviour change or for relationship building. You also have to influence across the organisation (your colleagues and peers) as well as up (your managers and executive). When it's tough to focus people's attention on important quality and safety issues, a well-honed influence skills set can help you choose an effective approach to getting your message heard.

Most quality managers find that, when tested, their circle of control is quite small. It is important to define exactly where it starts and ends so that you control the things you can, and don't waste valuable energy trying to control the things you can't, as seen in Figure 1.

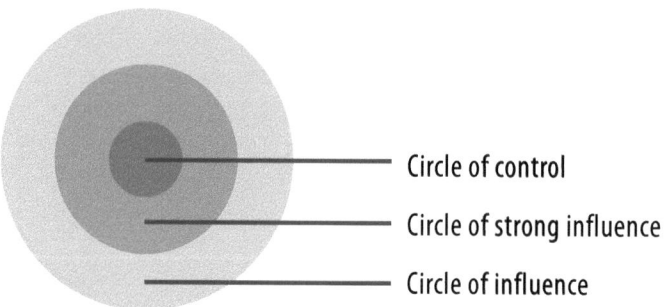

Figure 1: Circles of control and influence[29]

Much of what you need to achieve is outside your circle of control, so influence is your key tool for developing collaboration and cooperation. As we know, your organisation is populated with individuals and groups who are key gatekeepers and trendsetters, few of whom are under the quality manager's control. So what are your options for gaining their cooperation? Demanding anything of others, even those for whom we are operationally responsible, is not an option and is likely to backfire as people respond by more rigorously defending their position.[30] So you must use your influence. Your circle of influence must be as wide as you can possibly make it to work effectively within the web of relationships and norms that run your organisation. A savvy set of influence skills gives you a solid platform for engaging people in creating great care.

What is your natural or preferred influence strategy? Have you thought about it? If, for example, you wanted someone in your workplace to change their hair colour next weekend, how would you go about this? Bargaining? Pleading? Offering incentives? Guilt tripping? Exaggerating the positives? Offering to change your hair colour too? All of the above? We all have our natural influence styles, but as quality managers in complex systems, we need a broad range of influence tools at our disposal.

Relationship management

Perhaps the single most common influencing strategy successful managers use is relationship management. They work to develop a personal relationship with other parties to be able to influence their involvement in change and improvement. Relationship development and management should be a definite item on any quality manager's position description. You need it to gain cooperation on activities and projects, and you also need it to support others to enact their responsibilities for the quality of care their service provides. The bad news is that relationship management requires effort – and homework. You may feel you don't have the time and energy to develop this aspect of your toolkit, but the investment will pay you back in spades in terms of increased cooperation and less frustration when trying to engage people with your proposals.[32] Building your own credibility will also help build your influence. If people trust that you know your stuff, you follow through on promises and requests, you solve problems and advise constructively, and that your agenda is about better consumer care, then people are more likely to be willing to be influenced by you. Both your professional and personal power will grow from the way in which you are able to build relationships and influence others to act for the good of consumers and the organisation.

Don't dive into influencing without first getting the lie of the land. As we discussed in Chapter Three, dust off your binoculars and observe the locals in their natural environment before approaching them. What are the hot buttons of various key stakeholders? Where are the landmines buried? What are the loaded issues? Who are the powerbrokers? Where are the key relationships? What else is going on for these people at this time? Who do I absolutely positively have to get on board to make this change happen? Who can be neutral? Who needs to speak up for me? Who needs to agree not to interfere?

Understanding the politics

Although your health service may look very organised on paper, it behaves more like a small town than an organised collection of plans and policies. Like any town, organisations are filled with pragmatists and idealists, politicians and activists, optimists and pessimists. People chat over back fences and take a strong interest in the issues that affect them and their patch. Politics – both formal and informal – are part of everyday life. Successful managers know that politics are inescapable – they run through organisations of all sizes, from families to towns to corporations to

---

IDENTIFYING THE UNWRITTEN RULES: THE TEN COMMANDMENTS EXERCISE[33]

The 'Ten Commandments' exercise will help you understand the relationships in your organisation. You can do this exercise by yourself or with a trusted colleague to work out the mental models that you may have to influence in a given situation. The exercise works this way: if you were to hire someone new to get an urgent job done in limited time, what 'Ten Commandments of how this place really works' would you tell them so they could get the lay of the land quickly and get the job done without hitting too many brick walls? For example, what are the ways in which things get done in this service that aren't written down in any policy, procedure or job description, but that everybody knows and abides by? Is it that Thelma must be the first to know of any change? That you don't try to change anything on a Tuesday because that's when everyone is the most stressed? Don't teach people a new software program on a Friday afternoon as that's when there is a queue of people to use the computers? Always ask John the ward clerk to help with roster changes as he understands them better than anyone? Don't try to introduce a new training program without involving the HR manager?

nations. Politics themselves are not good or bad, but neutral. Politics involves knowing who to work with and how to work with them within the context of everything else that's going on. If you want to change the system, particularly a complex system like a health service, you have to understand how it works, where the power lies and where the key relationships are.[33]

Central to maintaining your integrity in dealing with the politics of an organisation is being very clear about your role and your goals, particularly as they link to the organisational goals for improving care and services for patients. Accept the reality of politics – they are what they are – but know your values and what you will and will not do. It may be useful to develop some personal ground rules for dealing with the politics of an organisation, such as:

- Deal face to face with the people you wish to influence. Politics is based on established relationships of loyalty and trust. Relations are best established one on one.
- Find shared objectives. These give people a reason to meet with you, so try to discover what it is that you both want.
- Take the big picture view. Remember that what you are trying to accomplish is improved patient care. Be open and share information as a means to this end.
- Tolerate ambiguity and try to find a way between either/or solutions where there are conflicting agendas. As we have seen, ambiguity is a key characteristic of complex systems, and polarised points of view are unlikely to be effective in this environment.
- Remind yourself that understanding does not mean agreement. It is possible for people to listen to each other, understand each other and still hold different points of view. In fact, when people of differing views try to get something done together, it is essential for them to hear each other in order to discover what they can do together. Disagreement does not preclude collaborative action.[30,34]

Flexibility and boundaries

You must also ascertain how flexible you are prepared to be to achieve your goals. People can easily lose influence by being too inflexible in the way they go about achieving their goals. Sometimes people with an exciting idea and strong commitment become more single-minded than is necessary. They lock in on the vision for change they have created and ignore other variations that could also work. Research shows that those without a lot of organisational power who have carried out important changes within their organisations are both highly persistent and highly flexible. They stick to the essence of their desired results, but are open to changing their approach to getting there as they deal with the many stakeholders whose cooperation they need.[33,34,35] They understand the concept of 'course correction'. Course correction can be challenging and frustrating, but it may increase your chances of arriving at your planned destination – even if you do have to take a different route to get there.

Similarly, when you approach an individual or group whose assistance you need, or to whom you are offering support for them to fulfil their quality governance responsibilities, it is important to be very clear about exactly what it is you are offering and what you need from them. Are you trying to gain agreement? Cooperation? Implementation? Or are you improving the working relationship for the future? Being clear about exactly what you need from people will help you identify your influencing strategy for dealing with them.[33,34]

Influencing starts with them – not you

When observing those you wish to influence, you are looking for a number of things. Some of these are essential to creating change in complex systems. As noted in Chapter Three, people generally value autonomy, interesting work, their boss's expectations and their peer's view of them. We're hoping in healthcare that they also value processes and outcomes for patients, but we know that this can sometimes get lost in the day-to-day demands of getting everything done. There will also be group norms and goals that are important to people, and it is important to identify these too.

One of the best tools to use when influencing others, to gain trust and build relationships, is empathy. Empathy is about SWTA: Start Where They Are, rather than where you are. Our natural inclination is to start our enthusiastic persuasion spiel with what we want and where we want to go. Unfortunately, this is really only of great interest to us. We point ahead and shout 'come on!' without knowing where those who we wish to follow us are starting from. Even if they want to follow, they may see themselves on the brink of a deep abyss that stands between them and your destination – with not a bridge in sight. If you have not first made a sincere effort to meet them on their starting ground, you cannot draw a map that enables them to move in the direction you want them to go. Always influence from the premise of Empathy + Sincerity = Persuasion.[35]

Influence is based on identifying the benefits for them – not you. It is almost impossible to communicate successfully with another person unless we're prepared to take their point of view seriously.[30] The secret to influencing others to get on board with your ideas is to ground your changes in their reality and to tailor your influencing approach to the individual. This takes a little homework, as with all skills, but the payoff should be worth it.

1. Clearly identify the issue and what you need from the influence. Ask yourself:
- What am I trying to achieve in my work?
- What is my vision for the future?
- What are the key tasks I need to undertake to achieve this goal?
- For each of these key tasks, whose cooperation will definitely be necessary and whose cooperation may be necessary?
- Whose compliance will definitely be necessary? Who can block or prevent me from achieving these tasks and goals? Who do I need to have agree, advocate for me, stay out of my way, or take action?
- What do I have to offer these people in return?

2. Gather information about the 'influencees' current state and environment.

3. Understand where they are coming from, be empathic, listen, understand.

4. Respect and accept their point of view and communicate that you have done this.

5. Decide the best course of action, assess whether or not you need to take active influencing steps and determine how to find a common way forward. [31,34]

Deal in their currency

Before selecting the appropriate influence tool, you must also be clear about what you have to offer the other party as a result of them cooperating with you – the influence currency. What do they value? The preferred influence currency of an individual in healthcare will depend on a range of factors, and may involve a mix of principles and practicalities, such as:

- improving patient care
- making processes easier, simpler and more efficient
- involvement in something new and innovative
- challenge, learning and making something happen
- recognition and reputation

- to be taken seriously and to have our views reinforced
- contacts and influence
- belonging to a group or team
- being useful and problem solving in areas in which we're skilled
- gaining resources
- controlling something.[30,31,34]

Part of your observation of the complex system in which you operate is identifying who responds best to which currency. Remember the Chapter Three discussion on engaging clinicians? The currency they like to trade in includes better patient care, more efficient processes, access to good data and sharing expertise.

Preparing the ground

Before you can offer currency, however, you must first get the attention of your 'target' and create a willingness to engage with you. This can be a difficult challenge for quality managers trying to get their issues noticed in an environment full of competing priorities – particularly if you need the other party to take action that adds to their already crowded list of things to do. So you have to be smart about how you approach people. Human beings respond to certain cues that influence their willingness to get involved, listen to someone's request or change their behaviour. And identifying which cues work for your influencees is an important part of your pre-approach observation. These cues include:

- reciprocation: people feel indebted to others who do something for them or offer them a gift. What can you do for them?
- commitment and consistency: people are more likely to follow through with something if they have previously committed to it verbally or in writing
- social proof: people look to others for cues on how to behave and what to believe
- liking: people prefer to engage with individuals they know and like
- authority: there is strong pressure in society for people to obey authority figures and experts
- scarcity: according to the scarcity principle, people assign more value to objects and opportunities that come in limited quantities or are more difficult to obtain.[36]

These engagement strategies can also be described as influence tools on a continuum, as seen in Figure 2. These apply whether influencing down, across or up in the organisation. If you are trying to manage up, which some people find the most difficult kind of influencing, it is even more important to do your pre-influencing observation and homework! Observe your boss and identify the best approach – that is, your engagement strategy – and which currency they trade in. Remember, start where they are – not where you are. The smart influencers are also able to link individuals' goals with organisational goals so that people feel they are gaining something personally as well as making a contribution to the organisation. This may be especially useful when managing up if engagement with your initiative also helps your boss to fulfil organisational goals they have some responsibility for. Yes, your manager also deals in a currency and it will serve you well to find out what it is and supply it, where possible.[33,34] Identifying the engagement strategy and currency for each individual you want to influence, and making the exchange a win-win, is a skill that makes organisational life easier, and requires a lot less energy than more common engagement strategies such as arguing or nagging.

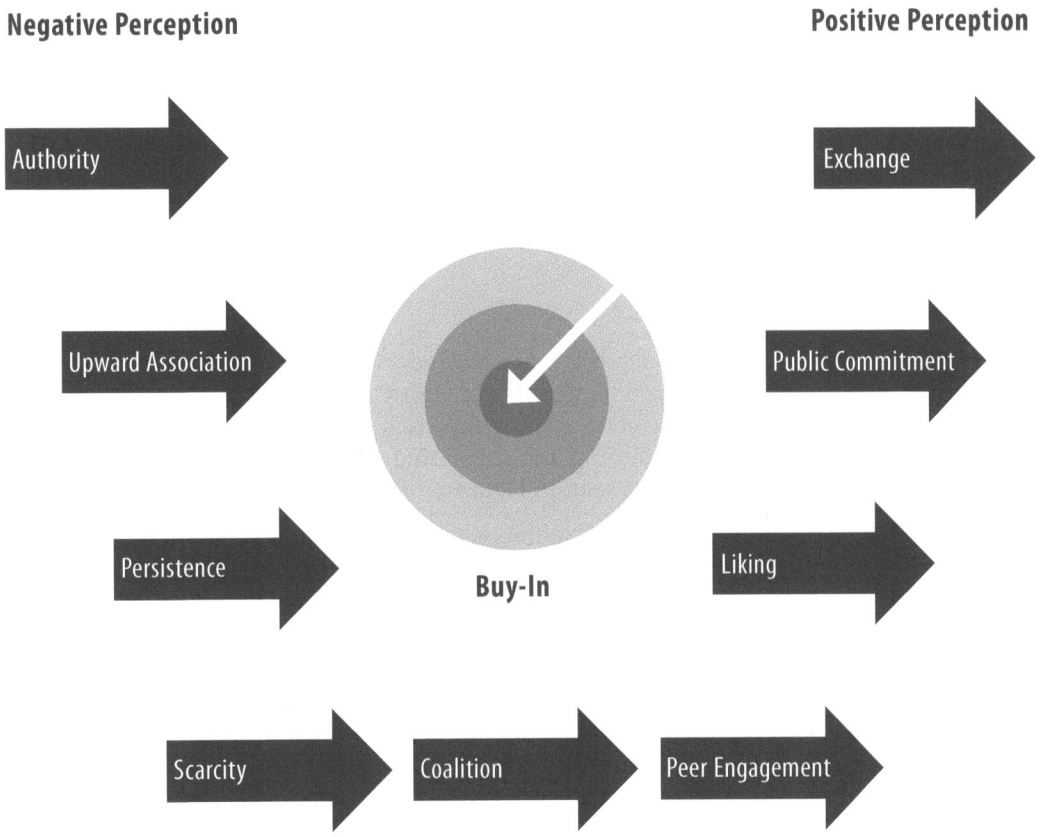

Figure 2: An influence tools continuum[33,34,35,36]

Separate the person from the transaction

One of the greatest difficulties of being a change agent is dealing with people whom you don't particularly like and who don't particularly like you. It's an unfortunate fact of life that you won't have a positive personal relationship with everyone you need to influence. It is easy to sabotage your own efforts by labelling these people as 'difficult' and using phrases such as 'how do I get them to change'? But how do you react when someone labels you 'difficult' or 'stubborn'? And it is unlikely that anyone likes to be forced to change, including you. People don't dislike change as much as they dislike being changed. Try to avoid the trap of easy labels that will lock you further into negative attitudes about these people. A less than positive attitude is usually obvious to others and will reduce your personal power generally and your effectiveness in dealing with these people specifically.[31]

Do your homework, establish the currencies they may be interested in, try a few different engagement strategies, and don't treat it as a personal thing. Find someone who gets on with that person or who views them positively. What do they see that you don't? What currency are they using in their relationship with that person that you haven't tried? Can this third party help you get through? The importance of being clear about your own goals and the organisation's goals for improving quality and safety is critical here if you are to have a chance of aligning your goals with the goals of the difficult person.[31,32,33] This is business with an important objective that is bigger than both of you.

That 'difficult' person may end up being an immovable object, but until you have thoroughly tested that notion, you can't know if this is true. If you can, approach that person and allow them to tell their story. Warning! This will work only if you are genuinely interested in what the other person has to say and not just going through the motions. False sincerity will get you nowhere. If this person is truly recalcitrant, or perhaps has a real problem, there are many useful resources on strategies for dealing with 'difficult' people and it may be well worth developing some understanding about different personality types.[31,36] But sometimes the timing is just not right. In organisational change, as in life, timing is everything.

The influence tools continuum [32,33,34,35,36]

Once you have done your ground work and you understand what is important to those people you need to influence, it is time to select the most appropriate engagement strategy and influence currency. There are many ways to approach people to gain their cooperation and collaboration. One way of exploring and organising your influence tools is to arrange them on an influence continuum, as seen in Figure 2.

These influence tools are really just different ways of gaining people's attention and buy-in, some of which are likely to be positively received and some more negatively, depending on your influencee and the situation. The purpose of the continuum is to expand your choice, as there isn't a 'one size fits all' approach to influencing. For example, the more coercive strategies on the left side of the continuum are more risky because they may invite retaliation. But occasionally the use of authority is the only thing that people will respond to, and it needs to come from an appropriate level of management – *not* from you![31] It is recommended, however, that you focus as much as possible on the right side of the continuum to find a strategy that fits your influencee; unless, of course, your information gathering has assured you that there is a certain type of influence you should use with a certain group or individual. The attitude you bring to the exchange is part of the influencing process and it is unlikely that you will receive a collaborative response if you can't offer a positive attitude and a serve of goodwill with your opening gambit.

You will already have one or two favourite tools from this continuum that you use constantly. Everyone has their own inbuilt set of influencing tools. Skilful use of these tools is an effective way of helping people to engage positively in organisational objectives and goals. But remember: influence is not about coercing or brainwashing! There should be a clear benefit for anyone whose cooperation and buy-in you seek. In the case of quality managers, in particular, the focus should be on building cooperation to improve the consumer experience.

Exchange
Most human beings will try to repay in kind what another person has provided. A sense of future obligation makes possible the development of various kinds of continuing relationships and exchanges that are beneficial to the relationship. The decision to comply with another's request is frequently influenced by the reciprocity rule. A useful tactic for people working in the area of compliance, in particular, is to give something before asking for a return favour. This can translate to making an initial concession that stimulates a return concession. It could also involve making an extreme request and then conceding and modifying it to a smaller request, which is likely to be accepted because it's a much better deal than the first offer.

Public commitment
There is a desire in most people to be consistent with their words, beliefs, attitudes and deeds. Good personal consistency is highly valued by society. Within the realm of influence,

securing an initial – perhaps small – commitment is critical. Once they have agreed to even part of your request, people are generally more willing to agree to further requests that are in keeping with the prior commitment. Thus, many compliance professionals try to induce people to take an initial position – even if only in a minor way – that is consistent with the behaviour they will later request from these people. These initial commitments are most effective when they are active, public, require some effort and are viewed as internally motivated.

Personal liking
Compliance professionals commonly increase their effectiveness by emphasising several factors that increase their overall attractiveness and likeability. One of the key ways to do this is through emphasising the similarities between you and the other person, as we like people who are like us and are more willing to say yes to their requests. Another factor that produces liking is praise, although this can backfire if it's not sincere. But we all like to be recognised for our skills and what we do well. Increased familiarity with a person is another factor that may facilitate liking, particularly where that has involved a prior cooperation.

Peer engagement
One way that people decide what to commit to is to look at what other people believe or are doing. The principle of social proof can be used to encourage compliance with a request by informing the person that many other individuals, particularly those who are respected and liked, are complying with it. The more ambiguous the situation, the more likely it is that social proof will be a successful strategy. People are also more inclined to follow the lead of others who are similar to them, such as those from the same professional group. We seem to assume that if a lot of people – or some people whom we respect – are all engaged in the same thing, they must know something we don't. So get as many people as you can to talk up your proposal!

Coalition
Some people enjoy feeling as though they belong to a group that has found alignment between individuals' goals and pooled its ideas and talents for a greater good. They enjoy the challenge of bringing people or professions together and finding a way to work collaboratively, despite the difficulties. This also satisfies a number of the influence 'currencies', such as belonging, recognition, challenge and making contacts.

Scarcity
People assign more value to opportunities when they are less available. This can be particularly true for certain types of information in organisations. Research indicates that the act of limiting access to information can cause individuals to become more interested in it. So messages may be more effective if they are perceived as consisting of exclusive or difficult to get information. As you know, some people find 'being in the know' particularly alluring. You may be able to bring people on board if your idea provides opportunities for accessing hard-to-obtain information through membership of committees, dealing with external groups and data collection.

Persistence
There is another word for this – nagging! For many quality managers, the 'friendly reminder' is their influence kit! This is not a fun approach for either party. There is nothing worse for a quality manager than to observe people actively avoiding contact with them, and not returning phone calls or emails. There is no doubt that reminders have a place in our busy healthcare world. People do forget their commitments and sometimes they'll be grateful for

a reminder, particularly if it's something they've omitted to do that will be exposed publicly, such as preparing for a meeting presentation. But as a primary tool of influence, the 'grind 'em down until they give up' approach is not sustainable – it will deplete your reserves of goodwill and is exhausting for both parties.

Upward association and authority
Some people enjoy fulfilling requests for compliance from people of authority. It has been shown that symbols of authority such as uniforms and titles can be just as effective in gaining compliance as the actual people in authority. Association with authority may work almost as well as the request coming direct from the authority itself. If you can say 'when I was meeting with the Executive Committee the other day they all thought this was a great idea', this will influence some people to participate. But for others it will be a turn off. And using authority as a threat by warning that a lack of participation will have adverse consequence from above, is definitely a last resort.

Leadership and influence are required for buy-in – and stay in

Every one of your requests for engagement and collaboration in change requires a core 'buy-in, stay-in strategy'. This will include the things they need to buy in to, the strategy for getting their attention and the currency they deal in. And it should also include the supports they need to stay in, such as DKRS. There's no point going to all the trouble of influencing people to engage with your improvement and then not following through on their involvement. It will damage your credibility and make it ten times as hard to work with them next time.

Human beings want to participate in activities that help them be autonomous, where they have freedom within a framework, and where they know what the boundaries of their decision-making are to make things happen in a way that suits them. This is why the goals and objectives of your quality program need to be cascaded from the strategic to the operational frontline of your organisation. People want to understand what the organisation is trying to achieve, and have some control over implementation in their environment. People also require tasks that are complex enough to be challenging and interesting but don't tip them over the edge into frustration and discouragement because they are unable to do them, the challenge is too great, or they don't make progress. People quickly lose interest in such tasks. You can equate this to playing video games, the designers of which have mastered the art of making the first two or three levels interesting enough to keep you engaged, challenging enough to make you feel you have achieved something when you pass each level, but not so impossible that you give up. If those first two or three levels are too difficult to get past, you are likely to give up and move on. If you can design your tasks in a similar way, you will greatly increase the pulling power of your initiatives, meaning you need to do less pushing.

A strong magnet for many people in the workplace is the link between their identity and their work.[37] People are more likely to engage with and continue with work that is meaningful, interesting, achieves something useful and gives them the freedom to have a say in how it's done. To stay on board, we need a clear set of goals, a balance between the perceived challenge of the task and our ability to meet it, confidence that we can produce results and constructive feedback about our performance and progress.[38]

Leadership and influence are key skills for quality managers. A leader for quality requires a range of competencies and knowledge to effectively play this role. Be clear and sincere about your motives and objectives, listen to those you are trying to influence and be prepared to be flexible, and you won't go far wrong.

Headlines: Chapter Five

- Leading quality requires the leaders to have a clear destination, and to define their role in getting there
- Effective leaders know their organisations as they really are
- Quality leaders should be developed in formal and informal roles at all levels of the organisation
- Influence is a key skill for quality managers and leaders
- Understanding and working with the politics in your organisation is as important to the quality manager's success as understanding and working with data
- Be clear about your goals, and be prepared to be flexible about how to achieve them in a complex environment
- Don't preach involvement in quality – lead by your actions!

References and Further Reading

1. Kouzes J, Posner B (1995) *The Leadership Challenge.* Jossey Bass, USA

2. Senge PM (1990) *The Fifth Discipline – The Art and Practice of the Learning Organisation.* Century Business, UK

3. Ovretveit J (2004) The Leader's Role in Quality and Safety Improvement: A Review of Research and Guidance. MMC Karolinska Institute and Association of County Councils, Sweden

4. Ovretveit J (2009) *Leading Improvement Effectively, a Review of Research.* The Health Foundation, UK

5. Boaden R, Harvey G, Moxham C, Proudlove L (2007) *QI: Theory and Practice in Healthcare.* University of Manchester Business School, UK

6. Young S, Bartram T, Stanton P, Leggat SG (2010) High Performance Work Systems and Employee Well-being: A Two Stage Study of a Rural Australian Hospital. *Journal of Health Organization and Management*, vol. 24, no.2, pp. 182–99

7. Balding C (2005) Strengthening Clinical Governance Through Cultivating the Line Management Role. *Australian Health Review*, vol. 29, no. 3

8. Berwick D, Ham C & Smith D (2003) Would the NHS Benefit From a Single Identifiable Leader? An Email Conversation. *British Medical Journal*, vol. 327, no.7429

9. Braithwaite J, Runciman WB, Merry AF (2009) Towards Safer, Better Healthcare: Harnessing the Natural Properties of Complex Socio-Technical Systems. *Quality and Safety in Healthcare*, vol. 18, pp. 37–41

10. Hardacre J et al (2011) *What's Leadership Got to Do With It? Exploring Links Between Quality Improvement and Leadership in the NHS.* The Health Foundation, UK

11. Reinertsen JL, Bisognano M, Pugh MD (2008) *Seven Leadership Leverage Points for Organization-Level Improvement in Health Care* (2nd edn). Institute for Healthcare Improvement, USA

12. Keroack et al (2007) Organisational Factors Associated with High Performance in Quality and Safety in Academic Medical Centres. *Academic Medicine*, vol 82, pp. 1178–86

13. Baker GR et al (2008) *High Performing Healthcare Systems: Delivering Quality by Design.* Longwards Publishing, Canada

14. Ovretveit J (2010) Improvement Leaders: What Do They and Should They Do? A summary of review and research. *Qual Saf Health Care*, vol. 19, pp. 490–92

15. Brand C et al (2010) *High Performing Healthcare Service Characteristics Literature Review: Executive Summary*. Monash University, Victorian Managed Insurance Authority and Department of Health, Victoria, Australia

16. NHS Confederation (2010) *Feeling Better?: Improving Patient Experience in Hospital*. The NHS Confederation, 2010

17. Luxford K, Piper D, Dunbar N, Poole N (2010) *Patient-centred Care: Improving Quality and Safety by Focusing Care on Patients and Consumers: Discussion paper*. Australian Commission on Safety and Quality in Healthcare, Australia

18. Hindle D, Braithwaite J, Travaglia J, Idema R (2006) *Patient Safety: A Comparative Analysis of 18 Enquiries in 6 Countries*. Centre for Clinical Governance Research, UNSW, Australia

19. Walshe K, Shortell SM (2004) When Things Go Wrong: How Health Care Organisations Deal with Major Failures. *Health Affairs*, vol. 23, pp 103–12

20. Plsek P, Wilson T (2001) Complexity Leadership and Management in Healthcare Organisations. *BMJ*, vol. 323, no. 7315, pp.746–49

21. Braithwaite J, Coiera E, (2010) Beyond Patient Safety Flatland. *JR Soc Med*, vol. 103, pp. 219–25

22. McGlynn, E, et al (2003) The Quality of Care Delivered to Adults in the United States. *New England Journal of Medicine*, vol. 348: 26, pp. 2635–45

23. Ehsani J, Jackson T, Duckett S (2006) The Incidence and Cost of Adverse Events in Victorian Hospitals, 2003–04. *Medical Journal of Australia*, vol 184 no 11, pp. 551–55

24. Øvretveit, J (2009) *Does Improving Quality Save Money? A Review of Evidence of Which Improvements to Quality Reduce Costs to Health Service Providers*. The Health Foundation, London

25. Berwick D (2008) Connecting Finance and Quality. *Healthcare Financial Management*, October

26. Kemp SM and Kemp S (2004) *Business Statistics Demystified*. McGraw Hill, USA

27. Gagliardi AR, Majewski C, Victor JC, Baker GR (2010) Quality Improvement Capacity: A Survey of Hospital Quality Managers. *Quality and Safety in Healthcare*, vol. 19, pp. 27–30

28. Jones C, (2006) *Retaining Quality Managers: the Recipe for Making Them Stay*. Paper presented at the 4th Australasian Conference on Safety and Quality in Healthcare and Personal Communication, Healthscope, 2010

29. Adapted from Covey SR (1989) *The Seven Habits of Highly Effective People*. Simon & Schuster Inc., USA

30. Mackay H (2010) *What Makes Us Tick? The Ten Desires that Drive Us*. Hachette Publishing, Australia

31. Kotter JP (1985) *Power and Influence*. Simon & Schuster, USA

32. McGrath H, Edwards H (2000) *Difficult Personalities*. Penguin Books, Australia

33. Cohen AR, Bradford DL (2005) *Influence Without Authority*. John Wiley and Sons Inc, USA.

34. Bellman GM (2001) *Getting Things Done When You Are Not In Charge*. Berrett-Koehler Publishers Inc, USA

35. Borg J (2004) *Persuasion – The Art of Influencing People*. Pearson Education Limited, UK

36. Cialdini RB (2009) *Influence: Science and Practice*. Pearson Education Inc, USA

37. Ariely D (2010) Behaviour. *Boss Financial Review*, October, Australia

38. Csikszrntmihalyi M (2010) Flow. *Boss Financial Review*. October, Australia

Q6 PLANNING FOR 'GREAT':
Creating a consumer centered quality system

'Vision without action is a dream. Action without vision is simply passing the time. Action with vision is making a positive difference.'

– JOEL BARKER

6. PLANNING FOR 'GREAT':
Creating a consumer centered quality system

Where do you start to define the care and services that your consumers deserve? Can your organisation develop a more strategic approach to achieving the quality of care and services your organisation wants to provide? How can you ensure your quality leaders have something tangible to lead? These questions are often not well addressed in health and aged care, resulting in quality systems heavy on tasks but light on purpose and direction. But if you aim at nothing, that's probably what you'll hit. Like a jigsaw puzzle without the box top, there will be many pieces, but they won't always come together to make a great picture. Creating great care requires more than a quality plan that is a list of tasks – it requires a consumer-centred quality system. You need a blueprint where goals, strategies, leadership and governance converge on a specific target – quality care for each consumer. This chapter works through a goal-based process of quality planning and implementation for creating consistently great care within the complex healthcare environment.

Strategic planning for great care – what are we talking about?

You might be wondering why the discussion on quality planning is contained in the penultimate chapter. Shouldn't it have been discussed earlier in the book? There is method in the madness – this chapter is about quality planning within the context of healthcare organisations as complex systems. As such, it builds on previous discussions about the importance of defining your quality system's purpose, how to lead change and the importance of a thinking organisation in creating safety and quality in this unique environment. As we've seen in previous chapters, life is different on planet healthcare. Quality care for each consumer at each encounter, even with the best intentions and people in the world, is not a given. Creating consistently good care in this environment requires a consumer-focused quality system that drives and pursues quality at all levels of the organisation in a way that fits with our complex healthcare world.

This requires a strategic, dynamic framework and plan to create the focus and guide the activity, but quality plans fitting this description in healthcare still appear to be the exception rather than the rule. Why is this? It could be that the purpose of engaging staff in a structured set of compliance and improvement tasks in health and aged care is often assumed and not explicitly expressed. Everyone holds a few pieces of the quality jigsaw puzzle, but few, if any, know what the overall picture is supposed to look like. Take a look at your organisation's current quality plan. If a new staff member read it for five minutes (which is, in reality, about the maximum time any frontline staff are going to give it) would they know exactly what quality of care the plan is designed to achieve – and their role in achieving it? Would it motivate them to want to be part of creating something special? Would it give them hope that it could be done? If not, your current quality plan, to them, is a list of tasks; important tasks, no doubt, but unlikely to drive staff to knock down your door in their haste to be involved.

Achieving consistently great care for each consumer requires the multi-faceted approach required to achieve change in a complex system. Your starting point is a clear and strategic purpose for the quality system, translated into measurable goals and objectives, and a plan that shows how the components of the quality systems framework will be activated and implemented to achieve the goals and objectives. Health service quality plans often comprise the implementation aspects (the 'how') without clearly defining the purpose (the 'why'). A strategic quality plan is goal based, the goals are focused on the consumer, and all initiatives and measures flow from and feed into achieving the vision for great care.

A goal-based quality plan should:
- help operationalise your organisation's strategic plan; specifically, the aspect of the plan that commits your organisation to providing quality care for each consumer
- define great care in your organisation expressed as quality goals that describe the quality of care and services that your organisation wants to be known for
- provide a roadmap and a vehicle for achieving great care
- motivate and enable consumers and staff to play their part in the journey towards great care for every consumer, every time
- support the development of cross discipline improvement initiatives
- track progress and keep the focus on the quality goals and priorities.

The importance of goal-based planning

So, what is goal-based quality planning – and why do we need it? Developing a quality plan and system without a strategic view of what's to be achieved is like building a house without a blueprint. Staff involved in healthcare quality systems are often frustrated because they don't understand why they are being asked to collect data, develop new processes or go to meetings. Simply, they can't see how these efforts fit into the bigger picture. All they see are tasks that interfere with their capacity to do 'real' work. This is no fun for either party and is one of the key contributors to quality managers' lack of enjoyment of their role. The goal-based quality plan is the blueprint for how the quality system components work together to achieve great care. A clear, focused plan can help quality managers to clarify and fulfil their role, and supports managers and staff to better understand their part in achieving great care. It also demonstrates that participation in the quality system is about a lot more than achieving accreditation.

There are three key aspects to your quality system, as discussed in Chapter 1:
- Maintenance – minimise risk, maintain processes and standards of care, detect problems, monitor compliance
- Improvement – identify and drive operational improvements in processes designed to solve problems and improve consumer experiences and outcomes
- Transformation – develop and pursue a strategic view of consistently 'great' care for every consumer.

Most quality systems address maintenance and improvement, but too few use their quality and governance structures and processes to pursue transformation. So how does goal-based quality planning address this? More importantly, how does it address this in a complex environment? Your quality plan and system are only as good as the extent to which they impact on the care the consumer receives – supporting it to be good today, and driving it to be great over the long term. Helping managers and staff understand this, and their role in it, is a key responsibility of the quality manager. And it's not just the managers and staff who need to understand it; a quality manager will often have to explain it to the organisation's executive and governing body. They may understand that they have a governance responsibility for the quality of care and services the organisation provides – but they may not be sure about what that really means. When it comes to quality, governing bodies needs something tangible to govern and leaders need something concrete to lead.

The strategic approach to quality planning and creating great care in this chapter is based on the characteristics of successful strategic planning processes used in healthcare and other industries, and is a good fit with complex systems characteristics. They include:

- the use of vision statements that inspire and stretch the organisation
- the development of revolutionary goals to achieve the vision
- a horizontal approach to the planning process where input and participation are equalised across the organisation
- using learning, information and rewards to increase the strategic view of the entire organisation
- encouragement and the cultivation of strategic thinking and culture change at all levels of the organisation
- having strategic decision making driven down to all levels of the organisation so that it is both ongoing and everyone's job.[1]

Organisations that use this 'dynamic' approach develop their quality plan as the platform for achieving the organisational strategic vision for quality, and the values that underpin it. The strategic planning process is managed centrally or corporately and the leaders, managers and staff who are closest to the consumer are the key implementers. As we have seen throughout the previous chapters, a goal-based quality plan must encompass the development and support of good people and good systems to achieve great care. It should also take an organisation somewhere better than where it is currently. A dynamic quality plan is a map and a vehicle for reaching a destination. That means that a strategic approach to maintaining, improving and transforming great care and services requires you to know the where (where are we now and where do we want to go?), the why and what (why are we doing this and what do we want to achieve?) and the how (how will we get there?).

Six steps to a consumer-centred quality system

This chapter walks you through a six-step process for identifying the where, why, what and how of creating great care, designed to be implemented within the complexities of the 'systems beings' that comprise healthcare organisations. The six steps combine planning, quality improvement and quality governance and point you in the right direction to build a great experience for every consumer, as seen in Figure 1 (and Sidebar).

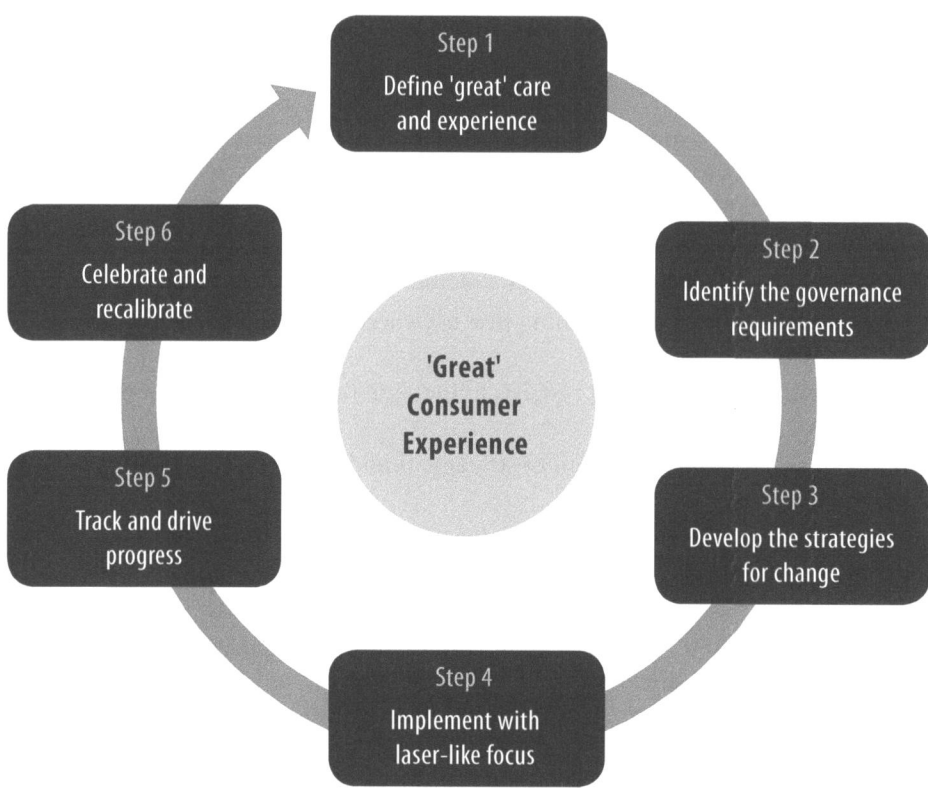

Figure 1: Strategic, goal-based quality planning in six steps

STRATEGIC, GOAL-BASED QUALITY PLANNING IN SIX STEPS: SUMMARY

STEP 1: CREATE A RICH PICTURE – DEFINE THE QUALITY OF EXPERIENCE, CARE AND SERVICES YOUR ORGANISATION WANTS TO PROVIDE FOR EVERY CONSUMER, EVERY TIME

1.1 Brainstorm the characteristics of a 'great' experience for your consumers (the 'why' we have a quality system), taking into account:
- How would we like each of our consumers to experience our care, services and organisation in three years time?
- How would we like to describe our care and services?
- How would we like our consumers to describe their experience with us?
- What would we like the media to be saying about us?

1.2 From these characteristics, develop strategic, aspirational and shared statements of intent and success – the 'goals for great care'.

1.3 What are the components of each goal from a consumer (subjective) perspective?
- Where is the line between acceptable and unacceptable care and experiences?
- What do we definitely not want to see?
- What behaviours, processes and outcomes should/should not happen?

1.4 What are the organisational (technical) components of great care for each strategic quality goal (the 'what' we want to happen at point of care)?
- What behaviours would we like to see from consumers and staff?
- What outcomes would we like to see for consumers and staff?

STEP 2: IDENTIFY THE GOVERNANCE SUPPORTS REQUIRED TO CREATE THE ENVIRONMENT FOR GREAT CARE

2.1 What governance systems and supports need to be in place to achieve great care from the consumer and technical perspectives and minimise the things that shouldn't happen (the 'how' we will achieve great care)?

2.2 What's the current status on organisational supports for great care?
- What do we currently have in place that supports great care as we've defined it?
- What do we need to enhance/change to achieve our quality goals?
- What new processes/supports do we need?

STEP 3: DEVELOP THE STRATEGIES FOR CHANGE

3.1 Develop SMART objectives, based on the components of great care for each strategic goal:
- How good do we want to be?
- By when?
- How will we know?

3.2 Select priorities: what do we need to do in the first year of the plan?
- To maximise the quality experience for the consumer
- To minimise and eliminate the things that shouldn't happen
- To solve current problems and manage key risks
- To meet legislative, policy and accreditation requirements
- Because they will take a long time to achieve and must be started in Year 1
- Because they cover a lot of the quality plan's intent, using the 80:20 principle.

3.3 Develop strategies/actions/activities for achieving the SMART objectives:
- Fit the strategies and actions to the environment: consider current norms and culture that support this and those that will need to be changed.
- Include the current governance structures and processes that need to be maintained or strengthened and those that still need to be developed and implemented to support the required changes.
- Categorise the strategies by 'maintenance, improvement and transformation' to ensure you consider all your policy, legislative and accreditation requirements as strategies for achieving great care.
- Ensure your objectives have matching qualitative and quantitative measures – how will we know we are making progress and moving closer to achieving our objectives and goals? How will we know if we're not?

STEP 4: IMPLEMENT THE PLAN

4.1 Allocate ownership and responsibility for achieving strategic goals, priorities and objectives to executive members and throughout line management, supported by relevant committees and working groups.

4.2 Translate the objectives and strategies for the local/service/departmental context and develop local plans for achieving them.

4.3 Ensure the changes are resourced.

4.4 Use effective change strategies tailored to a complex system that incorporate:
- clear first steps and messages
- influential leaders and relationships
- local ownership
- DKRS
- short cycle pilots of new initiatives
- sustain and spread.

4.5 Set up qualitative and quantitative data collection and create an easy way to track progress at point of care and channel this into the broader organisational view of progress towards the objectives.

STEP 5: TRACK, EVALUATE AND DRIVE PROGRESS

5.1 Line managers and sub committees monitor local/service/departmental progress towards achieving objectives, remove roadblocks, and re-think implementation strategies if they are not working.

5.2 The executive and organisation-wide committees regularly consider overall progress towards the objectives and act to drive progress:
- Are we seeing more of the behaviours and outcomes we want?
- Are we seeing fewer problems and behaviours from the 'unacceptable care and experience' side of the line?

5.3 The governing body tracks progress with the strategic quality goals:
- Are we moving towards our strategic quality goals and objectives?
- Is the executive supporting and resourcing the implementation of the plan and the achievement of 'great' care?
- Are care, services and experiences tangibly or visibly better for our consumers?
- Are our consumers better off because of the implementation of the strategic quality plan?

STEP 6: CELEBRATE AND RECALIBRATE

6.1 Share and celebrate the wins, however small.

6.2 'Course correct' if strategies aren't getting the desired results and as the context changes.

Let's take a look at each step in more detail.

Step 1: Define the quality of experience, care and services your organisation wants to provide for every consumer, every time

We discussed the concept of 'great' care in Chapter One as providing the essentials of great care to every consumer every time. That doesn't mean we can't also provide over and above the basics but part of your role as a quality manager is to support your organisation to define and provide the essentials for every consumer, every day while also pursuing optimum standards over the longer term.

So let's look at defining great care. As we saw in Chapter Five, a common characteristic of high-performing healthcare organisations is a shared dissatisfaction with the level of care they provide and a desire to do better. We know that there is much room for improvement – we have enough evidence from the statistics and the public inquiries into poor care to last us a lifetime of quality plans. No doubt there are desired improvements and targets identified in your current quality, operational or business plans. These are important quality jigsaw pieces. But we need more than this.

Do you really know what your organisation is trying to achieve? What do you want to be known for in terms of the quality of care and services you provide? Where do you stand in terms of the key quality and safety issues? The research points to the need for a shared purpose if real change is to be made. Engaging people's hearts and minds in a common purpose requires us to paint a rich, specific picture of what they will gain if they participate and what the end result will look like. This is a staple of effective strategic planning. But it is still rare to see health services with a specific vision for the quality of care and services they wish to provide for their consumers. The pressures of short-term budget cycles and political and corporate demands do not lend themselves to a comprehensive, longer-term approach. However, stretch goals can have a transformational effect on an organisation. A strategic approach should be designed to take your organisation somewhere better than it is now, and that requires a quality plan based on the vision of great care that your organisation wants to move towards. It must also be based on current reality, achievable enough so that people can believe it can happen and enough of an improvement that it is worth pursuing. If you want people to lay the quality bricks, you have to engage them in developing a rich picture of what the finished house will look like.

Creating the picture of great care

First, you must define great care from the consumer perspective. It is not an easy undertaking to pull the threads of your organisation together to achieve a common vision for the quality of care your organisation wants to provide. And it is likely to be nearly impossible unless it is clearly defined, ruthlessly prioritised and pursued with laser-like focus. It also needs to fit with existing system goals. To achieve all of this, plans should not contain too many ingredients and focus on achieving the essentials of great care for every consumer, every time. This means that these essentials must be defined. Engaging all levels in the organisation, including consumers to the governing body, is a good way to ensure this picture of great care is both aspirational and achievable. Frontline staff and 'frequent flyer' consumers are central to this process. No one understands the difference between great and unacceptable care like those engaged in the care and service delivery transaction. The conversation around developing the vision might go something like this:

RECAPPING 'GREAT' CARE

Remember the logic for using the term 'great' care outlined in Chapter One? The term 'quality' has become so compromised and has such negative, bureaucratic connotations that it is no longer effective as a magnet to attach to your goals. 'Excellent' and 'world's best practice' are admirable things to aspire to but they are difficult to achieve for every consumer at every encounter. And they may also have lost some of their ability to connect with staff and consumers due to overuse or ambiguous definitions. Achieving 'great' care for each consumer is a positive aim that is aspirational but achievable. It has some energy about it that staff can relate to. Even better if your organisation decides its own equivalent of the term 'great' – something that fits with your culture and values. I've seen health services describe their approach to the services they provide for their consumers as 'extraordinary', 'amazing' and 'impressive'. Or why not brand your model of 'great' care with your organisation's name? As long as it is clearly defined, it doesn't matter what it's called – the more creative and motivational, the better!

- How would we like each of our consumers to experience our care and services in three years time?
- How would we like to describe our care and services?
- How would we like our consumers to feel about our services and describe their experience with us?
- What would we like the media to be saying about us – or not saying?

There are many ways in which you can approach consumers and staff to be engaged in creating the vision for great care. An example is the 'VSP' exercise. You need to set the scene and tell a story. Let's give someone a visit to an emergency department – in another country, and alone. To make it more interesting, let's ask each person involved with this exercise to choose someone special to them – a very special person (VSP). If you are working with a group, ask them to brainstorm for five minutes. What do they hope is happening with their VSP in that emergency department in another country? What do they hope is not happening?

With a bit of preparation and practice, you should be able to organise the ideas emanating from the brainstorm into the dimensions of quality. This example can be applied to all sectors – just change the story to suit community health, primary care and mental health. This is an exercise I have used many times with many different groups of consumers, board members and health professionals, and, with only minor variations, the end product usually looks something like Table 1.

Another way to conceptualise aged and community services, where you tend to be working in more of a holistic way than in acute care, is to base your vision and goals on Maslow's Hierarchy of Needs, as seen in Figure 2.[2] Wouldn't you be pleased if your elderly relatives requiring care spent their time with people who understood their hierarchy of needs – and had a plan to give them every opportunity to meet them? Or that you community mental health service had a holistic approach for every consumer? This model can be used to develop strategic quality goals and objectives at each level of the hierarchy, and translates well to the concept of consumers achieving their potential through effective goal setting and associated strategies.

Another way to put staff in the consumers shoes is to ask them to imagine themselves in a high stress environment – outside of healthcare – that they cannot control. I find that asking people to relate an experience they have had with the legal system, such as a visit to court, gets people talking. What emerges is usually a discussion about how stressed they felt, how confusing it was and how they felt peripheral to most of the process because it was difficult to understand what was going on and if the right decisions were being made. If you have this conversation with a group of staff who have experienced this, they will be full of ideas about what they really wanted, how it could have been better and what the court could have done to have made it a simpler and less fraught process. I imagine that this is what at least some of our consumers feel like in our health services every day, and many of the generic 'solutions' generated in your discussion on the court process, particularly in the areas of clarity and availability of information, clear communication and valuing client input, are equally applicable to healthcare. Even if running this exercise with consumers and staff only raises awareness that your organisation can do better in these areas, that is a great start.

Person-centered	Safe	Effective and Appropriate	Continuous, Accessible and Efficient
• Translator available for consumer to communicate with health professionals • Someone is allocated to be with the consumer for emotional support who knows what's going on and can advocate for them • Consumer receives the same care and respect as locals • Care is responsive to the consumer's changing needs • The consumer is supported to be involved in their own care • Care is culturally appropriate • Consumer has a good experience • The environment is clean and comfortable	• Pain relief • No infection • No falls • No medication errors • No pressure ulcers or other skin problems • No clots • Correct consumer identification • Allergies are identified • Staff are not too tired to provide safe care • Consumer is not harmed • Consumer feels safe	• The consumer is cared for by competent practitioners who do what they are qualified, skilled and experienced to do • Treatment is administered when needed • The equipment is up to date and works • Health professionals seek and act on important information from the consumer • The treatment is right for the consumer • The best outcome for the situation is achieved • Basic care needs are attended to and chronic conditions are treated • Care is current and evidence-based and the level of care that the consumer needs	• The consumer can access the operating room and post operative care as required, and these services are coordinated • Health professionals collaborate and communicate effectively across groups and services to provide coordinated care • The family doctor is informed of the hospital episode • Information travels with the consumer around the hospital to support continuity and decrease duplication of questions and treatment

Table 1: Example of brainstorm on the components of great care grouped by dimensions of quality

Person-centered	Safe	Effective and Appropriate	Continuous, Accessible and Efficient
• The client feels welcome, safe, comfortable and respected at all times • Staff respond cheerfully and promptly to the client's requests and needs • Clients are able to freely express wishes • Orientation to facility and staff is undertaken promptly by both a staff member and another client • Care is planned and discussed with the client and their family if desired (including end of life care) • Rights and responsibilities are explained and enacted, and privacy and spiritual needs are addressed • The system of complaints and feedback is explained • Personal routines are respected • The client is comfortable to have family and friends in their lives • The client's independence is valued • The client enjoys the social, cultural and spiritual life they desire	• Pain free • No pressure ulcers • Medications are correct and administered correctly • Risk assessment regarding physical and mental safety are completed accurately and acted upon • Alerts regarding risk of falls are in place and effective • The client is not subject to physical, mental or emotional harm • The client feels safe in the environment	• Care plans are regularly implemented and assessed to see if they are achieving what they should be • The client's normal pattern of daily living and physical health is quickly established • The client is involved in their care to the degree that they are able • Chronic conditions such as diabetes are effectively addressed and monitored • There is an agreed plan to manage deterioration and end of life • Optimum physical ability and cognition are sought and supported.	• Assessments/appointments with allied health and doctors are made and occur when they are needed • The client is familiar with different staff and shift changes, and staff work collaboratively to ensure there are no surprises • The client is confident that their doctor and other health professionals are informed of any changes in their condition

Table 2: Example of components of great aged care and services

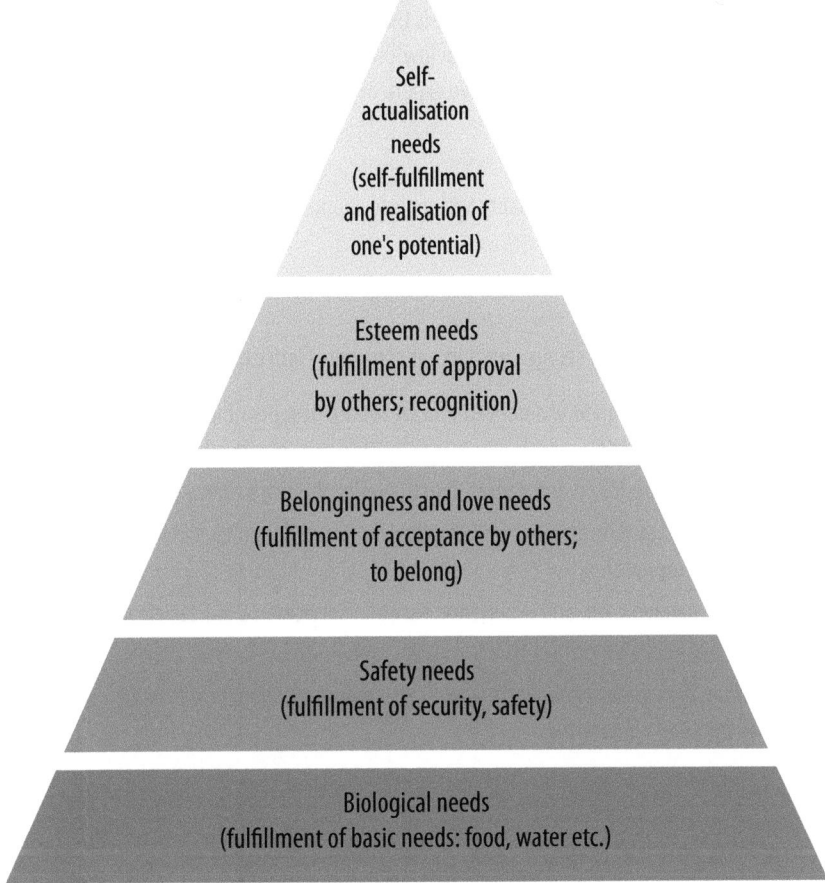

Figure 2: Maslow's Hierarchy of Needs[2]

Developing the goals for great care

So, you have identified what it is that your consumers should – and want to – experience in your service. But it is not always easy to take the next step and turn this rich picture of great care into concrete, strategic goals. This is where many organisations falter. Like a set of directions with no agreed destination, your quality plan may look like a long to-do list with no specific purpose and you may end up driving around in circles. So let's take a look at this next step. As we have seen, when discussing complex systems, without some tension between the way things are now and the way they could be, there will be no movement. So the vision for the care you want to provide must be rich, and also translated into concrete goals to describe the way things could be. Goals must be attractive and describe real, achievable changes that will elicit positive feelings. Identifying one key strategic goal per dimension of quality is a good and simple place to start, as in Table 3.

> Our definition of quality care at Super Health Service is that every consumer receives 'great' care that is safe, effective, appropriate and continuous (as defined below), that supports them to achieve their quality of life and quality of heath potential and enjoy a positive experience from our staff and services.
>
> The purpose of our Super Health Service Quality System is to support staff to provide consistently 'great' care for all consumers.
>
> Our strategic goals for the care and services each of our consumers will experience by the end of 20XX are:
>
> - Care and services are designed and delivered to create the best possible experience for each individual (person-centred).
> - Care and services are designed and delivered to minimise the risk of harm (safe).
> - Care is based around the consumer as an individual, and is designed to achieve optimal outcomes (effective and appropriate).
> - Consumers are provided with, and experience, care and services in a logical, clear and streamlined flow (continuous, accessible, efficient)
>
> Note: There are various 'dimensions of quality' models – the important thing is that you choose the one that best fits your consumers and organisation.

Table 3: Examples of strategic goals for your organisation's quality of care

Now you have an outline of your organisation's vision for quality care. This, combined with how it will be achieved, is the purpose of your quality plan and system. Although it sometimes feels like accreditation and compliance are the reasons you go to work every day, they are just part of the 'how' of your quality system, not the reason for it.

Quality plans can lack focus because organisations identify and attempt to address too many tasks, mix up subjective and technical issues and fail to clearly specify what the organisation is trying to achieve. Good strategic plans require tradeoffs and choices so that resources can be applied to the areas where they will yield the greatest return. That's why it's important to draw a 'quality line in the sand'. Identify the core things that all of your consumers should experience, develop your plan and commit your organisational energy and resources to first achieving that. Using the brainstorm as your raw material, distil what your organisation wants every consumer to experience as well as what they should not experience. For example, when we define great care from the staff and technical perspective, we would say that we'd like each consumer to experience a range of things such as:

- considerate, competent and proactive staff
- a safe environment, both physically and emotionally
- care based on the best available evidence
- good pain management

- proactive responses to requests or situations outside the norm
- clear explanations and opportunity for questions
- straightforward written information
- opportunity for involvement in care planning and decision making
- involvement of family and friends
- a sense of continuity and collaboration, including what happens before and after admission
- reliable, consistent, streamlined processes that make sense
- clean and comfortable surroundings
- staff who are good at what they do and do what they are good at. [3,4,5]

Whatever you decide are your 'non-negotiables', these become the priority components of each strategic quality goal to be achieved across the organisation. Once you've decided on what the strategic goals and priorities for great care look like, you need to explore how to make them real from the staff and organisational perspective.

Make it real

If your strategic goals are being met, what do they look like 'on the ground'? The answer to this is the description of quality care from the staff and technical perspective. This is the most common way in which quality is defined. If you ask a few people in your organisation to describe great care, you are likely to get a mixed bag of consumer and staff viewpoints. For example, some staff will say 'consumers should feel in the loop'. Others will say 'staff should communicate well'. In this example the same quality essential – communication – is being described from different perspectives. Most organisations that I've worked with tend to define quality care using the latter approach basically by defining what staff should be doing, and what should be happening – or not happening – at point of care.

But just describing great care as what staff should do, which is describing great care from the technical perspective, isn't quite enough to drive great care and an effective quality system. Developing a rich and attractive picture of great care requires the 'why?' or subjective perspective: what is it our consumers want and what do we want for them? Otherwise, quality plans soon become long to-do lists full of tasks such as credentialing and training and adhering to protocols and auditing – and it's hard to make the link between these tasks and their impact on what the consumer experiences. And from there, keeping staff motivated and engaged doesn't get any easier. Developing a rich picture of what the consumer experience will look like also helps to identify the culture required to drive the achievement of the quality goals; that is, the beliefs and attitudes that will shape the behaviours required to create great care.

So the quality goals are developed from what the organisation wants consumers to experience and what consumers themselves want to experience. Now you can link these to the technical perspective. How do we make it real? What has to happen at point of care to create this experience? What do staff have to do and say? How do our systems have to work? For example, a personal goal to 'get fit' is admirable but is difficult to achieve because you can't measure it, and therefore won't know when you've achieved it. You need to define what 'getting fit' means to you. What will it look like? What will I enjoy about it? What will need to change? What will be difficult and how will I tackle this? From this information you can set the measurable objectives and strategies that will help you make the journey (discussed later in this chapter). For example, if we were achieving the strategic quality goals described above:

- What would we notice that's different from the way things are now?
- What behaviours would we see from consumers and staff?
- Who would be doing what?
- What outcomes would we see from consumers and staff?
- Where is our line in the sand between acceptable and unacceptable care and experiences?
- What would we definitely not want to see?
- What behaviours, processes and outcomes would not happen?
- What supports do we need to make this happen consistently?

This is where you can link your organisational values or principles to the strategic quality plan. There should be nothing in the technical definition of great care that does not require an underpinning of strong organisational values, such as integrity and commitment. Staff at the front line (and many consumers – particularly the 'frequent flyers' with multiple or complex conditions) are well placed to help construct the 'technical' answers to these questions, and to link these to the organisation's values. One way of leading them through this process is described in Figure 3.

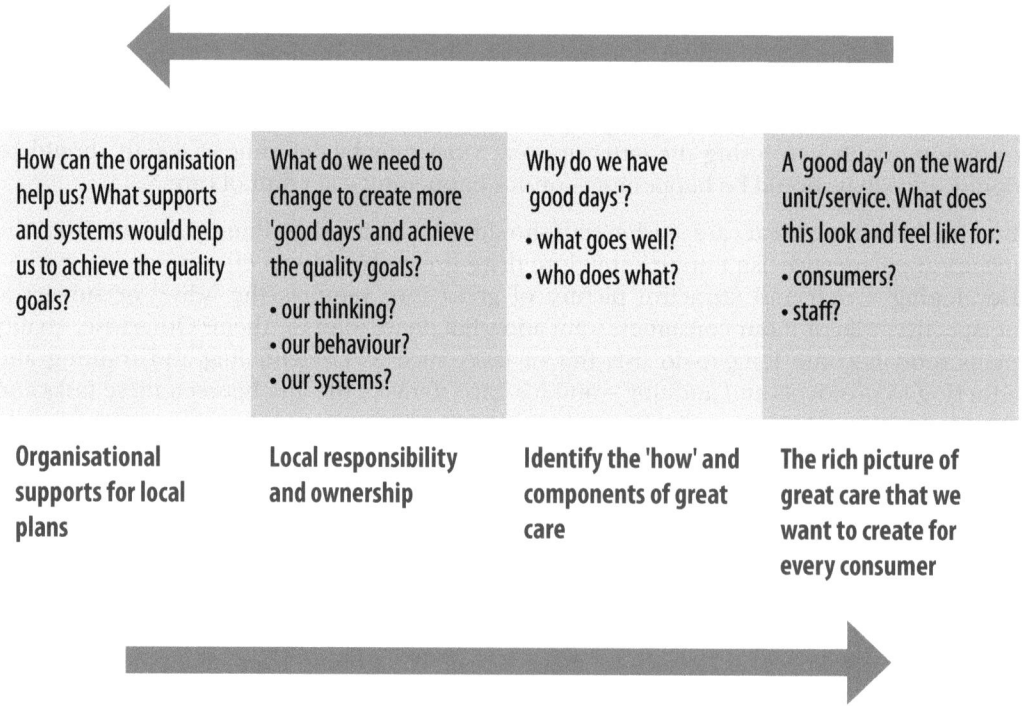

Figure 3: Example of a process for identifying technical components of strategic quality goals

Organisational/technical perspective on components of great care within each strategic quality goal			
Care and services are designed and delivered to create the best possible experience for each individual (person-centred)	Care and services are designed and delivered to minimise the risk of harm (safe)	Care and treatment is based around the consumer as an individual, and is designed to achieve optimal outcomes (effective and appropriate)	Consumers experience care and services in a logical, clear and streamlined flow (continuous, accessible and efficient)
<ul><li>Consumers are involved in decisions regarding all aspects of their care</li><li>Care is culturally sensitive and respectful of consumers' care goals</li><li>There is a planned process of communication between healthcare professionals, consumers and carers</li><li>Residents and families are treated with respect</li><li>Staff are responsive to changing consumer needs</li><li>Informed consent is always given, based on a real understanding of proposed treatment</li><li>Involvement of support persons/carers is facilitated</li></ul>	<ul><li>Risks are identified and managed to minimise harm to consumers</li><li>The environment is fit for purpose and promotes safety</li><li>Staff are clear about and enact their responsibilities for providing safe care</li><li>Care processes are proactively assessed for risk and effective controls put in place</li><li>Correct consumer identification processes are implemented and regarded as a key safety measure</li><li>Consumers are encouraged and supported to play their role in ensuring safe care</li></ul>	<ul><li>Staff are competent, credentialed, current and work within their scope of practice</li><li>Care is based on the best available evidence</li><li>Basic care needs are identified and met</li><li>The best possible outcome for each client is pursued through timely and accurate diagnosis and correct care and treatment</li><li>Evaluation of the care process and its effectiveness is regularly undertaken with each consumer</li></ul>	<ul><li>Health professionals, consumers and carers have a shared understanding of the care journey and consumer needs</li><li>Access points are clear and minimise waiting times</li><li>The system supports a multi-disciplinary approach to care to meet all aspects of consumer needs</li><li>Clear and planned processes for care are implemented consistently across services and professional groups</li><li>Planned and accurate communication/ information is shared between staff and consumers in response to changes in care status</li><li>The referral system between services within and outside of the organisation supports smooth transitions, reduces duplication and promotes uninterrupted care</li></ul>

Table 4: Examples of the technical components of great care within each strategic quality goal

Decide on the key components of great care

The components of each strategic quality goal will be derived from these brainstorms with staff and consumers. You can also draw on contemporary standards, literature and research. What you want to end up with is a set of components of each quality goal that cover both the subjective and technical aspects of care. What we generally find in quality plans and discussions about safety and quality in healthcare is great care described by the organisational, rather than the consumer, components. We miss the step that says 'this is why we want things to be this way, this is why we want staff to be credentialed and competent and effective communicators'. Without the 'why', quality systems become all about what staff have to do and achieve and the organisational processes for making this happen. This is where you end up with staff viewing your quality system as extra requirements with little purpose. So make this connection real. An example of some of the organisational components that make up each strategic quality goal is seen in Table 4.

These are the things you want every consumer to experience, described from an organisational perspective. This does not preclude the inclusion of innovative, transformational projects in your quality plan – the two are not mutually exclusive. In fact, you're likely to need significant innovation and transformation to achieve the essentials of great care for every consumer, every time. And policy, legislative, industry and accreditation requirements – your quality 'maintenance' activities – also need to be integrated into your quality plan and system. Accreditation, professional and industry standards fit well into both the technical components of great care and the governance supports.

Step 2: Identify the governance supports required to create the environment for great care

Once your organisation has determined what it wants to achieve, and why it wants to achieve it, the rest is just the 'how'. A challenging 'how'! It's not just about implementing improvement strategies and activities. Great quality care and services for every consumer cannot be achieved without great quality governance infrastructure.

The concept of quality governance is a relatively recent phenomenon. When I started working as a quality manager in the 1980s, we thought that if we were accredited, doing some auditing and clinical reviews and engaging staff in quality projects then we were doing well. We knew that leadership was important, but we didn't know how important it was or indeed how best to lead. It took the various studies and inquiries into suboptimal care and adverse events in healthcare to demonstrate that safe and high-quality care in a complex environment requires more than good staff trying hard. Of course, great care can't be achieved without good staff doing their best! But to create great care consistently, healthcare staff also need sturdy organisational supports behind them. Staff are 'front of house' – out there working with the customers. Governance is 'back of house' – the behind-the-scenes systems that support staff and enable them to provide a great consumer experience. Figure 4 gives a snapshot of the 3D quality jigsaw and shows how the goals, components and plan fit together.

To make the components of great care happen for every consumer, every day you'll need to ask:

- What do we currently have in place that supports great care as we've defined it?
- What do we need to enhance/change to achieve our quality goals?
- What new processes/supports do we need that we don't currently have?

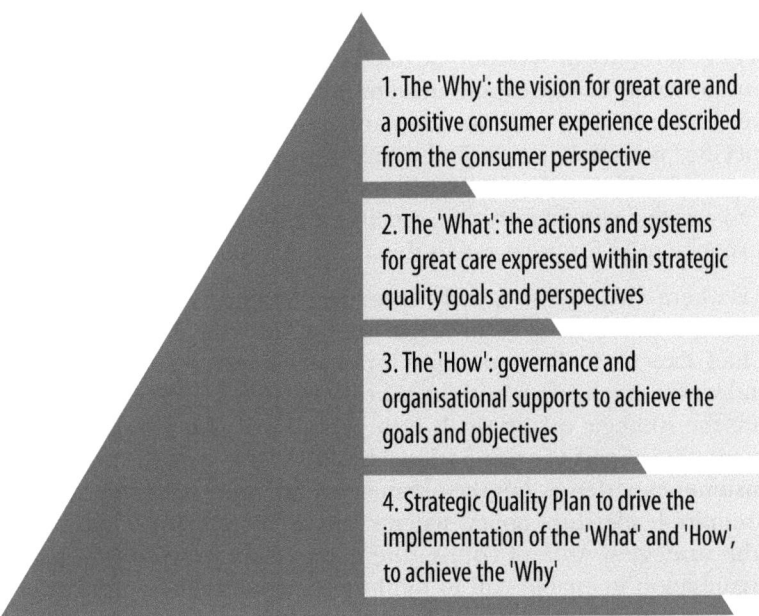

Figure 4: Overview of the '3D quality jigsaw puzzle' components

Providing great care and guarding against organisational weaknesses that allow poor care requires commitment and accountability to be embedded in the organisational structures and culture. Setting goals and targets for the quality of care your organisation wants to deliver, and implementing strategies to achieve them, is part of the core business (and governance) of any health or aged care organisation. A goal-oriented approach also unites the traditional silos of quality, risk, innovation and redesign in a common purpose, as they are all systems for achieving good quality care.

The emergence of clinical governance, over the past decade has been healthcare's approach to providing this accountability, planning and support. In aged and primary care, this can be reframed using more appropriate terms such as 'quality governance' or 'care governance'. The key components of governance can be organised into four generic cornerstones (see Appendix 2 for an example list of the key components within each of these categories):

- strategic leadership, planning and culture
- consumer participation
- effective and accountable workforce
- quality and risk systems.

These governance supports have been described in many publications and at many conferences, and can be designed and defined in many and varied ways. The importance of a quality governance system cannot be overstated; it provides the foundation for the myriad pieces of your quality system so that it can be understood by those operating within it, which in turn makes its implementation easier.

Understanding accountability

The concept of governance arose from the need to ensure greater and clearer accountability for the quality and safety of care experienced by the consumer. This is still a work in progress in healthcare. I have worked with many organisations where individuals are not aware of the clear, specific, personal responsibility they should have for the quality of care and services they provide. This makes it difficult for staff to carry out their responsibilities, and even harder to create a consistently safe, quality experience for consumers. An example of generic governance roles for great care is described in Table 5.

Governance is where the governing body, executives and managers play their critical role in creating great care. Accountability for achieving the strategic goals sits with the governing body and Chief Executive. Responsibility for operationalising the goals belongs to the executives and senior managers, who delegate this through line management. The executive must translate the strategic quality goals into operational plans and strategies to facilitate their implementation as part of organisational business. Those on the frontline of care create the great consumer experience, but the organisational supports for this must come from the top, as staff require leadership, policy, systems and an investment of time and resources to implement the strategies. And, of course, the quality manager provides technical support across the organisation to enable staff to fulfil their responsibilities, as discussed in Chapter One.

Governing Body

Accountable for the quality of care, services and consumer experience

- Make the achievement of great care a priority

- Set strategic direction and the line in the sand for the quality of care and services to be achieved

- Lead a just, proactive culture

- Ensure management provides the necessary system supports and staff development to provide great care for each consumer, and monitors progress towards achieving the strategic quality goals

Chief Executive and Executives

Accountable for and lead great care and services

- Make the achievement of great care a priority

- Set strategic goals for great care and operationalise them through effective governance: resources, data, plans, systems, support, tools, policy and people development

- Monitor and drive progress towards the strategic quality goals

- Develop a thinking organisation and a just culture, wherein staff are supported to take a proactive approach to achieving safe, quality care and services

Directors and Managers

Responsible for the quality of care in each service

- Make the achievement of great care a priority and take a proactive approach to achieving it
- Operationalise the strategic quality goals by translating them into local initiatives
- Understand the key organisational safety and quality issues and the broader quality agenda
- Identify local and service specific components of great care and support their development and improvement
- Monitor and drive progress by implementing the drivers of great care within their services
- Develop staff and systems to create quality care and services for each consumer
- Establish a system of quality leadership development across the organisation
- Make the right thing easy for staff to do

Clinicians and Staff

Responsible for quality of care at point of care

- Make the achievement of great care a priority
- Make evaluation and improvement a routine part of care delivery
- Identify and implement local requirements to achieve great care
- Develop, implement and evaluate initiatives to contribute to the organisational quality goals
- Support and enable all staff to create great care
- Create a great experience for each consumer through positive behaviours and attitudes and a proactive approach

All

- Scan for and act on safety and quality issues, model positive and proactive attitudes and behaviours
- Work towards the quality goals for creating a great consumer experience

Table 5: Example summary of governance roles for great care at each organisational level[6,7,8,9]

Quality-related committees

Another aspect of accountability is the way in which committees support the quality system. Driving the achievement of the quality plan through line management will generally occur in partnership with working groups or committees, particularly where implementation requires cooperation across staff groups or services. When committees are action focused they are invaluable in tracking and driving progress with the quality goals. When committees are just information recipients, staff will have difficulty understanding their purpose – and may try to avoid them.

Quality managers need to be alert to directionless committees – and get them on track before they erode the credibility of the quality system. Committees should take an active role in quality goal monitoring and action at the local department/service level (where they might take responsibility for driving one component of a goal) right through to board committee level (which monitors progress with achieving the quality goals). Committees that have an explicit responsibility for achieving a quality goal or key component are more likely to be proactive decision makers and less likely to be passive recipients of information. To be useful, committees need a clear purpose and something that they are responsible for so they can make decisions and take action. Giving a quality committee responsibility for driving and monitoring a quality goal, objective, strategy or governance support will add some life and energy to proceedings.

A clear purpose also helps determine a committee's agenda and membership. Quality committee agendas can be structured according to the quality goals and their objectives and components, which makes it easier to see how data monitoring and improvement activities link to the achievement of great care. For example, risk-related data such as adverse events and root cause analyses are reported under the 'safe' strategic quality goal. Information about a process for developing staff competencies would be reported under the 'effective workforce' governance cornerstone, as this is an organisational support for providing great care. All reporting should help a committee determine if progress is being made towards implementing governance cornerstones or achieving the relevant quality goals. (A sample generic health service quality committee reporting structure can be found in Appendix 3.)

Committee membership is always tricky to get right. Members can be invited on the basis of who has to be on this committee – there will always be political and relationship imperatives in a complex system – and who you need on the committee to fulfil its purpose. Some members may need to be there because they are decision makers and have formal power. Depending on the committee's role, you may also want people with informal power – the influencers. If the committee is responsible for addressing improvement in a particular area of the organisation, you will need some who have a deep understanding of the relevant systems, relationships and mental maps. Everyone on a quality-related committee should understand its purpose and exactly what each of their roles is – be it sharing their knowledge, experience or influence – and be invited to contribute to discussions and decisions on that basis. Remember our discussion in Chapter Five about the currencies of influence? Some people want to belong, others want information or to make a difference or to be known for their contribution. Committees are a great opportunity to offer all of these currencies in exchange for members' commitment to achieving a committee's objectives.

Step 3: Develop the strategies for change

You are now ready to plan your approach to achieving the quality goals for great care. You have identified what you want to achieve, why you want to achieve it and the governance infrastructure required to support it. The next step is to plan the journey to make it all happen. Your strategies are the maps and pathways for reaching your goals, and your objectives are the measurable milestones you must pass along the way to keep you on the road to your destination. Warning! Remember you are operating within a complex system and your path will not be straight and smooth. A more accurate description might be that you will have to weave your way towards the goals. Objectives are required to keep you travelling in the right direction, even though you may have to do many course corrections along the way.

To get specific results, you need specific objectives. Let's take our previous example of wanting to 'get fit'. What does that mean? What do you have to do to achieve it? How will you know when you get there? You are unlikely to make much progress unless you set a clear goal and some measurable objectives to work towards. Your overall goal might be to pass a certain fitness test at your gym within nine months. Objectives you will have to achieve to reach your goal may include things like 'increase my dead lift weight to 50 kg in three months' or 'improve my recovery time after a 1 km run by 20 per cent in six months'. Once you've set your objectives, you can develop your strategies – the training and nutrition in this case – you'll need to achieve these. Similarly, quality system goals also need to be broken down into tangible objectives. These objectives must be 'SMART': specific, measurable, achievable, realistic and time-bound. They must cover both people and process change as both of these are required to achieve change in a complex system. And your strategic quality plan is a plan about change.

Where possible and appropriate, measurable targets for achievement should be set for each objective. They will include both process and outcome targets: for how many consumers do we want this process to happen as we have designed it? What percentage of consumers do we want to achieve this outcome as a result of our new processes? How many staff should be demonstrating the agreed new behaviours? By when? You can set targets using your internal data and judgement and also by using benchmarking data from other organisations. Some targets will be set for you through funding, policy and corporate requirements. Some of the things you've identified as key components of great care will be '100 percenters' – you'll want these things to happen for every consumer, every time. I say 'some' because you can only achieve 100 per cent all of the time for something you have 100 per cent control over all of the time. And in healthcare, there are many outcomes that you don't have control over. Your organisation can control most of its processes, however, which is why your process targets will more often be '100 percenters' than your outcome targets.

Initially, achieving objectives derived from strategic, aspirational goals may seem impossible – or improbable. But you don't have to achieve it all by next week. That's why it's important to set manageable, achievable interim targets over time that will help you move towards your goals. You can also draw on national and international work on goals and targets to get an idea of what's doable. For example, the UK NHS[10] have pursued their 'no needless' list for a number of years: no needless pain, waiting or deaths. The US Institute for Healthcare Improvement (IHI)[14] advocates a number of safety goals in its 5 Million Lives campaign. How long a target will take to achieve will depend on where you're starting from and how much control you have over the outcomes. For example, if you have a problem with pressure ulcers and choose a 0 per cent stage 3 and 4 pressure ulcer target, you may start by setting a target of zero incidence of stage 4 pressure ulcers in the first three months and 50 per cent of the number of current stage 3 ulcers within six months. But if one of the components of your goal for continuous and integrated care requires major changes to professional communication systems across the organisation, this is likely to be a much longer-term goal, as you have less control over how people communicate. To keep on track you need to carefully track progress with both quantitative and qualitative data. We explore this further later in this chapter as well as in Chapter Seven.

Ensure you have a spread of 'maintenance, improvement and transformation' objectives to ensure you also consider all your policy, legislative and accreditation requirements as strategies for achieving great care. This also helps get around the problem of the ubiquitous 'ongoing' timeline seen in so many quality plans. An 'ongoing' timeline will not drive change or achievement! In reality, of course, quality systems are full of ongoing activities, particularly when it comes to meeting external requirements and managing risk. If your quality plan includes the three categories for your quality system purpose and objectives, however, the 'ongoing' activities can be organised under the goals and objectives as 'maintenance' activities. Even so, maintenance activities are not set and forget, and they should have timelines allocated for reviewing and refreshing these measures to ensure they remain current and relevant. And the improvement and transformational activities in your quality plan may sometimes be triggered by data from maintenance activities. Maintenance activities can also be used to monitor the effectiveness of improvement and transformational initiatives, so they are interdependent.

But setting objectives is hard…
Setting measurable objectives is difficult but worth it. Let's recap some of the essentials of setting effective goals and objectives.

Effective objectives are measurable, unambiguous, and behavioural. When an objective is clear and specific, with a definite time set for completion, there is less misunderstanding about what behaviours will be rewarded. You know what's expected and you can use the specific result as a source of motivation for staff. When the objective is vague, or when it's expressed as a general instruction, like 'be involved in activities to improve the quality of care', or, 'increase consumer participation in care planning', it has limited motivational value.

GOALS MAKE GREAT SIMPLE RULES

The success of goal achievement is all in the translation. Frontline staff may not be interested in goals and objectives and components – and the skill here will be to turn these into simple rules or principles on which they can base their everyday systems and behaviours.

So, for example, the strategic goal, 'Care and services are designed and delivered to minimise the risk of harm' may be translated at the frontline as:

'I speak up when I see something potentially harmful to a consumer', or

'Consumer safety is my business'.

The goal, 'Consumers experience care and services in a logical, clear and streamlined flow' may be translated at the frontline as:

'We don't change consumer care plans until after discussions with the consumer and other health professionals at the multidisciplinary handover', and

'We don't let one of our consumers leave our service to enter an aged care facility without calling the facility to brief them on the care we have provided', or

'When planning care, we think about the aspects of care we are directly responsible for, and also the steps in the consumer journey that occur before and after this.

This is further discussed in the selecting priorities section of this chapter.

If objectives are expressed as they are in the left column of the box below, staff will have difficulty understanding their purpose and what their role is in achieving them. In fact, it's easy not to have a role. And it's hard to measure – and therefore to show progress or achievement. To motivate involvement and improve performance, set clear objectives that use specific and measurable criteria, such as those in the right column. These are good objectives to start with and all answer the questions 'how good do we want to be? How soon do we want to be that good? And how will we know if/when we get there?' Then each of these objectives needs a set of strategies to achieve it.

As we've previously discussed, goals also have to be realistic, take account of where you are starting from and fit within your complex system. 'Stretch' is one thing, pie in the sky is quite another. Setting goals, objectives and targets that sound good but are impossible to reach will damage your credibility and make it difficult to engage people – now and in the future. But it is not uncommon to see organisational plans that state they are going to be the best in the world. Or even 'perfect'. If this is feasible in your organisation because you're starting from a high base – go for it! But if you are yet to eliminate suboptimal care and achieve consistently good care for each consumer, better to draw a line in the sand to say you'll first focus on achieving this; in a complex system, as we have discussed, this in itself will be challenging enough as a starting point.

Goals and objectives must also be understood and agreed upon if they are to be effective. Staff are more likely to 'buy in' to a goal if they feel they were part of creating it, as discussed in Chapter Three. Agreed goals and objectives lead to commitment. This doesn't mean that every goal has to be negotiated with and approved by staff, but it does mean that goals should be consistent and in line with organisational concerns, values, principles of great care and real issues – and not in direct conflict with the unwritten goals of local complex systems and relationships. Staff need to see that reaching the goals will make a positive difference for their consumers and that there will be corresponding support for achieving them. The whole point of goal setting is to facilitate success.

WHAT OBJECTIVES ARE – AND WHAT THEY ARE NOT

Objectives are NOT	Objectives ARE
• 'To hold meetings' • 'To raise awareness' • 'To improve the consumer's understanding of their condition' • 'To gather further information' • 'To continue to…'	• 'Reduce falls resulting in fractured neck of femur in the medical ward by 80 per cent within two years' • 'Zero complaints regarding poor pain management in residential care within three months' • '50 per cent of care pathways to demonstrate consumer participation in treatment options within 12 months' • 'All community aged care clients to receive a GP check-up at least every six months'

GOALS: CHALLENGING OR REALISTIC?

It's important to strike an appropriate balance between a challenging goal and a realistic goal. Setting a goal that you'll fail to achieve is possibly more de-motivating than setting a goal that's too easy. The need for success and achievement is strong; therefore people are best motivated by challenging, but realistic, goals. That's why 'achievable' must be balanced with 'realistic' – the goal may be technically feasible, but is it realistic?

People are motivated by achievement and they'll judge a goal based on the significance of the anticipated outcome: 'Can we make this happen? Will this really impact positively on consumer care? Will I see a positive difference in my daily work? Will I be regarded as successful? Challenging goals are very rewarding – if they can be achieved. And making it too easy doesn't work either. If a target is viewed as too straightforward and effortless, it may also be labelled unimportant.

Goal and objective achievement requires a clear means (the 'how') leading to a tangible end (the 'what'). Actions must directly pursue the achievement of the goals, objectives and priorities while also addressing the barriers and constraints. The ends must be definable targets at a point in time in the future so it is possible to measure progress, make adjustments along the way and allocate accountability for achieving them. What are the strategies we will need to put in place to achieve our objectives, and ultimately, our goals? What will it take to support and motivate staff to make good decisions and create great care? What are the governance structures and processes that need to be maintained, strengthened or developed to support the changes?

Planning for goal achievement – the Reverse Engineering Goal Planning Process[12]

Also known as 'backward goal setting', the Reverse Goal Planning Process is useful for developing manageable milestones and short-term goals to support long-term goal achievement. You start with what you want to ultimately achieve and work backwards – identifying the key milestone objectives you'll have to reach along the way. You might like to draw this as a timeline so that you can see what will be required when to achieve the objective.

Let's consider a SMART objective as part of the strategic goal to provide effective and appropriate care for each consumer:

Strategic quality goal: Care is based around the consumer as an individual, and is designed to achieve optimal outcomes (Effective and Appropriate).

Key component: Evaluation of care process and effectiveness is regularly undertaken for each consumer.

SMART Objective: By 1 July 20XX, a new collaborative model for evaluation of care process and effectiveness will be implemented for each consumer.

To achieve this objective by this date specified, what do you need to achieve six months before? For example:

Milestone: By 15 December 20XX, all consumers on Ward Zee and Eee will have their care process and effectiveness evaluated using the new collaborative model, and the success of the model implementation evaluated.

And in the three months before that?

Milestone: By 30 September 20XX, 25 per cent of consumers on Ward Zee and Eee will have their care process and effectiveness evaluated using the new collaborative model, and the success of the model implementation evaluated.

Then work backwards some more. What do you need to complete before that?

Milestone: By mid June 20XX, the plan for the pilot of the new model on Ward Zee and Eee will be ready for implementation on 1 July.

And of course that means…

Milestone: By the end of April 20XX the new collaborative model for evaluation of care process and effectiveness will be developed, ready for pilot testing.

And so on until you come to today's date and the first actions you need to take to achieve the first milestone objective. When you read a backward plan, it doesn't look much different from a traditional forward plan. Creating a backward plan, however, is a slightly different way of thinking about goal achievement. It can help you see things that you might miss if you use a traditional chronological process and highlights points of tension within the plan, showing where you'll need specific resources or strategies to make the next step successfully.

The milestone approach tells the story of the journey towards the objective and makes it easier to measure achievement and track progress. Your measures will comprise a mix of outcomes and processes. Are we meeting the targets and objectives we've set? Are they having the desired effect in terms of the consumer experience we want to create? Are we doing the things our plan said we'd do to achieve our targets and objectives? The ownership of these objectives, strategies and measures will sit at various levels of the organisation, as we saw in Step 2.

Select priorities – you can't do it all at once
A traditional problem with quality plans is that they are over ambitious. But it's far better to do fewer things and get them right. That's why any good plan has short, medium and long-term goals. Developing an annual Quality Action Plan, derived from the strategic quality plan, is a good way to keep the strategic quality plan current and dynamic. The annual plan contains the priorities to be achieved over the coming 12 months. It ensures the strategic quality plan can evolve with changing external and internal circumstances, while maintaining the overall direction towards achieving the quality goals over the longer term. So what should be done in the first year of the plan? Where do we need to start to:

- create a positive experience for each consumer
- maximise safety
- address components of great care that are currently suboptimal – or non existent
- minimise and eliminate the things that shouldn't happen
- solve significant problems and manage key risks
- meet legislative, policy and accreditation requirements
- get something going that will take a long time to achieve
- cover a lot of the quality plan's intent, using the 80:20 principle.

The 'first among equals' priority is safety and this requires robust processes across all services to reduce risk in key areas. Chapter Five lists a number of key causes of error and poor quality in healthcare, and these are good things to focus on in the first instance to make sure they're under control in your organisation. Priorities may also be selected based on safety and indicator data, consumer and staff feedback and identified problems in specific areas. Policy, funding issues and key risks must also be addressed as priorities – that's a reality. If compliance and safety issues are at the head of your quality priorities queue, try to also include some aspirational objectives for improving the consumer experience from other dimensions of quality on the Year One list, or you may lose the momentum and energy created by the planning process.

TARGET THE REAL ISSUES

All of this activity will be of little use if it doesn't have meaning to the people you need to enact these strategies. As covered in Chapter Three a few well-chosen, values-based principles that are consistent with staff values and norms will achieve more than pages of detailed to-do lists or a set of new rules and protocols. Managers and staff need to agree what success looks like. Relying on formal rules to achieve 'great' care will not result in 'great' anything.[17,18] Great care requires staff to be motivated to respond to consumers' needs. For example, take the strategic quality goal 'Consumers experience care and services in a logical, clear and streamlined flow (continuous)'. You might first re-visit the organisational/technical components identified by staff when developing the objectives for this goal. This will tell you a lot about what the staff think is important and, combined with what consumers think is important, can form the objectives and strategies. Staff may have identified simple rules such as:

- We communicate and coordinate with other departments every day and don't receive or send consumers to other areas without a handover.
- Every change to a treatment schedule is discussed with consumers at bedside handover.
- When a consumer asks when something will happen we won't guess, we'll find out.
- If the consumer requires an appointment with more than one health professional, the appointments will be made on the same day.

Simple rules such as these can be further distilled to make them easy to remember, for example: 'communicate, respond, streamline'. Of course, there will be some robust systems and governance strategies sitting behind this to support these things happening. But they should help staff focus on the principles that drive behaviour, not distract from them.

I'm not saying that staff shouldn't have to follow policies and procedures. I'm suggesting that you think carefully about how to translate these for the front of house staff. Policies should provide a foundation for behaviour, but not preoccupy staff to the extent that they are blind to the consumer in front of them. If creating a quality experience is equated with compliance, it is unlikely to happen – willingly or otherwise. The 'systems beings' that comprise your organisation run on simple rules. The more you can embed desired ways of thinking and acting in these simple rules, the more likely they are to happen. Shared norms and principles within subsystems influence staff decision making far more than formal rules. And great decisions are fundamental to great care. We need to develop 'thinking organisations'.

There is also now more external information than ever before to help you decide on priorities that you can match with your internal line in the sand. The published plans that lay out strategic priorities for achieving great care include the Scottish NHS Quality Strategy[3], the Australian Commission on Safety and Quality in Healthcare Safety and Quality Framework[7], the NHS No Needless System[10], National Quality Forum's List of 28 'Never' Events[13], the IHI Quality Map[14] and the World Health Organization WHO Patient Safety Program[15]. A recent addition to this mix is the Obama Administration Partnership for Patients[16], which is a three-year patient harm reduction strategy that aims to reduce preventable hospital-acquired conditions by 40 per cent and reduce readmissions relating to complications in transition between settings by 20 per cent.

Other organisations can also supply ideas for achieving your quality goals. Health services, professional associations, government and quality organisations all have a myriad of strategies, actions, initiatives, guidelines and standards for improving the quality of care in each dimension of quality. Internally, you will already have many activities in place that will help you achieve your goals. You could start by conducting a gap analysis to ascertain where current quality activities are or are not addressing or supporting the key priorities. Above all, don't get caught up in the detail of planning to the extent that you lose sight of your purpose. Keep the care you want every consumer to experience at the centre of your activities.

Step 4: Implement the plan

Effective implementation is fundamental to success. Many brilliant plans have sunk without trace in the swamp of implementation. It is better to have a basic but practical strategy that is well implemented than a world's best practice strategy that's poorly implemented or impractical.[18] The implementation of the plan to achieve the objectives and priorities takes us back to the chapters on change and creating safety in complex systems, and a brief recap of the key points of these reminds us that implementation, based on a complex systems change approach, requires a number of actions:

- Actively pursue the strategic goals for great care in the everyday routine of care and services through building or changing the norms and beliefs that drive behaviour
- Strengthen the key clinical governance cornerstones to support the quality priorities and goals for great care.
- Use the quality goals and governance cornerstones to structure meeting agendas and staff and manager roles. It must be clear how the various agenda items and quality activities contribute to each goal and to better care for consumers.
- Assign lead responsibility management and committee roles for each of the components and objectives, and establish regular reporting at all levels of the organisation.
- Develop implementation teams across services to address the objectives.
- Identify and supply the resources and support required by the implementation teams, both through line management and via the quality team.
- Ensure the implementation teams are empowered to achieve their priorities – they need DKRS.
- Engage all staff in the implementation of at least one component of great care.
- Monitor and respond to progress data.
- Respond to qualitative and quantitative information that indicates implementation is not progressing or has unintended side effects, and have contingency plans ready.
- Engage the finance team from the outset through implementation, monitoring and assessment of progress.
- Reinforce and spread the change.
- Keep your eye on the prize. Is all this activity moving us closer to achieving great care? [1,19,20]

Ideally, the implementation will be led by your governing body and executives. The quality manager has a role in facilitating and guiding this process. First and foremost, remember that change is about behaviours, and behaviours are more about culture than rules. Work with the local mental maps, values and norms to translate the goals and objectives for local use, as seen in Figure 5.

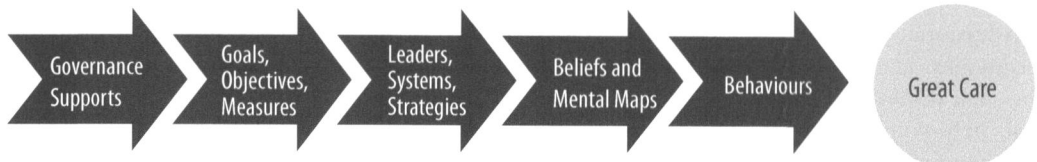

Figure 5: Drivers for creating great care from the wider governance supports to local behaviour

As discussed in Chapter Three, 'Start Where They Are', not where you are. Agendas that get implemented are not 'yours', but shared. Achieving the quality goals will require working across professional boundaries, whether inter-departmental, interdisciplinary, or across the sub disciplines of improvement, risk and transformation. This is where your quality leadership skills come in handy, as you facilitate discussions and help turn them into concrete quality plans. The time invested at this stage is essential to long-term organisational success. Where possible, develop and use 'change experts' to help implement your plan across the organisation – there is a skill and an art to this and you'll reduce your implementation woes considerably with some expert assistance! This is the 'teach people to fish' aspect of the quality manager role: it takes a little longer to support people to manage these processes themselves, but the local capacity, ownership and knowledge you are developing will save you a lot of work getting things back on track later.

Don't forget to support the middle managers, as they are the engine room of change and implementation – and your best asset when it comes to making objectives a reality. Build their resilience as well as the resilience of individuals and teams at point of care to create quality and safety. Work with the managers and their staff to develop the systems for supporting the components of great care.

Remember that standardising systems does not always standardise behaviour. If new processes don't make sense, or make life harder, you will hear – or see – the voice of the people, and you can wave goodbye to the implementation of your strategies. Managers and staff at ward, department and service level should be given both the opportunity and resources to collaborate on how they will adapt and achieve the quality objectives in their area over the short and long term, while the executives have responsibility for developing organisation-wide governance supports and systems to drive local actions. An example of what this might look like for one objective is seen in Table 6.

Finally, use your imagination – and others' – to make it fun. People naturally engage in activities they enjoy, that are challenging and that they have some control over. Quality managers, be brutally honest with yourselves: identify the paperwork and administration that must be done as part of the quality system – and ditch the rest. And then try to make this paperwork as easy as possible – for yourselves, and also for others. Make the right things easy to try and make it easy to do things right. Unhappy people do not create great care!

Step 5: Track, evaluate and drive progress

In addition to selecting the right type of goals and objectives, an effective goal-oriented program must also include monitoring, responsive action and feedback. Regular reviews of progress should take place at all levels of the organisation, with data differently configured and presented for each group: informal and formal at the local level, in corridors and working groups; and more formally at line management levels and committee meetings where key responsibilities for goal, objective and strategy monitoring sit, as seen in Figure 6.

Strategic Quality Goal: Consumers experience care and services in a logical, clear and streamlined flow (Continuous, efficient and accessible).

Objective: By the end of this year, all clients with multiple needs will be offered a care map to help them navigate around our services.

Organisation-wide governance supports

- Develop the procedure and link it to a policy
- Develop and support a pilot
- Identify required key staff roles and competencies
- Develop a generic care map template
- Provide education and briefing material for staff and clients
- Implement a monitoring and evaluation process
- Ensure relevant staff job descriptions reflect this goal and link to performance appraisal process
- Add to relevant clinical governance committee agenda.

Implementation through local strategies developed by X Department

- Determine the service specific content of the care map
- Revise the entry and assessment process to incorporate the care map development
- Work with consumers and relevant staff from other services to identify roles and input
- Adapt the generic template and process to the specific service
- Collect local monitoring data
- Add to local quality meeting agenda for discussion and monitoring.

Table 6: Example of the governance and local strategies for implementing a quality objective

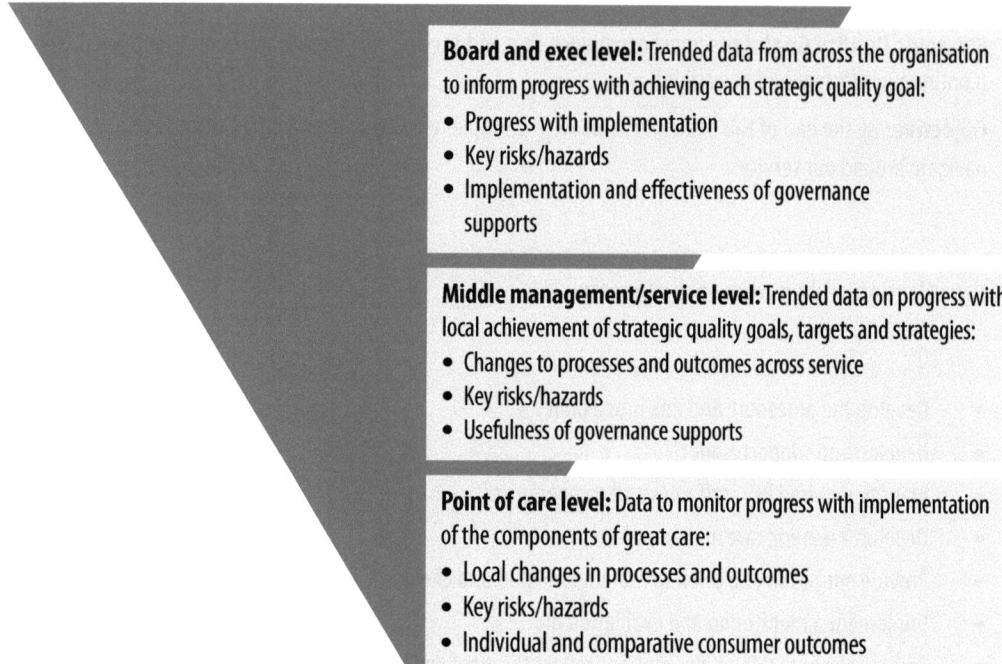

Figure 6: Monitoring and evaluating quality plan effectiveness at different levels in the organisation

Regular reports that measure progress with achieving the milestones within each objective are particularly important for long-term goals. Taking the time to have regular discussion about progress towards goals at all levels of the health service is a necessary factor in achieving long-term performance improvement. All safety and quality measures in the organisation should relate to at least one goal and objective. This focuses efforts across the organisation and supports the pursuit of common goals.[21] The data contained in progress reports provides opportunities to clarify expectations, adjust timelines and objectives if necessary and recognise achievement. In a complex system, it's also the time to identify the inevitable side effects of the changes put in place to achieve the goals. Data flow and corresponding responses will include the following activities at key levels of the organisation:

- Line managers and sub committees monitor local/departmental/service progress towards achieving objectives, remove roadblocks and re-think implementation strategies if plans are not working. They also report up, down and across the organisation on progress towards achieving the key objectives and outcomes.

Note that staff at the frontline generally prefer raw, real-time data on their consumers to high level percentages. It is more engaging for staff to know that three of their clients were readmitted or returned to the program unexpectedly, than to be confronted by a more abstract readmission rate from three months ago. Longer-term trended data is also important and useful for promoting healthy competition between like services and organisations.

The executive and organisation-wide committees regularly consider overall progress towards the objectives and act to drive progress by asking:

- Are we seeing more of the behaviours and outcomes we want?
- Are we seeing fewer problems and behaviours from the 'unacceptable care and experience' side of our line in the sand?
- Are we improving across the organisation?

The governing body tracks progress with the strategic quality goals and poses the questions:

- Are we moving towards our quality goals and objectives?
- Is the executive supporting and resourcing the implementation of the plan and the achievement of 'great' care?
- Are care, services and experiences tangibly better for our consumers?
- Are our consumers better off because of the implementation of the strategic quality plan?

These questions cannot be answered without the executive resourcing relevant data collection and analysis and then convening and supporting organisational committees to properly consider and act on the information. Data can be derived from administrative databases such as disease coding, or specifically generated indicators, auditing, direct observation and results of improvement activities. Quality committee members at all levels of the system should also consider the data within the context of the difficulties of trying to achieve consistently great care in a complex environment. This means that they must be open to data that identifies both successes and failures in quality systems, and be prepared to learn from both. Part of a quality committee's terms of reference should discuss how it will respond to problems and changing circumstances given that events are unlikely to always unfold as planned. Involving consumers and carers on these committees – something that must be well managed to be a positive experience for both parties – can provide a particularly valuable reality check for improvement actions and strategies, and help identify unintended flow-on effects from new systems, policies and processes. This also addresses the danger of health professionals developing complacency about the quality of care and services. Hearing bad news about your health service is uncomfortable, but it's part of developing a fuller picture of the quality of care that is being delivered, rather than the care you hope is being delivered. If you don't know, you can't act.

Step Six: Celebrate and recalibrate

Don't forget to celebrate the wins and acknowledge the hard work that goes into achieving them. This is something that often gets lost in the busyness of our healthcare world, but it's essential on many levels. Use appreciative enquiry to look into the reasons why implementation has gone right and staff will feel that their deeds have not gone unnoticed. Ask what can be learned from the way a strategy has been effectively implemented, a change sustained or an objective successfully achieved. Where things do not go according to plan, ensure that this is discussed in the context of a complex system, where the best laid plans may be hijacked by the web of complexity. This is not failure, as long as course corrections are made where necessary to continue to pursue the objective from another direction. Sometimes a strategy or objective has to be re-thought altogether due to unintended consequences or changing circumstances. Healthcare is a rapidly changing beast and sometimes events will overtake your objectives and plans. Be aware of dynamic environments and contexts, both internal and external, and be prepared to be flexible to achieve your quality goals.

Putting it all together – a framework for creating great care and services

Congratulations! You now have a system and a plan that connects the various parts of your quality and governance systems together into a coherent whole to achieve a clear purpose, as seen in the 'house of great care' in Figure 7. A quality plan is not just a list of improvement activities to be done over the coming year. It brings together your governance and quality systems to support the achievement of quality goals and objectives. All of these components should come together in your improvement plan – what you are trying to achieve and how you are going to achieve it. Evaluating the effectiveness of the quality system is not about how many activities have been completed, but about progress made towards quality goals, objectives and targets – and the degree to which this created great care and experiences for consumers.

The strategic level improvement plan for quality care may form part of your broader organisational business planning – or it may be a separate document linked to your organisation's strategic and business plans. Quality goals may be cascaded to the level of local point of care and service delivery via quality, operational or business plans. Or you may use another process entirely. The important thing is that the process is effective in supporting staff at all levels to contribute to achieving the quality of care your organisation has determined it wants to provide.

Whatever planning structures and processes you use, the success of your quality plan depends on the degree of understanding and ownership it achieves across the organisation. I believe it is more meaningful for consumers and staff to get the essentials right for every consumer, every time, and then build on that, than to plan for perfection that will require heroic efforts and enormous resources to achieve and maintain – and which may only be experienced by a few consumers at the expense of others. A great goal-based quality plan is one that enables everyone in the organisation to complete the sentences 'as a result of our quality plan…' and 'my role in creating great care is…' with something tangible and positive that reflects a real improvement for consumers and staff. Ultimately your organisation's quality plan should be judged on its ability to achieve this.

Strategic aim: great care for every consumer every time

The vision for great care: the rich picture of the quality of care and services each consumer will experience at point of care, linked to the organisational strategic plan and values

Organised into the dimensions of great quality care:

| Person-centered | Safe | Effective and appropriate | Continuous, accessible, efficient |

Strategic quality goals for great care and the 'quality line in the sand' for each dimension of quality

Key components of great care, that every consumer should experience, for each strategic quality goal

SMART prioritised objectives to drive the implementation of the key component

Strategies for achieving key objectives and goals implemented through operational plans and supported by four governance cornerstones:

Consumer and carer participation	Strategic leadership, planning, support	Effective and accountable workforce	Quality and risk systems
Partnerships	Goals and priorities	Accountability	Evidence/protocols
Policy	Leadership	Role clarity	Safety systems
Support	Resources	Proactivity	Dataset
Training	Information	Credentialing	Improvement/change
Communication	Culture	Scope of practice	Risk management
Care planning/processes	Delegation	Resilience	Implementation
Service improvement	Committees	Empowerment	Monitoring and response
		Support and skills	Evaluation

Figure 7: The 'house of great care'. A framework for planning and creating great care and services [22]

Headlines: Chapter Six

- A quality plan must be strategic to lead the quality of care and consumer experience through the complexities of health services to somewhere better than where it is now.
- The quality plan must include initiatives that maintain, improve and transform the quality of care and services, and focus on delivering the basics of good care for every consumer, every time.
- A key aspect of the quality plan is vision – the rich picture of great care that can be achieved when all the jigsaw pieces come together in the right configuration. Consumers and staff at all levels of the organisation should have input into this vision for great care.
- The vision for great care must be translated into tangible goals and objectives, implemented using a change model that works with complex systems characteristics, and pursued with laser-like focus.
- Staff should be able to implement the strategies for great care through behaviours based on simple principles and norms.
- The governing body and executive monitor and drive the plan through robust quality governance systems that support frontline managers and staff to create great care.
- Individuals must be adequately supported to implement the quality plan, and they must understand their specific responsibilities for providing great care.
- The quality manager maintains both a strategic and operational view and is able to articulate where the organisation is going and how it is getting there.
- Reporting on quality plan progress and the quality of care being achieved should happen at all levels of the organisation through line management and committees, and be linked with the quality goals and objectives.

References and Further Reading

1. Zuckerman A (2005) *Healthcare Strategic Planning.* Health Administration Press, USA

2. Maslow A (1970) *Motivation and Personality,* (2nd edn) Harper & Row, USA

3. NHS Scotland (2010) *The Healthcare Strategy for NHS Scotland,* www.scotland.gov.au/publications

4. Luxford K, Piper D, Dunbar N, Poole N (2010) *Patient-centred Care: Improving Quality and Safety by Focusing Care on Patients and Consumers: Discussion paper.* Australian Commission on Safety and Quality in Healthcare, Australia

5. Balik B, Conway J, Zipperer L, Watson J (2011) *Achieving an Exceptional Patient and Family Experience of Inpatient Hospital Care.* IHI Innovation Series white paper, no. 23, Institute for Health-care Improvement Cambridge, USA

6. Victorian Quality Council (2003) *Better Quality, Better Healthcare: A Safety and Quality Framework for Victorian Healthcare.* Department of Human Services, Victorian Government, Australia

7. ACSQHC (2010) *Australian Safety and Quality Framework for Healthcare: Putting the Framework into Action: Getting Started.* Australian Commission on Safety and Quality in Healthcare, Australia

8. Øvretveit J (2004) *The Leader's Role in Quality and Safety Improvement: A Review of Research and Guidance.* MMC Karolinska Institute and Association of County Councils, Sweden

9. Department of Health Victoria (2009) *The Victorian Clinical Governance Policy Framework.* Department of Health, Victorian Government, Australia

10. NHS Modernisation Agency (2004) *No Needless Framework: Creating Ambition in Health and Social Care.* NHS, UK

11. Committee on the Quality of Healthcare in America (2001) *Crossing the Quality Chasm: A New Health System for the 21st Century.* Institute of Medicine, USA

12. Adapted from McGrath M (date unknown) *Reverse Engineering for Goal Achievement.* Personal Development. www.personal-development.info (Accessed February 2011)

13. National Quality Forum (2006) *Serious Reportable Events in Healthcare.* NQF, USA qualityforum.org

14. Institute for Healthcare Improvement. www.ihi.org/IHI/Programs

15. World Health Organisation, *WHO Patient Safety.* www.who.int/patientsafety

16. Obama Administration (2011) *Partnership for Patients.* www.healthcare.gov/center/programs/partnership

17. Institute for Healthcare Improvement (2007) *Engaging Physicians in a Shared Quality Agenda.* IHI, USA

18. Chatman JA, Cha SE (2003) Leading by Leveraging Culture. *California Management Review,* vol. 45, no. 4

19. NHS (2002) *The Improvement Leaders Guide to Managing the Human Dimensions of Change: Working with Individuals.* NHS Modernisation Agency, UK

20. Adapted from Cameron E, Green M (2004) *Making Sense of Change Management.* Kogan Page Limited, Great Britain

21. Frankel A, Leonard M, Simmonds T, Haraden C, Vega K (eds) (2009) *The Essential Guide for Patient Safety Officers.* Joint Commission on Accreditation of Healthcare Organisations and Institute for Healthcare Improvement, USA

22. Adapted from Department of Health (2010) *Governing Quality in Public Sector Residential Aged Care: An Organisational Readiness Tool.* Aged Care Branch, Department of Health, Victorian Government, Australia.

Q7 BUILDING YOUR BRAND:
The quality professionals' 'essentials' kit

'We are what we repeatedly do. Excellence, then, is not an act, but a habit.'
– **ARISTOTLE**

7. BUILDING YOUR BRAND:
The quality professionals' 'essentials' kit

This chapter explores some of the most common quality manager questions and will help you assess the state of your quality toolkit to identify the gaps you'd like to fill. The information in this final chapter is primarily directed at those new to a quality role, but should also prove useful for the many people were thrown in at the deep end of a quality job at the beginning of their career, and feel they may have missed out on some of the basics along their journey.

Reviewing your current 'quality manager essentials' kit

Unpack your current quality tools and skills kit and spread it out on your desk. How many of the following do you see?

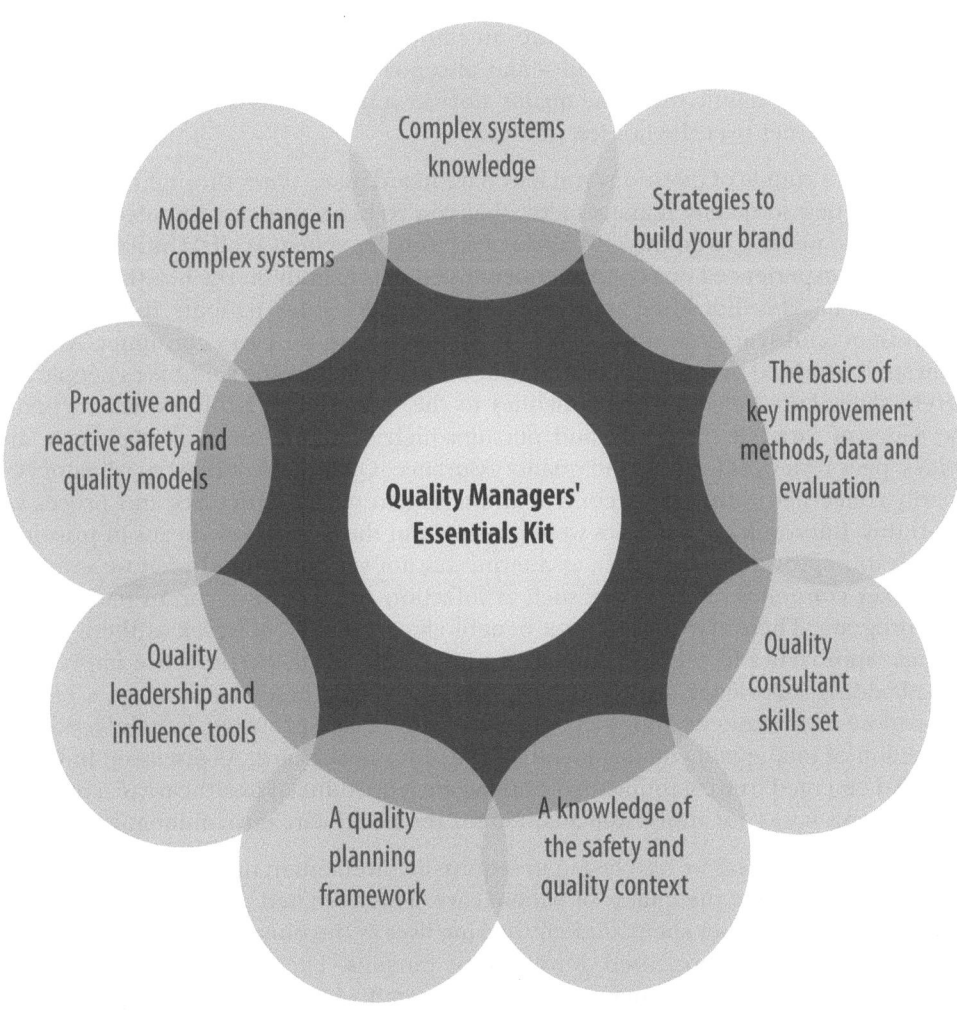

All of these skills and tools will help you develop a more strategic view of the quality manager purpose and role and together form the bulk of what this book is all about. This 'quality manager essentials' list does not represent a complete kit, of course; there will be many other tools you already use and others you'll collect and add as you develop your skills and experience. And the more knowledge and skills you have, the more confident you will feel; competence breeds confidence.[1]

This chapter gives a brief overview of key quality manager essentials that haven't been covered elsewhere in this book:

- the quality journey over the past two decades
- the characteristics of some of the most widely used quality management methods
- some important need to know aspects of data and evaluation
- building your quality professional brand (the ten point plan).

A small slice of the big picture – how we got here

Knowing a bit of history helps put things in context. If you ever have to teach the basics of safety, quality and clinical governance, it's handy to be able to explain why our quality systems ended up the way they did, what they are trying to achieve and why it can be challenging! Some personalities, in particular, require an understanding of context to learn and to commit to participation. So it's useful – and also not bad for your credibility as a quality 'expert' – to include a little bit of the quality story in your kit. This is one insider's snapshot of the quality journey over the last few decades.

Let's start with a couple of questions you may have heard many times throughout your career (or, if you're new to quality management, that you're likely to hear) expressed in various forms. 'Why do we have to do this?' 'Why do need a quality system at all?' Until the 1980s, the quality of care experienced by a consumer depended significantly on the health professionals caring for them. This individual approach, while great for some patients, did not translate to a consistent and systematic approach to high-quality care for every consumer. As long as healthcare is provided by humans and not robots, care will always be variable as people bring different skills, knowledge and personalities to the task. Health professionals recognised these issues of variability and risk and pursued high standards through their own audit activities, peer review, education and quality assurance. Quality assurance coordinators were primarily concerned with quality control and trying to set up structures and processes to support this. Improvement activities were pursued but there were few means of prioritising key issues to improve. Patient safety, as a term, was not yet born – and what we would now consider key consumer safety issues, such as infection control, were run in parallel to the quality program. These activities did not benefit all consumers, however, as there were few systematic approaches in organisations to learning from mistakes, proactive improvement and embedding knowledge. In the 1980s and 1990s, health service managers began to develop more organisational approaches to the quality of care provided, largely based on the introduction of total quality management (TQM) into healthcare. As discussed in Chapter Four, TQM emerged from manufacturing and while it introduced healthcare to a number of useful concepts it was not always well adapted for the healthcare environment and culture.

Somewhere along the way we also began to require involvement in programs such as TQM as proof of commitment to the quality of patient care. This alienated many staff – clinical staff, in particular – who felt they spent all their working lives in the pursuit of quality care without having to be involved in organised, bureaucratic pursuits. The word quality itself took on a negative connotation for the many clinicians and staff who found themselves involved in administrative quality management activities that did not appear to have direct connections with improving care for patients. And the quality manager, as bureaucratic keeper of the quality system, was increasingly labelled just as 'quality' and seen as responsible for all quality monitoring and improvement, rather than for the system to support monitoring and improvement by those responsible for the care. It is difficult to ascertain now whether TQM helped develop a more systematic approach to achieving consistently high-quality care or if it just created a quality bureaucracy. In reality, it was probably a combination of both. Towards the end of the 1990s, healthcare began to shape its own approach, based on a combination of the various tools and strategies used up until that time.[2] Terms such as continuous quality improvement (CQI), quality improvement (QI) and quality management (QM) gradually became part of the healthcare lexicon. Tools from manufacturing, such as Lean Thinking and Six Sigma continued to be used in healthcare but became better adapted to the healthcare environment.

Some of the early confusion and negative connotation around quality improvement is alive and well today. We can still mistake the quality manager's role for being responsible for monitoring and improving the quality of care provided, rather than for guiding the development and implementation of the quality system to support this. As discussed in Chapter One, if staff in your organisation think of 'quality' as you, rather than as something they are trying to achieve in their care and services, your culture and quality system both need an overhaul. Part of this problem stems from the difficulty many clinicians still have in seeing the impact of quality activities on patient care, and this remains as off-putting for clinicians as it ever was. Despite these difficulties, the range and type of quality knowledge and approaches has slowly grown into a large mass of quality jigsaw pieces, many of them quite sophisticated. But up until the late 1990s there was still no common understanding or definition of quality care in healthcare and how the various pieces of the jigsaw should fit together. We still had person-dependent quality systems that relied heavily on the enthusiasm and drive of quality champions in each health service.

The public inquiries into poor care and the early large-scale studies into adverse events in healthcare in various countries in the 1990s were much-needed circuit breakers. We found we weren't quite as good as we thought we were, despite our years of accreditation and quality programs. We discovered that errors and adverse events in care across the world were at unacceptably high levels. Estimates varied depending on study variables, but the rate was – and still is – in the order of 10 per cent of all admissions, with some studies estimating up to and beyond 30 per cent.[3] In about two per cent of these cases, major iatrogenic disability or death occurs. This equates to some 10,000 injuries per day that are the result of errors. It is estimated that only about half of all patients receive evidence-based care and that important diagnoses are undetected in about 30 per cent of cases.[4]

In the face of these data, we had to concede that our improvement efforts were not effective enough to prevent harm and poor care, seemingly for two key reasons: there was little formal governance of clinical care as there was for corporate matters, and our quality efforts were not focused enough on the right priorities. Safety became the dominant dimension of quality programs, and clinical governance was developed as a system of accountability for the safety and quality of care. There are many definitions of clinical governance, some of which are so wordy that the meaning can get lost. A short definition that is useful and easy to remember comes from the Scottish Office: 'Corporate accountability for the quality of clinical performance'.[6]

Over the last decade clinical governance has grown and developed into a framework that encompasses features of our previous quality programs, but with a broadened scope of accountability and support systems, including staff roles, organisational culture and consumer participation. The components of clinical governance target many of the organisational weaknesses uncovered by the various public inquiries into poor care around the world (as discussed in Chapter Five). The lessons from these inquiries emphasised the need for governance of the quality of clinical care that was as rigorous as financial governance, requiring corresponding systems of accountability, planning, leadership, policy and measurement.[5,7] In short, quality governance is now the comprehensive set of organisational supports for the creation of great care at the consumer interface that healthcare previously lacked.

The combination of hard data and public exposure was powerful enough to restart our quality engines and send us down a more focused and, seemingly, effective track.[2] We now understood the importance of clearly defining the quality care that we wanted to achieve, and we agreed on some dimensions of quality, such as safety, effectiveness, appropriateness, person-centredness, continuity, efficiency and accessibility (varying according to which dimensions model you use). The growing collection of valid and reliable data on adverse events meant that priority areas – such as medications, falls, pressure ulcers, blood, infections, wrong site procedures, poor communication and patient identification – were identified as requiring focus and resources. Key safety drivers that had never before been addressed on a large scale – such as open disclosure, credentialing, root cause analysis, redesign and human factors – were embraced by healthcare. We also learned the importance – from other high-risk industries – of recognising the inevitability of human fallibility; a difficult concept to accept in a healthcare system founded on professional, expert knowledge and skill. We began to accept that intelligent people with good intentions were not enough to guarantee safe and high quality care for every consumer, every time, and that a rigorous systems approach was also required.[2] State and national policy drivers and incentives, largely focused on developing these rigorous systems in safety and governance, were developed and strengthened.

Despite all this activity and focus, progress is slower than we would like. As discussed throughout this book, professionals' resistance to change, organisational complexity and perverse financial and political incentives make it difficult to achieve an agreed way forward.[8] Health and aged care are full of competing priorities, and are generally overstretched and under-resourced. Until we can clearly demonstrate that high-quality care and efficient and cost-effective care are not mutually exclusive, it will be challenging to get the attention of key decision makers and funding bodies. And without serious clarity of purpose and commitment from healthcare managers, clinicians and policymakers, and an understanding of how to effect change in the complex healthcare environment, the quest for great care for every consumer, every day will continue to be a 'wicked' problem.[9]

Quality management methods

As we saw in our history snapshot, we have progressed from clinical audits to clinical governance, from quality assurance to total quality management to continuous quality improvement – and we have adapted ever more sophisticated tools along the way. Keeping up with the latest 'new thing' in healthcare quality can require almost constant attention to journals, conferences, books and events. But while these quality improvement methods are often superficially different, particularly in language and terminology, there is a high degree of underlying commonality of approach. They all make use of the 'plan, do, study, act' cycle of improvement. Most make use of a common set of improvement tools and techniques such as cause and effect diagrams, process mapping, indicators and data analysis (see Appendix 4 for a map of quality tools linked to the quality cycle). They all acknowledge the need for supportive leadership and a clear organisational commitment to achieving quality care.

Most quality management approaches recognise the importance of the engagement of frontline staff, particularly clinical staff, in patient care improvement and the need for improvement processes to be grounded in the reality of staff knowledge and practice. The quality methods derived from manufacturing, in particular, focus on conceptualising the organisation as a series of processes and using and applying some basic principles in process flow analysis and design to make improvements. Proponents of Lean Thinking, for example, emphasise the importance of understanding process functioning and reducing or eliminating waste or unproductive effort. In contrast, adherents of Six Sigma focus on the use of statistical process control techniques and the reduction of variation.[10, 11]

A brief overview of some key improvement methods

Let's have a look at some of the popular tools for improvement to see where they are similar – and different.

Six Sigma is a rigorous statistical measurement method designed to reduce cost, decrease process variation and eliminate defects. At the level of Six Sigma, a process that has about 3.4 defects per million opportunities (DPMO) is virtually error free. Six Sigma is achieved through a series of steps: define, measure, analyse, improve and control. Control charts are created to monitor and study the process being improved. When the desired state of quality is achieved, the process is controlled by implementing policies and guidelines and error-proofing strategies to make reverting to the old process impossible. Quality controls are developed for ongoing monitoring of the new process.[11]

Lean Thinking is derived from the Toyota Motor Corporation approach to quality. It is driven by the identified needs of the customer and aims to improve processes by removing non-value-added activities. Lean tools maximise value-added steps in the best possible sequence to deliver continuous flow. To create an organised cost-efficient workplace that has clear work processes and standards, Lean experts often recommend the five 's' strategy: sort, shine, straighten, systemise and sustain.[11]

Statistical Process Control (SPC) is increasingly being used in healthcare to better understand the processes we have in place and the degree to which they drive good or poor quality for consumers. Identifying, understanding and reducing variations are keys to achieving consistently high-quality care and services in complex systems. The use of process control charts (also known as process behaviour charts) to understand our processes is a good fit in the complex healthcare environment where it can be difficult to work out what our data are telling us and when and how to act on them.[11,13]

We make many mistakes when reviewing healthcare quality data. Two common mistakes involve over-reacting and under responding, described as Type 1 (acting when not warranted, such as reacting to a blip in the data and fiddling with processes that don't need fiddling with) and Type 2 (not acting when it is warranted, leading to small problems going unaddressed and sometimes turning into big ones). The use of control charts helps us make improved decisions about the way in which we respond to data and, therefore, allocate our limited resources more effectively. It also helps us to better understand our processes and what they are really capable of achieving. Remember our discussion about processes only doing what they're capable of? This enables us to set realistic goals and targets to drive achievable change. More about the way in which these charts work is discussed later in this chapter[13]

Risk management is discussed in Chapter Four in the context of creating safety in complex systems. Although there are a number of methods for identifying risk and adverse events, no process on its own is sufficient to create an accurate picture of patient safety in an organisation. Studies have been undertaken to compare four commonly used methods of detection: incident reporting, coding data, indicators, and medical record review-based trigger tools/concurrent screening. Each method tends to identify different adverse events. No single method can identify all adverse events, and not all adverse events are identified by all four methods. It has been claimed that indicators and voluntary incident reporting can miss more than 90 per cent of the adverse events identified through record screening. And if we could have someone watching every patient around the clock we'd probably pick up on many more![3] The emphasis of the detection methods also differs. Administrative data appears to place more emphasis on problems occurring in surgical and procedural practices and detects fewer problems among medical patients. Issues identified through incident reporting tend to relate to events considered to be more nursing oriented; for example, wrong medication, falls and pressure ulcers. Concurrent screening and case review of medical records show the most promise in its ability to detect adverse events or sub-optimal care in a consistent fashion. However, this is a resource intensive method. These results suggest that combining approaches may be required to more fully capture the real status of your adverse event count – and of consumer safety in your organisation.[3,14,15]

So which method is best?

When faced with a new fad in quality improvement, we should first ask, 'is it really new?' and second, 'is it really an improvement on what we are currently doing?' It may be tempting to believe that the latest fashion in quality will be more effective than its predecessors, and some approaches are sold as a quick and simple solution to improvement. However, experience teaches us that worthwhile improvement in healthcare is usually slow. It could be argued that the use of a number of different quality methodologies in healthcare over the last 20 years has not led to sustained and continuing improvement.[10] The variable effectiveness of individual quality methodologies, and the fact that no one method appears to be superior to others in effecting lasting change, suggests that there is probably more to be gained by adopting a limited number of approaches that work in your organisation and sticking with them. This approach allows your organisation to develop skills and experience in their use and build up engagement, commitment and organisational capacity in their application. This may help avoid the organisational disruption caused by switching quality methodologies, which involves learning new processes for analysing, monitoring and embedding new ways of improving.[10,11]

Data and evaluation

There is a plethora of information about using data and evaluation to measure and monitor the quality of care (see the reference list for this chapter and the appendices for some useful resources). As this chapter is about highlighting some 'quality essentials', I have chosen to focus on three data areas that are particularly useful for quality managers to have in their kit.

Sample sizes

Deciding on the right sample sizes is always challenging for people collecting data. Unfortunately there is no correct answer to 'how many should I collect?' It depends on a range of issues from what you want to find out, to the size of the population, to how you intend to use the information. The trick is to be sure about exactly what it is you want to know in the form of a clear question you are trying to answer. This will help you determine what and how many to collect. For example, if you are trying to answer the question, 'what is the process of handover in X department?' you may decide to ascertain this through the use of qualitative, descriptive data, by observing handover and interviewing those involved. You will need to collect data over different shifts, including weekends and weekdays, to note any differences in the handover process. And you'll need to do these things until you start

NOT ALL QUALITY TOOLS ARE CREATED EQUAL

A review of the NHS approaches to quality improvement since the introduction of clinical governance identified some quality dos and don'ts. This is a particularly useful list for quality managers. No more arguing about what does and doesn't work — someone has done it for you!

- There is no one right way to improve quality. Improving quality requires a range of tools and approaches within a framework of clear goals, empowerment, capacity, development and data.
- Define quality first. Attempts to improve quality often fail to address clearly how quality is defined before starting to change organisations and processes. It is important to explore what is meant by quality before attempting to improve it.
- The process of implementation is more important than the approach. A great improvement idea or tool is no substitute for effective implementation.
- Adaptation of other organisations' tools, methods and approaches to your local needs is imperative. Use the right tool, and ensure that it is adapted to your local environment and needs.
- When attempting to improve processes, the clear identification of which process is being improved is a vital first step. The interdependence of clinical and administrative processes in healthcare must also be recognised. Processes are key determinants of outcomes, and their position as part of a wider complex system should be an important focus of your quality efforts.
- Don't exclusively promote one approach. Beware the person who appears more interested in promoting pre-determined tools and approaches than in solving organisational problems over the long term. Many tools dressed up as different approaches have the same characteristics of process control and redesign at their core.
- Understand the people. Quality will only improve when the behaviour of individuals within the system changes. Understanding and working with what motivates individuals within the healthcare system, especially those with a clinical professional background, is vital.
- Get data about quality before you start improvement activities. Data about performance and quality should enable improvement action. Evidence of success cannot be obtained without a baseline against which to assess progress.
- Recognise the importance of whole system leadership. Organisations need to be effectively led, and staff empowered, to improve quality. Quality will not improve throughout the system when the actions or words of those at the top do not support quality improvement. Effective change will only be achieved with whole systems approaches. In the long term, improvement has to be an integral part of what the organisation does, not an add-on. This means that targets for performance have to be translated into meaningful measures for different stakeholders and may be achieved in different ways within a complex system.[12]

to see a pattern. If your question is more definite and quantitative, such as 'what proportion of evening handovers follow the standard process?' you will have to decide how many to observe over what period to be able to accurately answer this. You can't observe every evening handover forever, so what sample size will you use? You may start with observing three in each department, for example, to see if that gives you a strong enough pattern to answer your question. If there isn't a clear pattern, you may need to observe more evening handovers over a set period, ensuring a mix of busy and quiet days until you can paint a picture of the current status of handover practice.

If you're asking a question about something involving large numbers – such as a large mental health service trying to ascertain the proportion of consumers over a year not followed up within a recommended time frame, for example – you will review a sample because you won't have the time or resources to review every record or ask every consumer (and these are the sort of data best collected concurrently). You might select ten per cent of the target mental health consumer records from a certain month to check for missed follow ups, and extrapolate your results from that. But, once again, the number and time period of your sample depends on the question you are trying to answer. As a rule of thumb, at least 30 samples are required to achieve normal distribution for your results. This allows you to be confident about how close the sample results would be to the broader population, were they to be extrapolated.[16] The important thing to remember when collecting data is that you are not doing research – you just need enough data to show a trend and tell a story. You do need to be able to defend your conclusions, however, so make sure that your data are reliable (collected in such a way that you can replicate the collection and get a consistent result) and valid (the data gives an accurate picture of what's actually occurring) so that good decisions can be made based on the results.[17,18] And when in doubt – ask an expert!

A note about observation as a data collection method. I believe observation is underused in healthcare, where audits tend to be king of the collection methods. But direct observation can be every bit as scientific and rigorous – and it is particularly useful when assessing safety issues such as use of protocols, resilience and teamwork. It must be done properly, however, to ensure it is not misinterpreted by staff. Observers should have had at least minimum training and practice. What is to be observed and how that will be assessed should be clear. And yes, staff should be warned! This is not about catching people out, but about collecting useful data for improvement. It's also an interesting, relatively easy way of gathering information that is more engaging to some staff than performing yet another record-based audit. There is a growing body of tools and research on direct observation for quality and safety in healthcare and I recommend you use this to inform your observation efforts.

Indicators

There are relatively few measures in healthcare that are absolutely accepted as unambiguous pointers to quality. If we had a set of universally accepted, valid and reliable data on safety and quality, a lot of quality manager problems would be solved. Despite the difficulties involved, indicators are widely used to monitor clinical quality. It is important to remember that indicators are only indicators. They do not purport to give absolute answers as to whether the quality of your care or services is good, bad or indifferent. Indicators are only useful to prompt further investigation, cultivate interest in improving an area and stimulate discussion. They can also indicate, by examining one aspect of a process, whether or not there may be quality problems in other, connected, processes. We can't measure every aspect of every area in healthcare. So we examine post-surgical wound infection as one indicator of the broader quality of surgical processes, for example. The usefulness of indicators is all in the way in which they are used. When an indicator result indicates something other than what is expected or desired, it is important to examine:

- data-related issues such as poor data quality
- differences in clinical practice
- external unusual factors that may have impacted on this particular sample
- whether this is common or special cause variation. Variation in and of itself is not necessarily a cause for concern.

Indicators can cause concern among clinicians and managers, particularly if decisions are based on indicator results. Indicators are not definitive measures; it's not the same as measuring the number of consumers on a waiting list for more than a month. Indicators are monitoring tools for key processes, designed to highlight areas where there might be a cause for concern and further investigation. Your data are compared to a set point, which may be an optimum result or a minimum standard. Be clear about whether you're comparing your data against the ideal or the minimum. Just maintaining your results above the minimum standard does not mean you are performing well or providing quality care – it might be OK, but there is always room for improvement. And issues flagged by indicator data should be further investigated before any conclusions are drawn about the quality of care being provided.

There are many valid indicators available for nearly all aspects of healthcare that you can use in your quality program. Don't invent them yourself unless you absolutely have to, as indictors that have been developed and tested by experts external to your health service are likely to have more credibility with managers and clinicians than your home-grown efforts. If you do develop and apply local indicators or introduce external indicators into your service, do so carefully. They are often regarded with suspicion by clinicians and managers. Don't try to use them for anything more than flags of potential issues, and be transparent about how they have been developed and how they will be used. Where indicators are well defined and the data are as reliable and valid as possible, indicators can be a critically useful addition to any quality program. But poor indicators that do not meet these criteria can do more harm than good. A small set of robust indicators that staff pay attention to is much more useful than a large set of indicators that no-one takes much notice of, or worse, that gives people ammunition to fire at your quality program.

Process control charts

Increasingly, indicator and other monitoring data are being presented on process control charts. Known also as process behaviour charts, which may better describe their purpose, these charts help us to better understand the processes we have in place to achieve quality care and how they are performing. One of the problems with comparing indicator data to one fixed point is that this does not allow for the natural variation in all systems – particularly complex systems. Your results will go up and down from day to day, week to week. Although this is well understood in other high-risk industries, we are only just starting to understand this in healthcare quality. Because normal variation in any process is greater than we think, we may waste time criticising staff and investigating processes on the basis of results that look bad, but which in reality fall within the range of normal variation, or are the result of a one-off event that may never occur again. To spend resources in response to a variation that falls within the normal range is needless fiddling. On the other hand, if results really do indicate a systems problem, they must be investigated as you could be headed for a systems breakdown.

Process control charts are developed by plotting results for one process, such as the number of falls each week over a number of weeks. They are really just run charts of trended data where we plot our results over time to look for trends. But rather than compare the data to a set point or to historical results, they are compared to upper and lower control limits set at two or three standard deviations from the mean, as seen in Figure 1. A number of rules are then applied to the chart to assess whether or not a process is deemed 'in control'.

The greater the number of data points, the easier it is to see the patterns, but it is generally recommended that at least 20 and preferably 30 data points are required to identify the mean and set accurate upper and lower limits for the data points. There are different types of control charts, depending on the type of data you are reviewing, and the upper and lower control limits are calculated differently depending on the type of data you are looking at. There are a number of free and commercial software packages that provide tutorials and make these calculations for you once you have inputted your data.[20,21,22] Once your data is plotted, there are a number of rules to apply to interpret the data and ascertain whether or not your process – such as your process for falls prevention – is in control and doing what you want it to do, or out of control and needs fixing.

Variations in the results of any process can be caused by special or one off events that interfere with the process. Variation can also be caused by the normal ups and downs of any process (particularly in a complex system), which is known as common cause variation. Indications that you may have a variation in your process caused by a 'special cause' are:

- a run of seven or more points all above or all below the centre line, or all increasing or all decreasing
- five diagonal points, up, down or across the mean
- a data point above or below the upper or lower control limits
- any unusual pattern or trends within the control limits.[13]

So in the example control chart in Figure 1, we see everything reasonably in control in this process in Year 1 (although the mean is constant, so performance is static rather than improving) but things look less controlled at the beginning of Year 2 – a trend worth looking into. What has changed in Year 2? Where the results indicate special cause variation, your investigation should be able to identify a specific event or change in the process that is producing these unusual results. The beauty of identifying special cause variation is that it helps to focus the analysis and investigation of problem data. It reduces the reactive, scattergun approach often initiated by suboptimal or unusual results, and reduces the likelihood that time and resources will be wasted 'fixing' a whole process that may not be broken. If we take falls data, for example, a few spiking results in a data table compared to the same month last year, might result in a flurry of activity to improve assessment, purchase more aids or review policies. If you are using a process control chart to monitor your falls data, however, these changes will be interpreted as special cause variation, focusing you and the falls committee on first looking for a specific cause (which could be that a consumer new to the facility had refused assistance with falls prevention and chosen to accept the risk of continuing her daily routine, followed by a number of frequent fallers leaving the facility) rather than placing time and resources into reviewing a falls assessment and prevention process that is actually working quite well. [13,17,18,23,24,25]

If your data variation is all common cause, however, that doesn't mean that the process can't be improved. Once you've accounted for the special cause variations, you can focus on improving your process. As the process becomes more controlled, the range of points above and below the mean should move closer to the mean. Even if your falls prevention process is in control, the falls rate and mean may still be too high, and improvements to the falls assessment and prevention process must be made. Depending on what you are measuring, your aim is to move the mean to as close to ideal as possible. [24,25]

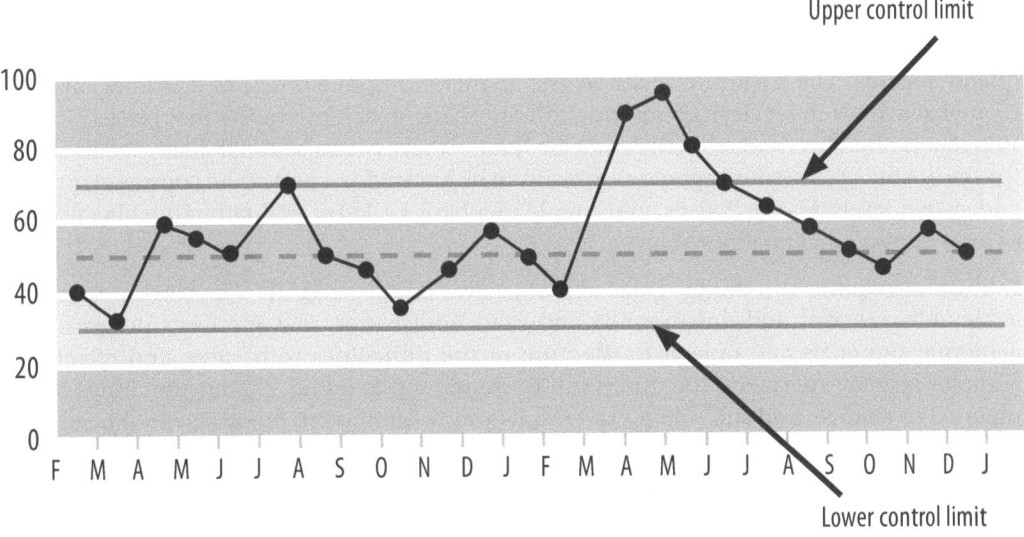

Figure 1: Example process control chart

ARE YOU REALLY BENCHMARKING?

People often use indicators, comparison and benchmarking inter-changeably. It's true that you need something to compare your indicator results against to know when they trigger the need for a response. This may be an internally set trigger, or threshold, or one provided by an external source. You might look at the literature to compare your organisation to those doing well or compare yourself to other organisations with a similar consumer mix to yours through formal or informal channels. It doesn't matter so much if you are comparing yourself to a larger or smaller organisation, with more or fewer staff or resources. Comparing 'apples to apples' is not so much about comparing similar organisations as it is about comparing similar consumers and using the same denominators and data collection processes. For example, if you are reviewing falls with fractures in aged care, you probably won't want to compare your high care consumer falls results with falls data in a community aged care service. This doesn't mean that you can't learn something from the community facility if they have a fantastic falls prevention program. But direct data comparison in that case may not be useful. You can, however, compare your high care consumer results to the high care consumers in any other facility — large or small, public or private — as long as the data have been collected in the same way, according to the same definitions, and as long as both organisations are using the same denominator to calculate their falls rate over the period. Small facilities may feel as if they don't have the same level of resources to tackle falls as larger facilities — but they may be more nimble and responsive in implementing solutions and therefore see faster rates of improvement.

Benchmarking is an important part of quality improvement, both within your organisation and with external organisations and data sets. The word benchmarking is not a synonym for comparison, however. Technically, comparison is only one component of benchmarking. True benchmarking is a proactive process that requires you to compare your results against the organisation or provider achieving the best results in a certain area, finding out how they achieve those results and applying that knowledge to your own organisation. Comparison alone may not be enough to result in improvement.

Evaluation

Evaluation causes much angst in healthcare, and never more so than in the evaluation of quality systems. The trick to evaluation and to measuring outcomes, as it is with any data-related activity, is to be clear about what you are trying to achieve in the first place. This is a step that is often overlooked at the strategic level – where organisational quality goals are set for the quality of care your organisation wants to be known for – and at the consumer, process and system levels. Figure 2 gives an example of a basic cycle for evaluating the effectiveness of an organisational quality system.

Evaluation requires two things: goals and objectives that are SMART (specific, measurable, achievable, relevant and time-bound) and valid information that monitors progress with achieving the goals and objectives. Because of the difficulties with cause and effect in a complex system, you can do the things you've committed to doing, change the things you've planned to change, and still not get the results you're aiming for. So often you'll need both quantitative and qualitative information on process and outcome changes to indicate the effectiveness of your quality plan and system. This information is collected through audits, indicators, results of improvement activities, direct observation, consumer and staff feedback, staff understanding and use of agreed strategies and processes, adverse events analysis, trends in incident rates and results of root cause analyses. Don't forget to also evaluate the usefulness and value of the 'ongoing' maintenance activities – and remember that 'ongoing' does not have to mean 'forever'. Ongoing monitoring and maintenance activities may only take up a section of the quality plan, but their contribution to achieving the goals should be routinely evaluated.

Building your quality professional brand

The final 'quality essential' for your kit is about who you are as a quality manager and how others perceive you in this role. We saw in the leadership chapter that people look for many characteristics in leaders, including credibility. As a consultant to staff at all levels of your organisation, especially if you have limited formal or positional power, credibility is 'essential' to your success. So if we ran the 'credibility meter' over you, what reading would we get? Do you know if the people in your health service or profession view you as the 'go to' person for quality knowledge and skill? It is particularly useful to have someone who knows how you operate – and who's not afraid to be honest with you – to help you reflect on your 'brand' and how to develop it. Mentors are particularly good for this – and highly recommended for anyone in a quality role. (And I hope that the experienced quality professionals reading this are already mentoring new recruits and supporting their peers!)

The more credible you are, the more respect you will earn and the easier it will be to do your job. Having credibility is critical to your quality professional 'brand' in addition to the other characteristics of effective leaders (as discussed in Chapter Five), who are commonly considered to be:

- honest – say what they mean, do what they say
- forward looking – have a clear view of the future as a better place and are prepared to do the work to get there
- inspiring – can engage people's imaginations in the view of the future and make it seem achievable
- competent – good at what they do
- empathic – clear about their own values, but understand that others may be driven by different values. [26]

As reiterated throughout this book, to develop and grow as a quality professional requires application and effort. What I'm talking about is a planned, proactive approach to building your 'brand'. Take a minute to answer a few questions (and if you can do this with a trusted mentor, you'll probably get even more out of it):

- What do I want to be known for as a quality professional?
- How do I want others to describe me – particularly those I need to influence?
- How would they describe me now?
- What do I need to do to get from how I am perceived now to how I would like to be perceived by my peers and colleagues?

You can also enhance your role and brand by developing some professional goals for your career in quality management. This helps give you a meaningful purpose beyond your current position, guides your professional development and career choices, and focuses you on the achievements you'd like to chalk up in your current job. In Chapter One, you completed these two sentences:

- My current purpose as the quality manager in my organisation/service is to [do what] to achieve [what].
- I would like my purpose as quality manager in my organisation to be [do what] to achieve [what].

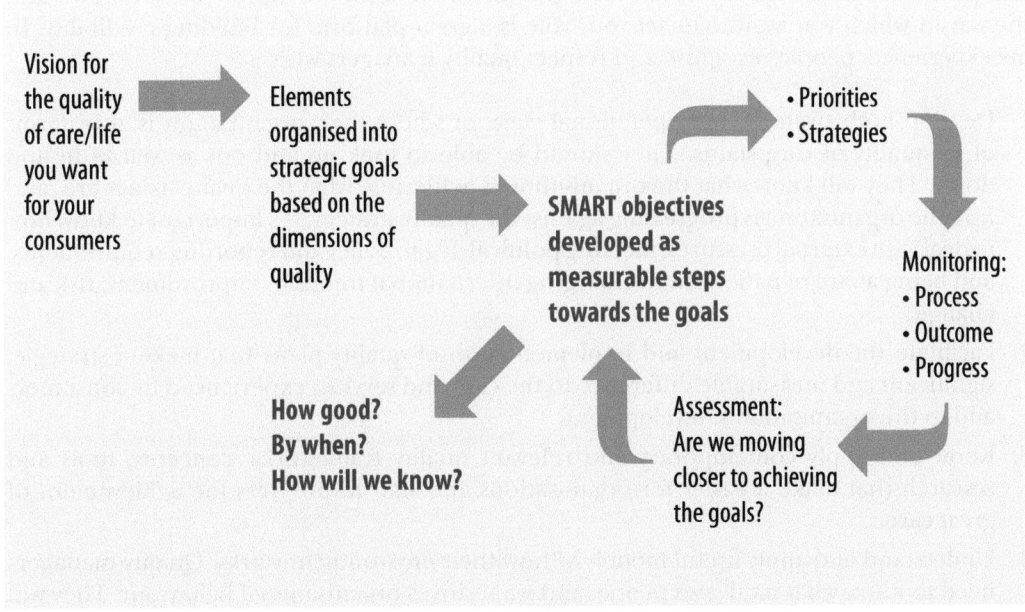

Figure 2: Example of basic steps in the evaluation of a quality system

Having now worked your way through this book, try completing these sentences again. Do they read differently? Do you have a different perspective? Then try these:

- To achieve this purpose I must be effective in the following key areas:
- My manager and I define success in each key area in the following ways:
- My current key responsibilities and tasks in each of these areas are (or should be):
- The measures and targets used to identify my effectiveness in each key result area are (or should be):
- My professional goals in quality management are (one year, three years and beyond):
- My current role assists me to achieve my professional goals in the following ways:
- I want to change my role to better achieve my professional and organisational goals in the following ways:
- The first thing I could do to make my role in this organisation more effective and fulfilling is:

The idea is to have your current role complement your personal professional goals, and support you to evolve professionally. If not, you need to re-shape your role to better align with your professional goals. Even small changes may help give your current role more meaning. Or, if the gap is wide, perhaps your professional goals need review. Or maybe your current role isn't the right role for you.

The ten point plan for building your brand

Being clear about your professional goals and direction, what you want to be known for and the way in which you want to enact your role is a great platform for building credibility. In my experience, people recognise and respect quality managers who:

1. Develop both strategic and operational views of where their organisation is at in terms of its quality of care status. They should be able to look up and out as well as in and down. They will know what the organisation is achieving, what the quality issues are, and how the organisation is progressing against the quality strategy. It's important to know how to deal with external pressures; meeting political, legal, policy and reporting requirements; and being aware of national and emerging international trends in improvement, risk and change.
2. Facilitate the development and implementation of quality plans that make a strategic, significant and measurable difference to the care and services experienced by consumers and to the organisation's development.
3. Know and apply contemporary and relevant quality frameworks, concepts, tools and research that make it easier for organisations and staff to progress the achievement of great care.
4. Understand and apply useful models of how their environment works. Quality managers need to know what motivates people and what drives organisational behaviour. They will know how to manage projects and how to influence and effect change in different environments.
5. Know useful quality facts and be able to apply them, for example:
    - The organisational characteristics that flag potential risks for the quality and safety of care, such as ineffective credentialing systems, poor quality monitoring and failure to address known problems.

- Standardising processes doesn't always standardise behaviour.
- Every system is perfectly designed to achieve the results it gets.
- Both robust systems and resilient people are required to create safety and quality.
- Key safety and quality problems in healthcare: for example, approximately 10,000 patients worldwide are harmed from error every day; incident reporting alone may miss up to 90 per cent of actual incidents; poor care may increase case cost seven times; in a complex system, policies and protocols are likely to drift and change over time.[3,4,15,27,28,29]

6. Know enough about 'everything' (the core tools and approaches required to do your job well) and a lot about one thing (develop expertise in one particular area). Real expertise in an area helps build credibility and confidence.
7. Have a neat, simple approach to clearly explaining the connection between the mechanics of the quality system and the achievement of great care, and are able to translate the improvement process into plain language.
8. Invest in developing training and communication skills to competently share and teach quality-related concepts and tools in meetings, presentations and publications.
9. Act as an effective consultant for the organisation, who:
    - understands and respects the definition of success from their clients', consumers', managers' and staff perspectives – and marry it to the organisation's definition of success for the consumer
    - cultivates relationships as the basis for collaborative change and improvement
    - uses skills, knowledge and the right tools for the job to pursue success
    - develops realistic and achievable aims
    - embeds robust project management into their every day work
    - supports and empowers staff at all levels of the organisation to enact their governance and professional roles in creating quality care in a way that is meaningful, enjoyable and positive for both parties
    - teaches people to fish by transferring skills and knowledge
    - is a problem solver rather than a problem creator
    - is clear about what they want to achieve, and flexible in their approach to achieving it.
10. Develop their personal resilience to bounce back from setbacks. The effective quality manager is also a consummate self-manager and takes a proactive approach to building their resilience within the challenging healthcare environment.

In the end, credibility is what you do. Do the things that you'd like to be known for. True credibility is like fitness: it's earned bit by bit and requires consistency and focus to achieve. It requires you to be clear about your purpose, know what you're talking about and be able to apply that knowledge in a way that adds value. The icing on the credibility cake may be a recognised professional profile, successful conference presentations and published articles. And yes, all these things help. But in the end, credibility is really about the things that you do well in the workplace day to day. The ways in which you develop your skills, solve problems, perform in meetings, show respect for other people and their opinions and, most importantly, the consistent way in which you apply these characteristics to make life easier and better for others: these are the building blocks of credibility. And credibility will make navigating your quality role a whole lot easier. These are the building blocks of credibility.

The last word

This seems an appropriate place to wrap up this conversation about navigating, developing – and surviving! – the quality manager role. This book has covered many topics, but at its core it is really all about credibility, effectiveness and fulfilment. As I've reiterated throughout, the quality manager often has to be the smartest person in the room to successfully inhabit a role in the harsh landscape of planet healthcare. It's not always easy. But it is incredibly important – and when you have a win for consumers, staff and the organisation, the satisfaction can be great.

This brings us to my final top tips. The first is 'sharpen the saw'[31] – keep learning and evolving. Knowledge is the best tool you can have in your kit to overcome the hazards you come up against every day. And you can help others sharpen their saws by sharing your knowledge and experience. My second tip is 'work hard to make it look easy'. Develop your expertise and practise your skills to make the healthcare quality journey easier for others – and yourself – not harder. The more strategic, proactive and knowledgeable you are, the more positive your impact will be on your consumers, your organisation and the health system. I hope that this book has added in some small way to the enjoyment of your professional journey, that it supports you to survive and thrive in the face of your challenges, and helps you to achieve your quality and professional goals. I wish you every success.

➡ TOP TIP: DEVELOP YOUR TRAINING AND COMMUNICATION SKILLS

For some quality professionals training, presenting and communicating is one of the hardest aspects of the job. But these are central to the quality manager's role. You don't have to be the world's best presenter or communicator, but to be an effective quality manager you do have to be competent in these areas. Do a course; read a book; watch others; practise, practise, practise – and learn from your mistakes.[30]

One of my first 'quality' presentations was to a group of chief executives and directors of nursing – many of whom did not know me – from across the large rural region in which I was a newly appointed quality coordinator. It was an hour-long talk explaining the Department of Health requirements for the development of quality systems in the region, and how we planned to achieve them. I was extremely nervous, but reasonably well prepared, so I stood up and plunged in. I realised after I'd finished and left that I hadn't introduced myself, and hadn't been introduced by anyone else. Most of the audience of 60 people probably spent the hour wondering who I was and where I'd come from, which may have detracted somewhat from the credibility of my message. For many years after that, when giving a presentation I would write at the top of my notes: 'INTRODUCE YOURSELF'.

When starting out as a quality manager I would always review my presentations and write down anything I wish I'd done differently or better. For the first few years, these lists were usually long, and ranged from 'take a printed copy of your presentation in case the computer crashes', to reminding myself of a joke that had worked well, to suggesting a different order for some key points. When preparing my next presentation, whether it was for a small group or a large conference, I'd pull out the list and make sure I applied all the relevant points in my new presentation. It's simple, and it works – my presenting improved and I became more confident. I believe it's called continuous improvement.

Headlines: Chapter Seven

- Effective quality managers build their quality essentials kit throughout their career.
- It's not the number of tools in the kit that counts, but knowing, and skilfully using, the right tool for each job.
- Develop a sound understanding of the basics: measurement and evaluation, quality methods, change, influence, planning and implementation.
- Adapt your skills and knowledge to the environment rather expecting the environment to adapt to you.
- A key aspect of the quality professional role is to use and to effectively transfer quality skills and knowledge to managers and staff to support them in their quality governance roles.
- Building a positive, credible quality professional brand takes effort and focus, but can make the quality role much easier.
- Be clear about your professional direction, and proactive about shaping your knowledge, skills and role to achieve it. Learn, evolve and share.
- Be strategic and keep your eye on the big picture: navigate the difficulties, celebrate the wins and enjoy doing great work!

References and Further Reading

1. Argyris C (1996) Actionable Knowledge: Design Causality in the Service of Consequential Theory. *Journal of Applied Behavioral Science*, vol. 32, no. 4

2. Balding C (2008) From Quality Assurance to Clinical Governance. *Australian Health Review*, vol 32, no 3. pp.383–91

3. Classen et al (2011) 'Global Trigger Tool' Shows that Adverse Events in Hospitals may be Ten Times Greater than Previously Thought. *Health Affairs*, vol.30, no. 4, pp. 755–63

4. Braithwaite J, Coiera E (2010) Beyond Patient Safety Flatland. *JR Soc Med Volume*, vol. 103, pp. 219–25

5. Department of Health, UK (2001) *The Report of the Public Inquiry into Children's Heart Surgery at the Bristol Royal Infirmary 1984-1995: Learning From Bristol.* London: Stationery Office, UK

6. NHS Scotland (2010) *The Healthcare Strategy for NHS Scotland.* www.scotland.gov.au/publications

7. Walshe K, Shortell SM (2004) When Things Go Wrong: How Health Care Organisations Deal with Major Failures. *Health Affairs*, vol. 23, pp.103–12

8. Grol R, Berwick D, Wensing M (2008) On the Trail of Quality and Safety in Health Care. *BMJ*, vol. 336, no.74–76

9. Westbrook JI, Braithwaite J, Georgiou A, Ampt A, Creswick N, Coiera E, Iedema R (2007) Multimethod Evaluation of Information and Communication Technologies in Health in the Context of Wicked Problems and Sociotechnical Theory. *J Am Med Inform Assoc.*, vol.14, no.6, pp.746–55

10. Walshe K (2009) Pseudo Innovation: The Development and Spread of Healthcare Quality Improvement Methodologies. *International Journal for Quality in Healthcare*, vol 21, no. 3 pp. 153–59

11. Varkey P, Reller MK, Resar RK (2007) Basics of Quality Improvement in Healthcare. *Mayo Clin Proc.* vol 82, no. 6, pp. 735–39

12. Boaden R, Harvey G, Moxham C, Proudlove L (2007) *QI: Theory and Practice in Healthcare.* University of Manchester Business School, UK

13. Ragush S, McAuliffe J (2005) *The Quality Improvement Toolbox.* Health Quality Council and National Primary Care Development Team, Canada

14. Naessens JM, Campbell CR, Huddlestone JM, Berg BP, Lefante JJ, Williams AR, Culbertson RA, (2009) A Comparison of Hospital Adverse Events Identified by Three Widely Used Detection Methods. *International Journal for Quality in Healthcare*, vol 21, no. 4, pp 301–07

15. Akbari Sari AB, Sheldon T, Cracknell A, Turnbull A (2007) Sensitivity of Routine System for Reporting Patient Safety Incidents in an NHS Hospital: Retrospective Patient Case Note Review. *BMJ* 2007, vol. 334, no. 79

16. Kemp SM and Kemp S (2004) *Business Statistics Demystified*. McGraw Hill, USA

17. Victorian Quality Council (2008) *A guide to using data for health care quality improvement*. Department of Health Victoria, Australia

18. Australian Commission on Safety and Quality in Healthcare (2006) *Measurement For Improvement Toolkit*. ACSQHC, Australia www.safetyandquality.gov.au (Accessed November 2010)

19. Frankel A, Leonard M, Simmonds T, Haraden C, Vega K (eds) (2009) *The Essential Guide for Patient Safety Officers*. Joint Commission on Accreditation of Healthcare Organisations and Institute for Healthcare Improvement, USA.

20. SQC Online: *Online Statistical Calculators for Acceptance Sampling and Quality Control*, www.sqconline.com

21. Lean Six Sigma Software. *Training and Consulting: QI Macros*. www.qimacros.com

22. National Services Scotland (date unknown) *Tutorial Guide: Statistical Process Control for Monitoring Quality in Healthcare*. Clinical Indicators Support Team, NHS Scotland. www.indicators.scot.nhs.uk/SPC/

23. Schmaltz S (2009) *A Selection of Statistical Process Control Tools Used in Monitoring Healthcare Performance*. National Quality Measures Clearinghouse, USA

24. Tague NR (1995) *The Quality Tool Box*. ASQC Quality Press, USA

25. Wolff A, Taylor S (2009) *Enhancing Patient Care*. MJA Books, Australia

26. Kouzes J, Posner B (1995) *The Leadership Challenge*. Jossey Bass, USA

27. Vincent C (2007). Incident reporting and patient safety. *BMJ*, vol. 334, no. 51

28. Dekker S (2006) *The Field Guide to Understanding Human Error*. Ashgate Publishing Company, UK

29. Ehsani J, Jackson T, Duckett S (2006) The Incidence and Cost of Adverse Events in Victorian Hospitals, 2003–04. *Medical Journal of Australia*, vol. 184, no. 11, pp. 551–55

30. Weeks C (2010) *Handy Hints for the Novice Conference Presenter*. The Junction, Australia

31. Covey SR (1989) *The Seven Habits of Highly Effective People*. Simon & Schuster Inc., USA

APPENDIX 1:
Quality Manager Skills and Knowledge Framework

APPENDIX 1: Quality Manager Skills and Knowledge Framework[1]

Quality System Component	QUALITY MANAGER CAREER PHASE		
	Foundation (maintenance and local improvement)	Development (maintenance and improvement across the organisation)	Established (maintenance, improvement and transformation)
Area 1. Planning, creating and monitoring quality care and services			

Define the desired quality care and services and develop a plan to achieve it	• Identify the legislation, policy and standards to be met by the organisation and develop an organisation-wide plan to monitor and achieve them
	• Help service managers define the quality of care they want their consumers to experience and organise this using the dimensions of quality
	• Assist department managers and staff to plan maintenance and improvement initiatives:
	  - Use data analysis and problem identification tools to identify relevant activities
	  - Define the activity purpose
	  - Set 'SMART' objectives and corresponding evaluation processes
	  - Advise on data collection
		• Facilitate interdisciplinary approach to an organisational definition, or vision for quality care, described in terms of the desired consumer experience and organised by the dimensions of quality
		• Frame the achievement of the quality vision in terms of a proactive 'creating safety and quality' approach
		• Develop interdisciplinary, organisation-wide improvement initiatives to achieve the vision for quality
		• Adapt initiatives from key external safety and quality organisations
		• Develop organisation-wide goals and 'SMART' objectives for creating great care that can be pursued by a range of services
			• Facilitate the involvement of all staff in setting the organisational goals and priorities for great quality care
			• Guide and support managers and staff to adapt and implement the strategic improvement plan and goals at a local level to drive great quality care

Identify and analyse quality of care status and problems	• Identify organisational gaps in meeting mandatory requirements and standards • Assist service managers to identify their quality status and issues: - Teach the PDSA cycle - Use quality analysis tools - Participate in data collection, analysis and presentation, using qualitative and quantitative data (including validity and reliability) - Simple survey design and analysis - Presentation and analysis of trends in basic risk and quality data - Measures of process and outcome - Sourcing and use of existing indicators to monitor and identify issues	• Identify organisational quality gaps and problems: - Develop and use performance indicators, other qualitative and quantitative data, internal targets and external benchmarking to identify opportunities for improvement - Use lean methodology, FMEA and other contemporary methods to review current practice and identify areas for improvement • Assist managers and staff to identify appropriate and effective solutions and improvements by using problem identification and analysis methods • Use control charts to monitor and improve processes • Develop organisation-wide surveys and corresponding analysis	• Diagnose organisational gaps and problems using robust quantitative and qualitative data, current research and tools relating to characteristics of high and poor performing organisations, and national and international benchmarking • Use appreciative enquiry to identify and spread areas of excellence in care and services

| Implement strategies and manage change to achieve high quality care and services | • Assist managers to effectively implement quality initiatives using basic change management methods
• Review and develop policies, protocols and processes to support change | • Facilitate the implementation of organisation-wide improvement initiatives, using a project management approach
• Develop and evaluate short cycle pilots to test changes
• Understand and work with theories and models of change in complex healthcare systems
• Use influence skills to gain staff buy-in
• Prepare funding submissions and recommendations for allocation of resources
• Design and implement systems to support change and improvement
• Use process redesign and lean methodology to improve processes and systems
• Advise on adapting, developing and implementing evidence based guidelines and protocols for improved quality and safety
• Sustain and spread successful local initiatives across the organisation
• Communicate effectively at all levels of the organisation | • Develop relationships and partnerships across internal and external services to achieve organisational change
• Source evidence based, effective approaches and models from research and other organisations and industries
• Empower and enable managers and staff at point of care to enact their responsibilities for developing local strategies and activities to pursue, monitor and measure progress towards the organisational quality goals and objectives
• Use a change model that is effective in the healthcare environment and takes into account the characteristics of complex healthcare organisations
• Use a mix of systems and people change to achieve improvement
• Sustain and spread complex initiatives across the organisation |

Monitor and evaluate the quality of care and services	• Identify, monitor and analyse key quality and risk indicators and provide corresponding advice to managers and committees • Develop, implement and analyse consumer feedback • Participate in clinical audits • Participate in case reviews • Assist managers and staff to evaluate the effectiveness of improvement initiatives	• Develop, source, implement and monitor a dataset that measures key aspects of each dimension of quality • Assist managers and staff to manage their risks and monitor and evaluate improvement initiatives • Implement a variety of techniques to seek consumer feedback • Advise on adapting, developing and implementing targets for improved quality and safety • Use control charts and dashboards to monitor and improve key processes and risks • Provide advice to committees and managers about the effectiveness of organisation-wide activities • Ensure rigorous mortality, morbidity and clinical review processes are in place and feed back into systems improvement	• Participate in state, national and international data comparison and improvement initiatives for local improvement • Source, participate in, lead and apply research for improvement of systems and outcomes

Area 2. Developing and implementing organisational governance systems to support and drive quality care and services

| Leadership, governance and culture | • Advise managers and staff on the legislation and policy requirements governing the way in which care and services are delivered in your organisation, and perform corresponding gap analysis

• Advise on and assist with implementing basic clinical governance structures and processes:
- Committees
- Governance roles and responsibilities at each level of the organisation
- Components of clinical governance

• Lead small quality related groups and manage sub committees:
- Chairing
- Agenda
- Minutes
- Follow up

• Prepare reports on various aspects of quality and risk for quality committees | • Develop an organisational quality plan that identifies key improvement goals, priorities and quality governance supports, and describe how these will be achieved to drive great quality care for consumers

• Develop position descriptions that clearly define governance roles and responsibilities for safety and quality at each level of the organisation

• Support quality leaders across the organisation to develop relationships and partnerships for improvement

• Support high-level quality committees and review their effectiveness

• Prepare reports and commentary for organisational quality, safety and governance committees on progress with the achievement of organisational quality goals and management of risk

• Advise on quality system resourcing

• Source and develop strategies for measuring and improving the safety and quality culture

• Advise and support organisational leaders to promulgate a 'just' and 'safety' culture | • Facilitate the development of a strategic quality plan that links to the organisation's strategic and business plans; identifies annual priorities and drives maintenance of standards, improvement of processes and outcomes; and transforms the consumer experience

• Guide the implementation of an organisational leadership structure for leading quality care and services and achieving the quality goals at all levels of the organisation

• Provide education and support for role redesign to support managers and staff to enact their safety and quality governance roles

• Develop internal and external business cases for large scale investment in transformation and improvement

• Develop relationships and partnerships for improvement across the organisation and with external organisations

• Influence and empower staff at all levels of the organisation to participate in and support creating quality care

• Participate in external expert panels and committees, and influence corporate and government quality-related policy |

Consumer Participation	• Set up systems to ensure consumer rights, responsibilities, feedback and complaints are supported and acted on where necessary • Use external and internal consumer and carer satisfaction and feedback to improve the quality of care and services	• Ensure there are policies, protocols and organisational structures in place to drive consumer and carer involvement in their care and participation in service improvement • Ensure consumer and carer perspectives are integrated into care pathways, service planning, risk management and care improvement • Identify barriers to consumer and carer participation, and make recommendations to appropriate committees and executive • Ensure training, orientation and mentoring are provided for consumers to support their membership of organisational committees • Ensure consumer and carer rights and responsibilities are understood and supported by staff at all levels of the organisation through active and ongoing staff development	• Develop processes to support consumers, carers and community groups to partner with the health service to identify and better communicate needs

Area 2. Developing and implementing organisational governance systems to support and drive quality care and services cont.

Effective workforce	• Advise on credentialing, scope of practice and performance management systems • Ensure staff compliance with standards of care, policies, guidelines and protocols is supported and evaluated as a key platform for safe and high quality care	• Support and advise on the development of clear role expectations for safety and quality at each level of the organisation • Ensure clinicians and staff have timely access to relevant data about the quality of the care they provide and are supported to understand and act upon their data • Design and participate in workforce training to support the development of core competencies to provide safe and quality care across the organisation	• Ensure staff recruitment and retention processes consider safety and quality issues to source appropriately skilled, qualified and experienced staff to provide quality care • Ensure there is a process for workload and skills mix management to create safe and quality care, and that this is regularly reviewed in light of changing casemix and consumer needs • Implement a professional development pathway for quality managers
Quality systems	Implement and maintain a quality system that: • supports improvement in each dimension of quality and meets accreditation and policy requirements • determines required resources Provide education to: • explain the components of the quality system, and connection between the quality system and quality of care basic quality tools	Participate in, implement and maintain a quality system that: • sets and achieves quality goals for great care • clearly connects the organisational goals for quality care, the supporting governance systems and accreditation requirements • encompasses contemporary national and international quality and risk initiatives	• Ensure the quality framework links quality activities and roles to the organisation's strategic plan and business plans, and clearly demonstrates the connection between these and the achievement of the quality goals and governance supports • Adapt or develop and implement an IT solution that integrates quality and risk initiatives, automates as much of the

and skills to define, identify, analyse, and improve the quality of care
- explain the basics of the reactive and proactive aspects of risk management

Coordinate accreditation and external quality reviews to:
- Develop and monitor a yearly schedule of preparation activities
- Explain accreditation to staff and how it links to the quality system
- Assist managers to perform a gap analysis in their service against the standards
- Advise executive and managers on accreditation issues to be addressed and delegation of responsibilities for meeting standards
- Prepare documentation to be sent to the accrediting body

- includes a minimum dataset reporting on key aspects of each dimension of quality, key risks and external reporting requirements that is regularly reported to relevant committees and the executive and governing body
- Adapt or develop an IT solution for capturing and organising improvement initiatives and corresponding data across the organisation, and linking these to accreditation requirements
- Evaluate the effectiveness of the quality system in achieving safe, high quality care and a positive consumer experience
- Advise and assist managers on various approaches to identify and present appropriate evidence to meet and exceed accreditation requirements

Provide education across the organisation, including:
- Quality system structure, function and responsibilities to all levels of the organisation
- Use systems theory for improvement
- Application of redesign and lean methods
- Quality and risk systems and tools
- Demonstrate effective skills transfer, equipping staff to be competent in basic improvement skills

data collection, analysis and reporting as possible, and demonstrates progress against quality goals and objectives
- Synthesise initiatives, measures and results from across the organisation to build a picture of the quality of care experienced by consumers
- Understand and be able to articulate the organisation's position in terms of the quality of care it provides
- Link relevant functions and programs in different parts of the organisation – such as redesign, finance, IT and risk management – to pursue the strategic quality goals

Area 2. Developing and implementing organisational governance systems to support and drive quality care and services cont.

Risk systems

- Implement a risk management system, comprising reactive and proactive risk approaches that identifies and monitors key risks, including:
  - An incident reporting and analysis system that encourages reporting and drives response to adverse events
  - Responds effectively to medico legal issues
  - Use of incidents to learn and improve
  - An active risk register
  - Proactive identification of risk and harm through auditing and monitoring
- Contribute to root cause analyses of sentinel events and critical incidents
- Provide data to department managers, organisational committees, the executive and governing body showing issues and trends in key risks and identifying priorities for action
- Provide education for small groups that explains how the organisation's quality system works, staff roles and responsibilities to

- Develop, implement and evaluate a risk management framework and system that identifies, rates, prioritises and controls clinical and non-clinical risk across the organisation
- Pursue safety through a combination of proactive aware staff, robust systems and valid data
- Implement human factors related solutions to creating safety
- Implement an IT solution to monitoring and reporting on proactive and reactive aspects of risk and safety management
- Produce comprehensive and informative reports for committees, the executive and the governing body on the organisation's risk status and priorities, and advise on investment in risk reduction
- Lead analysis of critical incidents
- Provide education at all levels of the organisation that explains how enacting clinical governance roles at all levels of the organisation will drive safe care, how international

- Provide high level advice to executives and governing bodies on proven strategies to minimise risk and improve safety
- Implement proven initiatives from relevant organisations and techniques from other high risk industries to manage risk and create safety
- Develop a system for creating safety and managing risk that combines robust systems, human factors, technology and development of individual and team resilience
- Understand and advise on the use of technology to improve safety
- Provide education at all levels of the organisation including context and rationale of the difficulties and complexities of improving quality, change and managing risk; training in building resilience and developing robust systems to create safety; and strategies for creating safety in complex systems

the quality system, cause and prevention of error and harm, incident reporting and management, and the systems you will develop to support safety

safety data can inform your organisation's risk management system, how safety can be created through applying human factors' engineering theory, and training staff in the basics of improvement, change and implementation skills

Area 3. Key areas for quality manager self management and development

Fundamental	Intermediate	Advanced
• Managing people up, down and across the organisation: - Basic understanding of control and influence, and how this relates to the quality manager role - Basic understanding of collaborating with staff (including medical staff) - Involvement in creating quality care and services • Sound knowledge of the PDSA cycle • Basic knowledge of change, project management, quality tools and collecting valid and reliable data	• Develop own leadership skills and quality expertise to build credibility: • Show examples of successful change and improvement that measurably improve care and services for consumers • Publications and presentations • Develop or adapt a change model that fits with your organisation and encompasses techniques that work in complex care organisations	• Develop leadership and credibility through expert knowledge of the internal and external quality position and context, quality and safety research and theory, and ability to effect successful and participative change across the organisation • Review, clarify and develop own role to meet the needs of the organisation • Scan for and identify emerging knowledge and initiatives in quality and safety • Develop skills to be able to successfully influence staff at all levels of the organisation, and external bodies,

Area 3. Key areas for quality manager self management and development cont.

	Fundamental	Intermediate	Advanced
	• Connection with a mentor and/or network of colleagues for support and advice • Effective time management • Demonstrate behaviour that models leadership, positive safety culture and practice • Model proactive and positive work attitude and develop personal resistance	• Apply contemporary quality tools and knowledge for monitoring, analysis, improvement and evaluation • Understand statistics and data systems to support the collection of valid and reliable information that effectively informs decision making for quality improvement • Develop influence and motivational skills • Lead the coordination, management and empowerment of the quality team • Mentor new quality managers and contribute to collegial networks • Develop and deliver quality and risk skills and tools training • Synthesise initiatives across the organisation to demonstrate impact on consumer care and experience	to contribute to the achievement of the quality goals • Apply techniques for change in complex systems • Represent the organisation at major industry conferences and meetings • Effectively coordinate, manage and empower a large, complex quality team across a range of services and sites • Mentor and lead other quality managers and collegial networks • Lead research in the areas of safety and quality improvement

Using the Quality Manager Skills and Knowledge Framework[1]

The structure of the framework is based on the 'House of Quality' framework discussed in Chapter Six. It organises skills and knowledge into three phases of a quality manager's career (Foundation, Development and Established) and across three areas of the quality manager role. The first two areas of the quality manager role are based on the key components of an organisation-wide quality and clinical governance system and the third addresses a range of self management and professional development aspects of the quality manager role, as follows:

- **Area 1:** the 'front of house' actions associated with planning and implementing improvement initiatives and systems at point of care delivery to support the creation of a great consumer experience
- **Area 2:** the 'back of house' actions involved with working with executives and managers to support staff to provide great care through the development and implementation of governance structures and systems.
- **Area 3:** these are broader areas for quality managers' self-development. They encapsulate the skills required for the components in Areas 1 and 2.

There will be topic overlap between areas 1 and 2. For example, in Area 2 under the 'Established' phase for the 'Leadership, governance and culture' governance pillar, the 'Facilitate the development of a strategic quality plan that links to the organisational strategic and business plans' is also seen in Area 1, but here it is to 'Support managers and staff to adapt and implement the strategic improvement plan and goals...' These are two aspects of the same component; the systems aspect that requires strategic planning knowledge and skills, and the implementation aspect that requires translation and change knowledge and skills.

The framework can be used to guide professional development and career planning. It is designed to motivate and guide life-long learning and different aspects will apply at various phases in a quality professional's career. The 'Foundation, Development and Established' phases are cumulative and designed to build on each other, although they are not linear and it is likely that aspects of each phase will be learned and applied in different settings as required.

The framework can also be used as an organisational framework:

- If used as an organisational instrument to guide quality manager recruitment, development, retention and succession planning to meet organisational needs, the framework must be adapted to fit with the organisation's workforce, organisation and people development services. The language should be also modified to fit with the organisation's culture.
- The way the framework is used as an organisational tool will depend on the size of the facility and the number of quality managers involved. Careful consideration should be given to the components of each of the three areas that need to be applied to best meet the organisation's needs. For example, a sole quality manager in a small organisation should not necessarily have mastery of all the skills and knowledge components, although they should be supported to identify and close their skills and knowledge gaps in their ongoing professional development. But the priority in this situation should be to identify the components across the three developmental phases that are key to supporting the organisation's quality and clinical governance program, and to ensure that these skills and knowledge areas are recruited or developed by linking to position requirements and descriptions.

- In a larger organisation where there is a quality team, it is likely that particular components will be relevant to specialist quality, risk or governance roles, although mastery of the 'fundamentals' phase may be seen as a baseline expectation for recruitment or professional development in a large, complex health service.

The framework is not exhaustive, and is proposed as a guide to be adapted and modified to meet the needs of individuals and organisations.

APPENDIX 2:
Example of Four Pillars and Components of Quality Governance

APPENDIX 3:
Example Quality Governance Structure and Reporting

APPENDIX 2: Example of Four Pillars and Components of Quality Governance [2,3,4,5,6,7,8,9]

Consumer Participation System	Planning, Leadership and Culture System	Effective and Accountable Workforce System	Quality and Risk Systems

• Consumer and carer rights and responsibilities are understood and supported by staff at all levels of the organisation through active and ongoing staff development
 	
• Consumers and families have access to responsive advocacy and complaints mechanisms
 	
• Policies, protocols and organisational structures for consumer participation in care and support service improvement are in place and understood and enacted by staff
 	
• Consumer and carer perspectives and feedback are consciously sought and integrated into care pathways, service planning, risk management and care improvement
 	
• Consumers and families are encouraged to participate in processes to improve their personal safety, eg, identification of correct medication, where possible
	• There is a planned approach to governance, risk management and improvement that ensures:
	  - improvement priorities are identified and resourced
	  - data informs risk management and prevention strategies
	  - compliance with legislative requirements and industry standards
	
	• Organisational quality goals and priorities are developed and translated into business and operational plans, and resourced for implementation
	
	• Staff are involved in development and achievement of quality goals priorities through strategic and business planning
	
	• There is a system of leadership development that promotes:
	  - Clarity of expectation of staff responsibilities for safe and high quality care
	  - Planning, mentoring and training to fulfil these roles
		• Credentialing, scope of practice and performance management systems are designed in line with legislative and professional standards
		
		• There is investment in the professional development and support of staff, clinicians and managers, including key skills development in communication, teamwork and creating safety and quality
		
		• Workload and skills mix management are regularly reviewed in light of changing case mix and consumer needs, to assess the risk to consumer safety
		
		• Clear role expectations are designed to drive high quality care; are supported by supervision, training and development; and linked to a regular performance review system
		
		• Compliance with standards of care, evidence-based policies, guidelines and protocols is supported and evaluated as the basis for safe and high quality care
		
		• Staff and clinicians are supported to access, use
			Quality System
			• There is a planned approach to achieving quality goals and priorities within each service and across the health service that includes monitoring, feedback, service redesign activities and innovation in each dimension of quality, using a variety of quality tools
			
			• The quality system supports staff to achieve goals and priorities for safe and quality care for each consumer
			
			• A safety and quality minimum dataset is developed that monitors the achievement of the quality goals and key risks, processes and outcomes at each stage of the consumer journey, using both quantitative and qualitative data
			
			• There is a clear and effective organisational system for responding to data indicating sub-optimal care
			
			• Research, industry measures, benchmarks and internal data are used to evaluate and improve care and services
			
			• The quality system is regularly evaluated to assess its effectiveness in improving care, support and services
			
			• Quality and safety are improved using a mix of quality improvement, systems redesign and development, human factors

Consumer Participation System	Planning, Leadership and Culture System cont.	Effective and Accountable Workforce System cont.	Quality and Risk Systems cont.
	- Identification and removal of barriers to staff participation - Intra and inter service partnerships - Empowerment of managers and staff to lead and drive the monitoring, improvement and provision of quality care • Leaders promulgate a 'just' and 'safety' culture throughout the organisation • The organisational climate is measured, including staff perception of consumer safety, risks and management attitudes towards safety • Key improvement drivers such as human factors, systems review and change management are understood and used by improvement leaders • An effective committee structure is in place to monitor and drive the quality plan and to oversee key quality processes such as monitoring areas of risk, credentialing and scope of practice	and evaluate evidence, standards and protocols and guidelines in their practice • Staff and clinicians have access to relevant data about the quality of the care and outcomes experienced by their consumers, and are supported to act upon this data • An understanding of risk and error, and commitment to report incidents and improve practice is supported and encouraged • The healthcare record is integrated and accurate and supports the healthcare team to provide safe and quality care • Staff and clinicians are encouraged to speak up for safety, knowing that they will be protected when they do so • Building staff and team communication and resilience is recognised as an important aspect of creating safety • Staff and clinicians have access to support after critical incidents	and staff development, using contemporary improvement tools and science **Risk System** • Incidents are reported, investigated and underlying systems issues and root causes are identified – and used as opportunities for learning, staff development and systems improvement • There is a proactive program of audit and review to identify risks and to evaluate the effectiveness of the risk management system • There is a system for addressing and responding to complaints and medico legal issues regarding risk • Risk information is considered in setting goals, priorities and developing business and strategic plans • There is a proactive system of risk identification and response for both individual consumer risk and broader systems risk • Staff are encouraged to create safety through an understanding of risk error and proactive initiatives to create safety through systems and resilience • Clinical processes and technology supports are designed to minimise error and ensure clear, unambiguous communication

APPENDIX 3: Example Quality Governance Structure and Reporting

Governing Body
Overall accountability for the safety and quality of care and consumer experience

Governing Body Quality Committee
- Accountable for safety and quality of consumer experience
- Sets strategic quality goals and priorities, and monitors their progress
- Monitors and oversees key risk and quality of care issues
- Oversees governance systems

Chief Executive
- Leads organisational climate and strategic quality goals
- Provides governance supports and resourcing to achieve quality goals and priorities
- Leads a just culture

Operational Quality Committee
- Drives leadership and culture
- Drives implementation of the Strategic Quality Plan and Governance systems
- Reviews risk and safety trends and sentinel events, and recommends action
- Reports progress to the Board Quality Committee
- Provides feedback to staff
- Drives accreditation

Line Management: Senior Staff
- Lead and drive operationalising of quality goals and priorities
- Track progress and review data
- Develop, implement and evaluate systems to support great care and services

Issues-related Committees: eg, Infection Control, Clinical Review
- Lead relevant quality goals and priority achievement
- Analyse risk issues and data, and implement appropriate action
- Implement relevant Quality Plan Activities
- Meet accreditation and other standards
- Develop, implement and evaluate policies and procedures

Line Management: Staff Teams
- Implement relevant quality plan priorities and actions locally
- Review local quality data
- Local improvements and monitoring
- Input into the development and implementation of policies and procedures and other relevant standards and protocols

Quality Systems Support
- Quality plan and system leadership, facilitation, coordination and synthesis
- Methods for improvement change, implementation and evaluation
- Governance systems support
- Education and training
- Data analysis and reporting
- Risk management support

APPENDIX 4:
A Quality Cycle and Tools Map

APPENDIX 4: A Quality Cycle and Tools Map [9,10,11,12,13]

Examples of improvement tools that can be used at each quality cycle step

- Strategic goals vs practice
- Standards/policy vs practice
- Performance indicators
- Sentinel/adverse events and incidents
- Complaints/consumer feedback
- Recommendations from accreditation survey/other review
- Routine data collection/monitoring

- Team meeting process
- Brainstorming
- Process mapping/FMEA/Lean Thinking
- Data collection, analysis and presentation:
  - Audit/checklist
  - Bar/Pareto charts
  - Run/control charts
  - Flow charts
  - Comparative data
- The 5 'whys'
- Sharing stories, listening and observation

- Brainstorming
- Nominal Group Technique
- Force Field Analysis
- Standards and benchmarks
- Evidence-based practice
- Data collection

- Short and long term project management
- Change, spread and sustainability management
- Team process
- Quality training
- Process review and evaluation
- Listening and observation
- Data collection, analysis and presentation tools

Improvement process steps

1. An improvement opportunity is identified from routine data collection, a problem arising, anecdotal reporting or a desire to improve the quality of a particular area.

2. Analyse the problem/issue. Who needs to address it?
   - An individual or department? A multidisciplinary team?

   Answer the 4Ws and 1 H – when, who, what, why, how?
   - When and how often does the problem occur?
   - Who does it affect?
   - What are the consequences of it happening again? Or continuing to perform poorly?
   - Why does it happen?
   - How are the people involved feeling?

   It may be necessary to collect some baseline/further data at this stage to answer these questions before proceeding.

3. Develop ideas for solving the problem/improving the area. Ask:
   - What are we trying to achieve? (aim)
   - How will we know that a change we implement has led to an improvement? (how/what will we measure?)
   - What changes to we need to make to effect these improvements? (what action do we need to take and who do we need to involve?)

4. Put ideas into action using the Quality Cycle.
   1. Plan the change
   2. Action the change
   3. Review the result
   4. Follow up to ensure change works long term

Appendices' References and Further Reading

1. Southern Health and Balding C (2011) *A Quality Manager Skills and Knowledge Framework.* Southern Health, Australia

2. Australian Commission on Safety and Quality in Healthcare (2010) *Australian Safety and Quality Framework for Healthcare: Putting the Framework into Action: Getting Started.* ACSQHC, Australia. www.safetyandquality.gov.au

3. Department of Health (2009) *The Victorian Clinical Governance Policy Framework.* Department of Health, State Government of Victoria, Australia. www.health.vic.gov.au

4. Department of Health (2010) *Governing Quality in Public Sector Residential Aged Care: An Organisational Readiness Tool.* Aged Care Branch, Department of Health, State Government of Victoria, Australia. www.health.vic.gov.au

5. National Quality Board (2011 Refresh) *Quality Governance in the NHS – A Guide for Provider Boards.* NHS, UK

6. Baker, GR, et al (2008) *High Performing Healthcare Systems: Delivering Quality by Design.* Longwoods Publishing, Canada

7. Yonek J, Hines S, Joshi M (2010) *A Guide to Achieving High Performance in Multi-Hospital Health Systems.* Health Research and Educational Trust, USA

8. Boaden R, Harvey G, Moxham C, Proudlove L (2007) *QI: Theory and Practice in Healthcare.* University of Manchester Business School, UK

9. Langley GL, Nolan KM, Nolan TW, Norman CL, Provost LP (2009) *The Improvement Guide: A Practical Approach to Enhancing Organizational Performance* (2nd edn). Jossey-Bass Publishers, USA

10. Deming WE (2000) *The New Economics for Industry, Government, and Education.* The MIT Press, Cambridge, USA

11. Tague NR (1995) *The Quality Tool Box.* ASQC Quality Press, USA

12. Australian Commission on Safety and Quality in Healthcare (2006) *Measurement For Improvement Toolkit.* Commonwealth of Australia. www.safetyandquality.gov.au

13. Victorian Quality Council (2008) *A Guide to Using Data for Health Care Quality Improvement.* Department of Health, State Government of Victoria, Australia. www.health.vic.gov.au/qualitycouncil/

Printed by Libri Plureos GmbH in Hamburg, Germany